General Editors: J. R. MULRYNE
and J. C. BULMAN
Associate Editor: Margaret Shewring

Henry V

Already published in the series

J. L. Styan *All's Well that Ends Well*
Jill Levenson *Romeo and Juliet*
Graham Holderness *The Taming of the Shrew*
Roger Warren *Cymbeline*
Alan Dessen *Titus Andronicus*
J. C. Bulman *The Merchant of Venice*
Hugh M. Richmond *King Richard III*
Alexander Leggatt *King Lear*
Scott McMillin *Henry IV, Part One*
Bernice Kliman *Macbeth*
Barbara Hodgdon *Henry IV, Part Two*
Miriam Gilbert *Love's Labour's Lost*
Hugh M. Richmond *King Henry VIII*
Geraldine Cousin *King John*
Jay L. Halio *A Midsummer Night's Dream*
Anthony B. Dawson *Hamlet*
Margaret Shewring *King Richard II*

Volumes on most other plays in preparation

Of related interest

Duncan Salkeld *Madness and drama in the age of Shakespeare*

Michele Marrapodi, A. J. Hoenselaars, Marcello Cappuzzo
and L. Falzon Santucci, eds *Shakespeare's Italy*

Alison Findlay *Illegitimate power: Bastards in Renaissance drama*

Jonathan Dollimore and Alan Sinfield, eds *Political Shakespeare:
New essays in cultural materialism, 2nd edition*

B. J. Sokol *Art and illusion in* The Winter's Tale

Kate Chedgzoy *Shakespeare's queer children:
sexual politics and contemporary culture*

Ann Thompson and Sasha Roberts *Women reading Shakespeare
1660-1900: an anthology of criticism*

John J. Joughin *Shakespeare and national culture*

Henry V

JAMES N. LOEHLIN

Manchester
University Press
Manchester and New York

Distributed exclusively in the USA by St. Martin's Press

Published by
Manchester University Press
Oxford Road, Manchester M13 9NR
and Room 400, 175 Fifth Avenue,
New York, NY 10010, USA

Distributed exclusively in the USA by
St. Martin's Press, Inc., 175 Fifth Avenue,
New York, NY 10010, USA

British Library Cataloguing-in-Publication Data
A catalogue record for this book is available
from the British Library

Library of Congress Cataloging-in-Publication Data
Loehlin, James N.
    Henry V / James N. Loehlin.
        p. cm. — (Shakespeare in performance)
    Includes bibliographical references (p. 170).
    ISBN 0-7190-4623-8 (hardback)
    1. Shakespeare, William, 1564-1616. Henry V.
2. Shakespeare, William, 1564-1616 —Stage
history. 3. Shakespeare, William, 1564-1616—Film
and video adaptations. 4. Henry V, King of
England, 1387-1422—In literature. 5. Historical
drama. English—History and criticism. 6. Kings
and rulers in literature. I. Title. II. Series.
PR2812.L64 1997
822.3'3—dc20   96-31545
                                                    CIP

ISBN 0 7190 5944 5 *paperback*

First published 1996
Reprinted in paperback 2000
04 03 02 01 00   10 9 8 7 6 5 4 3 2 1

Typeset by
Koinonia Limited, Manchester
Printed in Great Britain
by Biddles Limited, Guildford and King's Lynn

CONTENTS

List of figures   *page* vi
Series editors' preface   vii
Acknowledgements   viii

I   Introduction   1

II   This star of England: Laurence Olivier (1944)   25

III   We band of brothers: Terry Hands (1975)   49

IV   Flat unraisèd spritis: BBC TV (1979)   72

V   Rainy marching in the painful field:
         Adrian Noble (1984)   84

VI   These English monsters:
         Michael Bogdanov (1986)   107

VII   Let there be sung 'Non nobis':
         Kenneth Branagh (1989)   128

VIII   Wish not a man from England:
         Henry V outside the United Kingdom   146

         Bibliography   171
         Appendix   176
         Index   179

FIGURES

1 Lewis Waller as a heroic Edwardian Henry V, *c*. 1910.
Billy Rose Theatre Collection, New York Public Library
for the Performing Arts, Astor, Lenox and Tilden
Foundations.   *page* 22

2 The Salic Law scene in the Globe Theatre, from
Laurence Olivier's 1944 film. Courtesy of the Rank
Organisation Plc and the British Film Institute.   32

3 Olivier's Henry V at the battle of Harfleur. Courtesy of
the Rank Organisation Plc and the British Film
Institute.   40

4 The rehearsal-clothes opening of Terry Hands's 1975
RSC production. Joe Cocks Studio Collection,
Shakespeare Centre Library, Stratford-upon-Avon.   55

5 Alan Howard as Henry, from Terry Hands's 1975 RSC
production. Joe Cocks Studio Collection, Shakespeare
Centre Library, Stratford-upon-Avon.   64

6 The execution of Bardolph, from Adrian Noble's 1984
RSC production. Joe Cocks Studio Collection,
Shakespeare Centre Library, Stratford-upon-Avon.   92

7 Kenneth Branagh on the walls of Harfleur, from Adrian
Noble's 1984 RSC production. Joe Cocks Studio
Collection, Shakespeare Centre Library, Stratford-upon-
Avon.   99

8 John Woodvine's Chorus in Michael Bogdanov's 1986
English Shakespeare Company production. Courtesy of
Laurence Burns.   115

9 Henry (Michael Pennington) threatens Montjoy (Donald
Gee) in Michael Bogdanov's 1986 English Shakespeare
Company production. Courtesy of Laurence Burns.   118

10 The young King Henry at the opening of Kenneth
Branagh's 1989 film. Courtesy of Artificial Eye/Mayfair
Films and the British Film Institute.   135

11 Henry after the battle of Agincourt, from Kenneth
Branagh's 1989 film. Courtesy of Artificial Eye/Mayfair
Films and the British Film Institute.   142

12 Len Cariou's Henry surrounded by his 'hawkish' advisers, from Michael Kahn's 1969 production in Stratford,
Connecticut. Martha Swope, ©Time, Inc.   160

SERIES EDITORS' PREFACE

In the past two decades, the study of Shakespeare's plays as scripts for performance in the theatre has grown to rival the reading of Shakespeare as literature among university, college and secondary-school teachers and their students. The aim of the present series is to assist this study by describing how certain of Shakespeare's texts have been realised in production.

The series is not concerned to provide theatre history in the traditional sense. Rather, it employs the more contemporary discourses of performance criticism to explore how a multitude of factors work together to determine how a play achieves meaning for a particular audience. Each contributor to the series has selected a number of productions of a given play and analysed them comparatively. These productions – drawn from different periods, countries and media – were chosen not only because they are culturally significant in their own right but also because they represent something of the range and variety of the possible interpretations of the play in hand. They illustrate how the convergence of various material conditions helps to shape a performance: the medium for which the text is adapted; stage-design and theatrical tradition; the acting company itself; the body and abilities of the individual actor; and the historical, political, and social contexts which condition audience reception of the play.

We hope that theatregoers, by reading these accounts of Shakespeare in performance, may enlarge their understanding of what a play-text is and begin, too, to appreciate the complex ways in which performance is a collaborative effort. Any study of a Shakespeare text will, of course, reveal only a small proportion of the play's potential meaning; but by engaging issues of how a text is translated in performance, our series encourages a kind of reading that is receptive to the contingencies that make theatre a living art.

J. R. Mulryne and J. C. Bulman, General Editors
Margaret Shewring, Associate Editor

ACKNOWLEDGEMENTS

Among the many people I wish to thank for helping me with this book are my editors, James Bulman and Ronnie Mulryne; John Banks, Anita Roy, Stephanie Sloan and the Staff at Manchester University Press; Sylvia Morris, Marian Pringle and Mary White of the Library of the Shakespeare Centre in Stratford; Betty Corwin of the Theatre on Film and Tape Archive of the Billy Rose Theatre Collection at the New York Public Library for the Performing Arts; and the Departments of Drama at Stanford University, Dartmouth College and Colorado College. I am grateful to Michael Bogdanov, John Dougall, Barry Edelstein, Michael Kahn and Kevin Kline for talking to me about their work. Among those who have given me special help with the manuscript are Charles Lyons, Stephen Orgel and Peter Saccio, and I am grateful for the critical, editorial and practical advice of Lynda Boose, Helen Brooks, Rishi Goyal, Alice Rayner, William Worthen and David Ziegler. I want to record a special debt of gratitude to James B. Ayres, who got me started in this area.

My deepest thanks go to my family: to my wife Laurel, for her encouragement and love; to my sister Jennifer, for moral support and German translations; and to my parents, for everything. This book is for all of them.

Permission to reproduce photographs has kindly been granted by the Shakespeare Birthplace Trust, the British Film Institute, Rank Film Distributors, Artificial Eye film Distributors, Laurence Burns, Martha Swope, Time/Life and the New York Public Library.

I am indebted to the excellent recent editions of the play by Andrew Gurr (Cambridge) and Gary Taylor (Oxford); however, because their textual innovations do not correspond to the texts used in most productions, I have used J. H. Walter's 1954 Arden text for references and lineation.

CHAPTER I

Introduction

The modern performance history of *Henry V* may be summed up by the playwright John Arden's comment that Shakespeare seemed to have written a 'secret play within the official one' (Berry, *Changing Styles*, p. 77, see also Arden, p. 196). Before the twentieth century, even those critics, such as William Hazlitt, who disapproved of *Henry V* had no doubt about the sort of play it was: 'a very splendid pageant', a straightforward, nationalistic celebration of a great warrior-hero (p. 286). That tradition continued into the twentieth century, of course, culminating in Laurence Olivier's 1944 film, but by that time critics and directors were conscious that the play contained a great deal more: not only a complex and troubling analysis of war, leadership and heroism, but (as Olivier recognised) a sophisticated meditation on the nature of theatre. Innovations in theatrical theory and techniques, changing attitudes to war and politics, and new ideas about Shakespeare's histories have all served to *complicate* the play and make an 'official' heroic version increasingly untenable. Modern performance has discovered or created a wealth of hidden secrets in *Henry V*, and rendered what was perhaps Shakespeare's most straightforward and tradition-bound play one of his most theatrically provocative.

The 'official' *Henry V* is the story of one of England's greatest military triumphs, a young and valiant king leading a badly outnumbered army to victory over the French at Agincourt. It is the story told by the Chorus, when he instructs the audience how to respond to 'the mirror of all Christian kings' (II.Chorus.6):

> O now, who will behold
> The royal captain of this ruined band
> Walking from watch to watch, from tent to tent,
> Let him cry, 'Praise and glory on his head!'
>
> (IV.Chorus.28-31)

The official version focuses on Henry's courage in adversity, on his heroic speeches before Harfleur and Agincourt, on his concern for his soldiers, on his charm in wooing the French princess. It glorifies an ideal king, a divinely sanctioned victory, and a courageous and unified nation:

O England, model to thy inward greatness
Like little body with a mighty heart.

(II.Chorus.16-17)

By contrast, the 'secret' play undermines the Chorus's account with scenes of betrayal, loss and cruelty. This other play reveals a world of political chicanery, where the heads of the Church urge Henry to invade France as a diversionary tactic in order to protect their own wealth from the hungry Commons. It reveals a world of civil discord, where Henry's soldiers fight among themselves, and where his cause in France and his title at home are both subject to scrutiny. It reveals a world of ruthless expediency, where friends and enemies alike are sacrificed to the bloody demands of conquest. In the secret version, the son of a usurper goes to war in order to 'busy giddy minds with foreign quarrels' (*2 Henry IV*, IV.5.213-14), he wins a battle by cold-bloodedly slaughtering enemy prisoners and he marries the enemy princess in order to secure his spoils. For most of its production history, only the official version of *Henry V* was ever seen. The twentieth century has challenged it with a 'secret play' that is complex, disturbing and continually rewarding.

The 'official' and 'secret' versions of the play are not, of course, fixed entities; they are poles of interpretation. *Henry V* is a location for the production of meaning, a site where text, performance, history and culture intersect. Neither the 'original' text nor any 'definitive' performance has unique authority in establishing the play's meaning: *Henry V* is a battleground of interpretations. The official and secret versions crystallise the problems the play raises, but don't solve them. Indeed, though the twentieth-century tendency has been toward the secret play, many modern productions partake of both.

The most obvious area in which modern productions have complicated the traditional *Henry V* is in their presentation of war. In eighteenth- and nineteenth-century England, the battle scenes were occasions for patriotic spectacle and stirring rhetoric, sometimes involving literal calls to arms against the persistent

French foe. By contrast, modern directors have tended to deglamorise war, shaping their depictions of it for a public familiar with television images of Vietnam. Many productions question Henry's motives and condemn the cynical self-interest of the bishops who encourage him. The unity of Henry's army and the justice of his cause may be undermined, especially by his argument with the soldier Michael Williams, who reminds him of the 'legs and arms and heads chopped off in a battle', and the widows and orphans war creates (IV.i.137-8). The French, in production, can range from decadent fops who deserve to lose to a proud nation beset by brutal invaders. The battle scenes, once displays of medieval pageantry, are often grim evocations of combat recalling twentieth-century wars. Many productions of *Henry V* emphasise elements of ruthlessness that were once suppressed, such as Henry's threats before the besieged Harfleur, or the executions of Bardolph and the French prisoners. Nevertheless, such productions often employ counter-strategies for valorising Henry and his victory. Kenneth Branagh's 1989 film is perhaps the clearest example: the savagery of battle is tempered by Branagh's penitent tears, while Henry's rape of France is negated by his charming wooing of Princess Katherine. The epithet 'anti-war', applied lightly to many modern productions, is generally inadequate to both the text's complexities and the conflicting sympathies engendered by even the most radically revisionist productions.

Other important ways modern productions have complicated the text involve the performance of the lead role, the relation of the play to Shakespeare's other histories and the self-conscious exploration and exploitation of the performance medium. Many of the 'secrets' discovered in the character of Henry have resulted not so much from changes in political attitudes as from changes in acting style. In the Stanislavskian tradition of acting that dominates Western theatre, actors require internal as well as external conflicts. Thus many modern Henrys, most notably Alan Howard in Terry Hands's 1975 production, have seized on and expanded the moments of self-doubt, guilt and moral crisis the text provides and made them the basis of the character. The soliloquies of the night before Agincourt have become central to the complex modern Henry. The responsibilities of kingship, the telling arguments of Williams and the inherited guilt of Richard II's murder are all occasions for giving psychological depth and nuance to the character. Henry's inner struggles may also inform such moments as the initial decision to go to war, the executions of the traitors and Bardolph, even the public pronouncements to the French herald. What read in the text as straightforward orations may, through the opposition of intention and obstacle central to modern acting, become personal ordeals shot through with conflict.

Henry's moments of crisis often involve the personal and political inheritance from the *Henry IV* plays and *Richard II*, which have weighed heavily on *Henry V* in this century. Since the publication of Tillyard's *Shakespeare's History Plays* in 1944, it has become increasingly common to view the plays as parts of a grand historical cycle, and to play them as such. Scott McMillin and Barbara Hodgdon, in their volumes on the two parts of *Henry IV* for this series, reveal the prevalence of cycle-thinking and the impact it has had on all of the English histories in modern performance. Several modern Henrys (Richard Burton, Ian Holm and Alan Howard at Stratford, Michael Pennington for the English Shakespeare Company, David Gwillim on television) have played the part in conjunction with the younger Prince Hal. This gives the actor a broader canvas on which to develop the role, and myriad opportunities for fore-and-aft-shadowing. Howard's Hal, for instance, consciously anticipated the hanging of Bardolph during the jesting on 'halter' in *1HIV* 2.iv. Two important cycles, those of Peter Hall (1964) and Michael Bogdanov (1987-89), performed *Henry V* in the midst of both historical tetralogies – thus contextualising Henry's adventure in France not only with the political strife leading up to it but with its eventual disastrous outcome. While production as part of a cycle can fill out *Henry V*, it can also in some ways limit it. Most of the modern cycle-productions including *Henry V* been influenced by sweeping critical interpretations of the histories as a whole. The two most prominent rival theories in the twentieth century have been those of Tillyard, who saw the histories as a great lesson in a Tudor ideology of order and obedience, and Jan Kott (*Shakespeare Our Contemporary*), who reinterpreted them as a cynical criticism of that very ideology. Of the major twentieth-century cycles involving *Henry V*, Anthony Quayle (Stratford 1951) and David Giles (BBC 1979) essentially followed Tillyard; Peter Hall and Michael Bogdanov essentially followed Kott. In all cases *Henry V* was in some ways constrained and reduced by the cyclical presentation. None the less, the connections between *Henry V* and its companion plays have been a strong feature of twentieth-century performance. Even productions that present *Henry V* independently, such as the two films and Michael Kahn's 1969 Connecticut version, tend to inject material from other history plays in flashback or voice-over.

Finally, modern productions have often used the text's self-reflexiveness and acknowledgment of theatrical convention to question the limits and practices of their own media, whether stage, film or television. The Chorus's apologies for the theatre's limited powers of representation, ignored by Victorian actor-managers, have strongly influenced modern versions in spite of the contemporary possibilities for visual spectacle. Olivier, Kahn and Terry Hands (Stratford 1975) all explored the play's self-awareness in ways thematically relevant to their examinations of the theatrical construction of Henry's authority. In this approach, the Chorus becomes a central figure, whether the production illustrates or contradicts his rhetoric. The play includes several episodes wherein the Chorus's version of events can be called into question, as when the assertion that 'honour's thought / Reigns solely in the breast of every man' (II.Chorus.3-4) is followed by scenes of Pistol's cynical profiteering and the nobles' treachery. The Chorus repeatedly points out the gap between the story he wishes to tell and the play the audience sees. For many modern directors, the text's frequent references to the theatrical event produce a kind of Brechtian estrangement that allows a complex and critical interpretation of Henry's ostensibly heroic triumph.

The twentieth-century performance history of *Henry V* records a swing of 180 degrees, from patriotic heroism to bitter irony. This change is reflected in the modern critical history of the play. Mid-century historicist critics like Tillyard and Lily B. Campbell felt *Henry V* was part of a series of plays designed to reinforce Tudor ideology, stressing the dangers of dissension and the virtues of a strong and stable monarchy. These critics saw the Tudor state as essentially homogeneous and coherent, with its cultural productions reflecting a totalising 'Elizabethan world picture'. According to this reading, Henry V is an idealised ruler who prefigures Elizabeth in achieving domestic harmony and foreign triumph. More recent critics, especially those associated with the schools of American New Historicism and British Cultural Materialism, have read the play's politics as more complicated and contradictory, encompassing challenges to the Tudor orthodoxy. Stephen Greenblatt, in *Shakespearean Negotiations*, has argued that any official Tudor ideology the plays presented was bound up with subversions of it in the unstable, problematic medium of theatrical representation. Jonathan Dollimore and Alan Sinfield ('History and Ideology') similarly read the play as an ideological myth about national unity which cannot contain the centrifugal tendencies it includes. These readings stress the oppositional elements in *Henry V* – the embittered Williams, the treacherous nobles, the transgressive comics, the self-interested churchmen, the unruly regional characters – and the play's failure to conform to the idealised history promised by the Chorus.

Recent scholarship on the history plays has linked the modern critical debate about *Henry V* to an Elizabethan debate about historical causation. Phyllis Rackin, among others, argues that Shakespeare's text inherits, from its chronicle sources, two conflicting views of history, one medieval and providential, the other humanist and Machiavellian. In the former, exemplified by Edward Hall's *Union of the Two Noble and Illustre Houses of Lancaster and York*, history is seen as the unfolding of God's plan on earth, a view the Tudor state encouraged as a way of legitimating itself. The latter method, practised by humanist authors like Francis Bacon, John Hayward and Samuel Daniel, approached history as *Realpolitik*, the product of human manipulations of power, knowledge and force. According to Rackin, both approaches are inscribed in Shakespeare's texts, providing rival explanations for the same events. The nationalistic rhetoric of the Chorus and of Henry's own speeches tells the 'official', providential version of the story, as the play's narrative arc carries Henry through a series of victories to his final triumph: hero of Agincourt, heir of France, 'mirror of all Christian kings'. Several episodes along the way, however, tell the story differently, presenting a series of oppositional voices and critical undertones. In I.ii, the Archbishop of Canterbury quotes scripture to give Henry's invasion divine sanction; but I.i has already shown that his motive is to protect the wealth of the Church. Similarly, the episode of the three English nobles executed for plotting against Henry may be read from either a providential or Machiavellian point of view. Henry himself gives it the former interpretation:

> We doubt not of a fair and lucky war,
> Since God so graciously hath brought to light
> This dangerous treason lurking in our way.

(II.ii.184-6)

[6]

Yet the confession of one of the traitors, Richard, Earl of Cambridge, hints darkly at another side to the story.

> For me, the gold of France did not seduce,
> Although I did admit it as a motive
> The sooner to effect what I intended.

(II.ii.155-7)

What he intended, as some in Shakespeare's audience would have known, was to advance the Yorkists' title to Henry's crown, as his son York and grandsons Edward IV and Richard III finally succeeded in doing. Shakespeare had already dramatised the York takeover in the *Henry VI* plays and *Richard III*. The hint here serves to remind the audience of the shakiness of Henry's hold on the crown and the civil strife by which his son lost it. Henry's providential claim thus comes in a context of *Realpolitik* that contradicts it. Likewise, Henry's final victory at Agincourt is overdetermined. On the one hand, it can be attributed (by Henry) to the divine will: 'O God, thy arm was here' (IV.viii.108). On the other, it can be interpreted as the result of superior English tactics, exemplified by Henry's ruthless expediency: 'The French have reinforced their scattered men. / Then every soldier kill his prisoners' (IV.vi.36-7).

Henry's order to kill the French prisoners provides a good example of the complexity of the play and the interpretive decisions it forces on any production. It is the turning point of the battle in Shakespeare's play, which makes no mention of the archers and stakes that ensured the historical English victory, and which shows no actual fighting save that between Pistol and le Fer. The first question facing a director is whether to include the killing at all; productions accepting the divine explanation of Henry's victory often cut the massacre altogether. Even if the killing is retained, it is shrouded in ambiguities that demand theatrical resolution. Does it occur on stage or off? What is its temporal and causal relation to the French attack on the boys guarding Henry's baggage train? Does Henry make the order in cold blood, as his lines suggest, or in revenge for the French murder of the boys, as Gower interprets it? Is Henry's order 'justified' in either case? The principal productions covered in this book all made strikingly different and significant decisions regarding this moment. In keeping with the providential, heroic version of the play, Laurence Olivier's 1944 film cut the massacre entirely, moving directly from the killing of the boys to a tournament-style single combat between Henry and the Constable of France. Terry Hands's 1975 Royal Shakespeare Company production showed the boy killed on stage, and then deleted lines to make Henry's order a direct, angry retaliation. Hands frankly stated that he altered the textual order so that 'Henry's action seems less harsh' (Beaumann, *Henry V*, p. 199). In David Giles's 1979 BBC television version, Henry' s order was a quick, matter-of-fact instruction, barely noticeable in the scrum of battle. In Adrian Noble's 1984 RSC production, the order was likewise a tactical move unrelated to the attack on the camp. Nevertheless, Noble and his Henry, the young Kenneth Branagh, did much to condition audience response. Because the audience had seen the boy killed on stage, and because after learning of the boy's death Henry tearfully attacked, and then spared, a French prisoner, the brutality of Henry's order was to some extent tempered, and the emotional involvement of the audience remained with Henry. By contrast, Michael Bogdanov's 1987 modern-dress English Shakespeare Company production did not show the boy killed on stage, and Bogdanov stated that he wanted to present the French attack as a response to Henry's massacre: 'It is quite clear that the French action is a retaliation for the English action' (Bogdanov, *ESC*, p. 47). Henry issued the order with cool resolve, and a reluctant Pistol slit le Fer's throat in full view of the audience.

These differing treatments reveal the way a single textual moment can serve very different interpretations of the play. The instances cited above show a progression from a denial of the more unpleasant aspects of war, and of Henry's character, to an outright condemnation of them. Interestingly, with Branagh's 1989 film, the wheel seems to have come full circle: in this ostensibly anti-war production, self-consciously opposed to Olivier's film in other ways, the killing of the prisoners is once again suppressed.

Henry V is filled with events and characters that demand such interpretation, that can be made to serve either a heroic, providential view of Henry's victory or a cynical, Machiavellian one. The coexistence of the 'official' and 'secret' versions of the play reveals both the political oscillations of this century and a fundamental ambiguity in the play itself. In one of the most important modern essays on *Henry V*, Norman Rabkin compares it to an image from E. H. Gombrich's *Art and Illusion*, the 'rabbit/duck'. This simple line drawing, like the play, can be perceived in one of two distinct ways, alternately, but not simultaneously. *Henry V* can be either the story of an ideal king leading a unified nation to a glorious victory, or the story of a crafty and unscrupulous politician embarking on a cynical war of aggression in spite of its human costs. Rabkin's polarisation is perhaps too absolute; most modern productions have tried to incorporate aspects of both readings. But the play none the less contains incompatible and even irreconcilable elements. Every production will place its emphases differently, but we can briefly summarise the crucial issues around which modern productions have defined themselves: the character of the King; the reliability of the Chorus; the treatment of the bishops and the justification of the war; the depiction of the French; the executions of the traitors, Bardolph and the prisoners; the King's argument with Williams over the justice of his cause; the representation of battle; the wooing scene; and the production's relation to other Shakespearian histories. The text's own internal argument about the nature and causes of Henry's victory charges key moments in the play with interpretive tension. The selective emphasis and suppression of different kinds of evidence have given *Henry V* a varied and vigorous history on the stage.

What would an Elizabethan audience have made of *Henry V*? Would they have applauded the 'official' version or had any sense of the 'secret' play? We know that history plays were perceived as highly political works. Thomas Heywood, in his *Apology for Actors*, defends history plays as patriotic propaganda with the 'power to new-mold the hearts of the spectators and fashion them to the shape of any noble and notable attempt' (quoted in Worthen, p. 14). Thomas Nashe specifically mentions 'what a glorious thing it is to have Henry the Fifth represented on the stage, leading the French king prisoner, and forcing both him and the Dolphin to swear fealty' (p. 213). Nashe was referring to an earlier play on the subject; in the years of Elizabethan nationalism following the defeat of the Spanish Armada in 1588, at least four plays celebrated England's great triumph at Agincourt. On the other hand, history plays also had a reputation for political subversiveness, especially in so far as they seemed to comment on contemporary events. When *Richard II*, Shakespeare's play beginning the series leading to *Henry V*, was first printed in 1597, the scene of Richard's deposition was absent; presumably it was

[9]

deemed too provocative to be printed or played. When the Earl of Essex staged his abortive coup attempt in February 1601, his followers arranged a performance of *Richard II* the day before. Queen Elizabeth, in conversation with the antiquary William Lambarde, famously commented on the relation between history play and history:

> 'I am Richard II, know ye not that?'
> W.L.: 'Such a wicked imagination was determined and attempted by a most unkind gent. the most adorned creature that your majesty ever made.'
> Her Majesty: 'He that will forget God, will also forget his bene-factors; this tragedy was played forty times in open streets and houses.' (Salgado, p. 22)

Henry V was written before the Essex rebellion, but the unfortunate Earl plays a significant role in its political background. There are two early texts of *Henry V*, the Folio of 1623 ('F'), which seems to have been based on Shakespeare's autograph manuscript, and a heavily cut Quarto of 1600 ('Q') which is probably an actors' memorial reconstruction. The date of the first performance is generally agreed to be in the spring or summer of 1599, based on the Chorus's lines referring to Essex's ill-fated expedition to put down an Irish rebellion:

> Were now the General of our Gracious Empress
> As in good time he may – from Ireland coming,
> Bringing rebellion broachèd on his sword,
> How many would the peaceful city quit
> To welcome him!
>
> (V.Chorus.30-4)

Essex left London on 27 March, and returned on 28 September to face charges about his disastrous mishandling of the Irish campaign. If F indeed reflects an authorial manuscript, the play was written, and probably performed, in that interval. The 1600 Quarto text, published after the Irish fiasco but before the 1601 rebellion, omits all mention of Essex, along with the rest of the choral speeches. One theory about the Q cuts is that they were intended to dissociate Shakespeare's company from the Queen's former favourite. This argument, first advanced in the 1920s by Evelyn May Albright, has recently been convincingly developed by Annabel Patterson. Patterson contends that the Folio version of *Henry V* was written in 1599 in the midst of an ongoing public relations skirmish between Essex and the Queen. Essex's good looks, military successes and masculinity had captured the popular imagination in ways that the Queen's image-makers were anxious to control. Shakespeare's choral speeches share the enthusiastic tone of many contemporary encomia of Essex, who had himself led a flamboyant expedition into Normandy a few years before. With an aging spinster on the throne and no named heir, England was fraught with anxiety about its future leadership, and the original version of *Henry V* may have played into this anxiety with its political ambiguities and Essex-like young hero. Too much praise of Essex could be dangerous, however. In February 1599 John Hayward wrote a humanist history of *Henry IV*, which included justifications for the deposition of *Richard II* and a dedication to Essex. The dedication was immediately censored by the authorities, and the book was later called in and burned. In July 1600, after Essex's failure in Ireland, Hayward was committed to the Tower. When the Quarto of *Henry V* was published a month later, it not only contained no references to Essex, but 'presented an almost unproblematic view of a highly popular monarch whose most obvious modern analogy was Elizabeth herself' (Patterson, p. 46).

It is impossible to be certain what relation the Quarto text bears to Shakespearian authorship or the performances of the Lord Chamberlain's Men. The frequent corruptions suggest memorial reconstruction, but the more substantial cuts may well reflect stage practice or Shakespeare's own editing. Q is definitely a more compact text, requiring about half as many actors and half the playing time. From a purely dramatic standpoint it holds together fairly well: the main story-line is stressed, subordinate scenes curtailed, long speeches trimmed or cut altogether. Some of the cuts, however, suggest ideological as well as practical motivation. While Patterson has pointed out the removal of possible Essex associations in the choral speeches, Gary Taylor has more generally argued that the effect of the cuts is 'to remove almost every difficulty in the way of an unambiguously patriotic celebration of Henry and his war' (*Henry V*, p. 12). The Quarto omits the opening scene revealing the ulterior motive of the churchmen, as well as Canterbury's offer of 'a mighty sum' to Henry in I.ii; it removes all reference to Henry's personal responsibility for Falstaff's decline; it greatly reduces Henry's threats before Harfleur; and it eliminates Burgundy's description of the desolation of France by Henry's war. If Q indeed reflects stage practice, it suggests that the tendency to edit the play to fit a heroic, patriotic interpretation began in Shakespeare's lifetime. It must be said, however, that Q's excision of the choral speeches seems unlikely to have been motivated by a desire to make the play more patriotic, unless one assumes they were designed as overblown rhetoric to be contradicted by the stage action. The awkwardness with which they relate to the scenes surrounding them – especially the choruses preceding Acts II and V – suggests that they were not written together with the first draft of the play; but the Essex reference argues convincingly for an early date. For the present study I am assuming that they are an essential part of the play's design, and were, in some form, a part of Elizabethan performances.

The first performances of *Henry V* took place either at the new Globe, which opened some time in the summer of 1599, or at the Curtain, where the Lord Chamberlain's Men performed after the Theatre, their original home, was dismantled. The Chorus's apologies for the inadequacies of the 'wooden O' suggest the old Curtain, but the lines could just as easily be false modesty about the splendid new Globe (Gurr, p. 6). At any rate, the choral speeches repeatedly stress the necessity for the audience to 'piece out our imperfections with your thoughts' (I.Chorus.23). These speeches are usually taken as a fundamental expression of the verbal and imaginative nature of Shakespeare's theatre, which depends on language and thought rather than spectacle. On the other hand, Shakespeare hadn't shied away from spectacle in his earlier histories, which feature battles, processions, dumbshows and even apparitions. For that matter, the text of *Henry V* seems to require a certain amount of spectacle: the entries of the English and French courts include several non-speaking characters, who presumably are there only for show; the French comment on the splendour of their armour; and the battle of Harfleur requires cannons and scaling ladders as the English are driven back from the French wall. Nashe's memory of the earlier Henry V play is a strikingly visual one: 'What a glorious thing it is to have Henry the Fifth represented on the stage, leading the French king prisoner' (p. 213). Shakespeare doesn't include this moment, to be sure, and his battle of Agincourt is mostly unstaged: the encounter of Pistol and le Fer is fairly close to the 'brawl ridiculous' the Chorus promises (IV.Chorus.51). But it seems that the Chorus's modesty is largely a rhetorical gesture designed to magnify his own epic version of the events of the play, rather than a genuine apology for unusually minimal staging.

Audiences coming to *Henry V* in 1599 would have been familiar with the story; three other versions had played on the London stage in the 1590s, including the bluff and hearty *Famous Victories of Henry V*, which is a source for Shakespeare's play and was once considered an earlier version of it. Moreover, the Lord Chamberlain's men had promised a Henry V play in the epilogue to *2 Henry IV*:

> If you be not too much cloyed with fat meat, our humble author will continue the story, with Sir John in it, and make you merry with fair Katherine of France. Where, for anything I know, Falstaff shall die of a sweat, unless already 'a be killed with your hard opinions, for Oldcastle died a martyr, and this is not the man. (24-30)

The Epilogue seems partly designed to defuse the controversy over Shakespeare's original name for Falstaff, Sir John Oldcastle. As an advertisement for Shakespeare's play, the Epilogue is somewhat misleading. Spectators expecting to see the story continued, 'with Sir John in it', would have been surprised to get only a report of his death, though the Epilogue jokingly refers to Falstaff's passing as a possibility. Much critical discussion has focused on why Shakespeare removed Falstaff from *Henry V*, if he ever intended to place him there. In *Shakespeare's Clown*, David Wiles argues that Falstaff's disappearance was occasioned by the departure of Will Kempe from the company. On the other hand, there is no dramatic necessity for Falstaff in *Henry V*; in a structural sense, his part has ended with Hal's rejection in *2 Henry IV*, and the off-stage account of his death has been praised for centuries.

The merry-making with fair Katherine would have been a familiar scene from *The Famous Victories*, and in the wooing scene Shakespeare's play more or less lives up to this promise. But the degree to which *Henry V* really 'continues the story' of the *Henry IV* plays is debatable. In many respects it is a different kind of play. Hal's past life with his low companions, so large a feature of the earlier plays (and of the Epilogue's promise) is alluded to, and summarily dismissed, in the first scene with the bishops. Henry's transformation is virtually complete. As far as we know, he never hears of Falstaff's death, and his one scripted encounter with his former friends consists of a few lines exchanged with

Pistol while in disguise. For that matter, only Pistol, Bardolph, Mistress Quickly and the Boy carry over from *Henry IV*; Poins and Peto have vanished, Doll Tearsheet is mentioned but never appears, and Nym is borrowed from *The Merry Wives of Windsor* (assuming it predates *Henry V*). Moreover, the civil unrest that loomed so large in the earlier plays is reduced to the single reference to Cambridge's treacherous motives. None of the nobles is recognisable from the earlier plays. The Duke of York, who dies leading the vanguard at Agincourt, is the rebellious young Aumerle from *Richard II*, but the connection is never made. The Duke of Bedford, who played a large and unpleasant role as Prince John in *2 Henry IV*, is completely uncharacterised, and indeed doesn't appear in the Quarto. The virtual interchangeability of the King's various brothers and uncles is a marked departure from the earlier plays. *Henry V* recalls the earlier plays at certain moments, but the degree to which it is really connected to them is a function of production. We do not know, for instance, whether they remained in the repertory at the time when *Henry V* was introduced; if so, the connections between the plays would have been more apparent. We can presume that the same actor played Henry as had played Hal, and there is no reason to doubt that it was Richard Burbage, who had made his name in such heroic parts.

We don't know how long *Henry V* remained in the repertory after its initial performances, but the reprinting of the Quarto in 1602 suggests it was a popular play. There is a record of a performance at court before King James in the Christmas revels of 1604-05. This performance would likely have eliminated not only the old reference to Essex but the remarks about the dangers of 'the weasel Scot' and quite possibly the comically accented Scottish Captain, whose name, at the very least, would have been altered from James (Gurr, p. 4). This court performance is the last record we have of *Henry V* before the closing of the theatres in 1642.

After the Restoration, Shakespeare's *Henry V* received few performances until the later eighteenth century. In 1666, Pepys mentions seeing a court performance of a play on the subject. His main impressions are of the royal occasion and the actors' finery:

> to Whitehall, and got my Lord Bellassis to get me into the playhouse; and there, after staying an hour for the players, the King and all waiting, which was absurd, saw Henry the Fifth well done by the Duke's people, and in most excellent habits, all new vests,

being put on but this night. But I sat so high and far off, that I missed most of the words, and sat with a wind coming into my back and neck, which did much trouble me. (28 December 1666, quoted in Salgado, p. 51)

The version Pepys saw was probably a play by the Earl of Orrery, which centred on the friendship between Henry and Owen Tudor and their mutual love for Catherine, whom Owen married after Henry's death. The great Thomas Betterton played not Henry but Owen, in which part he had considerable success. The play made for a curious conflation of real king, historical king and player king: in the first performance Henry and Owen wore the actual coronation suits of King Charles II and the Duke of York (Cole, p. 349).

In 1723 Aaron Hill published a version of 'KING *HENRY* THE FIFTH; OR, THE CONQUEST OF *France*, By the *ENGLISH*. A TRAGEDY. As it is Acted at the Theatre-Royal in *Drury-Lane*, By His MAJESTY'S Servants'. This remarkable adaptation combines the Restoration tendency to tailor Shakespeare to fit contemporary tastes with the beginnings of an antiquarian approach to history-play staging. A few lines from the prologue give the general tone:

> *Hid, in the cloud of Battle,* Shakespear's *Care,*
> *Blind, with the Dust of War, o'erlook'd the* Fair:
> *Fond of* their *Fame, we shew their Influence, here,*
> *And place 'em,* twinkling *through War's smokey Sphere.*
> *Without* their *Aid, we lose* Love's *quick'ning Charms;*
> *And sullen* Virtue mopes, *in* steril Arms.
> *Now, rightly mix'd, th'enliven'd Passions move:*
> *Love* softens *War, — and War* invigo'rates *Love.*

> (Hill, Prologue)

With the advent of actresses after the Restoration, many of Shakespeare's plays were found wanting in female roles and love-interest. Hill's promised love-intrigue involves Harriet, a vengeful mistress discarded as part of Hal's reformation ('Has he not left me, like a common Creature, / And *paid* me, like a Prostitute? – Death find Him!', p. 10). The niece of Lord Scroop, Harriet joins the traitors and the Dauphin in a plot to bring about Henry's ruin. She later dresses as a man to dissuade Princess Catherine from a proposed marriage to Henry which would end the war. The Princess, for her part, objects strongly to her father's plan to 'Hang me out, / Like a shook Flagg of Truce!' (p. 18). However, it transpires

[15]

that the real reason for Catherine's reluctance is that she is already in love with an anonymous English gentleman who visited the French court the year before – and who naturally turns out to have been Henry himself. The disguised Harriet is captured and brought before Henry; love prompts her to reveal the treason, and stab herself. The Dauphin's pride and vanity break off the peace negotiations and bring on the battle of Agincourt.

Interestingly, Hill, unlike Shakespeare, spells out the tactics which brought the historical English victory. Anticipating the Victorian fashion for authenticity, Hill carefully researched his battle scenes:

> The Ground, we cover, by yon Village fenc'd,
> Secures our Rear; – On either Flank, strong Hedges,
> And deep-trench'd Ditches, guard us from Approach:
> Line these with chosen Bands of *English* Archers,
> And let *Sir Walter Orpington* command them.

(p. 55)

Hill was also ahead of his time in his insistence on historically accurate and realistic costuming. When his play *The Generous Traitor*, or *Aethelwold*, was to be staged at Drury Lane in 1731, he carefully documented the style of dress he desired, and in his theatrical paper *The Prompter* he published a manifesto advocating accurate costuming. 'An old Roman cou'd never with any Propriety, be made to look like a Modern Frenchman', and therefore when 'Persons of Rank and Figure are introduc'd upon the stage, they shou'd be cloath'd so as to represent Themselves, and not the Patchwork Inconsistencies of their Management' (Nagler, pp. 391-3). It is likely that the productions of Hill's *Henry V* were in keeping with his historical sensibilities, despite the absurdity of the love-plot.

Hill's adaptation reflects the anti-French feeling that ran high in England after the War of the Spanish Succession. France and Scotland played key roles in the series of Jacobite rebellions which ran through the first half of the eighteenth century, despite the Act of Union between England and Scotland in 1707. At the battle of Agincourt the Genius of England sings a song which concludes with a pointed ideological message:

> *Hark! Hark! – 'tis done!*
> *The Day is won!*
> *They bend! they break! the fainting* Gauls *give way!*

And yield, reluctant, to their Victor's Sway!
Happy Albion! – *strong, to gain!*
Let Union teach Thee, not to win, in vain!

(p. 57)

Hill's adaptation clearly tailors Shakespeare's play not only to audience demands for romantic intrigue, but to the volatile political situation of the time. Hill exhorts eighteenth-century England to remain firm in its relations with its fifteenth-century enemies, the French and the Scots. In 1746 Hill's version was adapted as a one-act play, *The Conspiracy Discovered, or, French Policy Defeated*, which made explicit links between the three traitors and the Lords Kilmarnock, Cromarty and Balmerino, then on trial for their roles in the Jacobite rebellion of 1745 (Gurr, pp. 43-4).

In terms of its political message, Hill's version was unquestionably conservative; however, the play has some surprisingly transgressive aspects, particularly in the female roles. Notwithstanding their fates, both Harriet and Catherine have strong rhetoric resisting the male exchange of women's bodies for political purposes – and the epilogue, spoken by the actress of Catherine, is startlingly subversive. Like Shakespeare's Chorus, Mrs Oldfield reminds the audience of the loss of Henry's gains under Henry the Sixth – but she places the blame on the former Henry's sexual inadequacy:

Tho' bold, in War, *His Feats, in* Love, *were faint!*
And this fam'd Champion *gave the world a* – Saint!
There *was a* Bliss! – *Oh! How was* Kate *mistaken!*
Such thund'ring Fame *must* mighty Hopes *awaken:*
But, tir'd with Action, Her Heroick *Lover*
Was found, in Peace, *and* Wedlock, *no great* Mover.

(p. 67)

Perhaps one-third of Hill's version is Shakespeare's text, liberally altered and redistributed. The comics are cut; the Chorus's speeches are shared among Henry, Exeter and even the traitors; Catherine gets a version of 'Upon the King'; and the defeated Dauphin suffers the indignity of saying Henry's 'Heaven, thy arm was here'. Some of Hill's adaptation is indisputably awful, as for instance Henry's response to Harriet's death: 'Her straining Eyes half burst their watry Balls! / Vainly they glare, to snatch a parting Look! / And Love, convulsive, shakes her struggling Bosom' (p. 43). Yet the play on the whole stands as a fascinating instance of the way Shakespeare is refashioned in performance in response to changing cultural values.

[17]

Hill's *Henry V* enjoyed revivals in 1735-36 and 1746; and while Shakespeare's *Henry V* was revived in 1738, it was not a particular success in the first half of the eighteenth century. David Garrick, the leading actor of the period, never played Henry, although he took the Chorus's speeches (as himself) for five performances at Drury Lane in 1747. Spranger Barry and William 'Gentleman' Smith both played Henry successfully at Covent Garden, but the first actor since Shakespeare's time to place a real stamp on the part was John Philip Kemble. He eliminated the choruses entirely in his version, but played a fairly full Shakespearian text. His was what A. C. Sprague has termed a 'pre-archaeological production', with modern furniture, anachronistic costuming, and inaccurate weaponry (p. 93). The production, revived several times between 1789 and 1806, was tailored to make Henry as attractive as possible: the threats to Harfleur were all but eliminated, Henry gave no sanction to Bardolph's reported execution, and the prayer before Agincourt ended with 'More will I do', removing Henry's acknowledgement of the worthlessness of his penance. Kemble played the part with a dignified royal bearing, but his biographer James Boaden noted that 'his occasional reversions to the "mad wag," the "sweet young prince," had a singular charm' (Shattuck, *Henry V*, in *Promptbooks*, p. i). Kemble played up the patriotism in response to war with France, donating box-office receipts to the Patriotic Fund and ending performances with an 'Occasional Address to the Volunteers' which blurred actor and character, play and history. For maximum histrionic effect, Kemble moved the Harfleur speech to the Battle of Agincourt and added some ringing patriotic rhetoric:

> Were the French twice the number that they are,
> We would cut a passage through them to our home,
> Or tear the lions out of England's coat.
>
> (Shattuck, p. 36)

Such additions were not uncommon during the threat of a French invasion. In 1804, the actor playing Henry in Manchester, one Mr Huddard, made a slight textual emendation to give the play extra patriotic force. According to the Manchester *Townsman*, Huddard's Henry rallied his troops before Harfleur with the cry, 'God for Harry, England, and *King George!*' (Sprague, p. 92).

During the Romantic period, *Henry V* and its hero came under attack from iconoclastic young critics like William Hazlitt and

Leigh Hunt. Hazlitt's denunciation, published in 1817 in *Charac-ters of Shakespear's Plays*, is the first powerful statement of the opposition view of Henry:

> Henry V is a very favourite monarch with the English nation, and he appears to have been also a favourite with Shakespear, who labours hard to apologize for the actions of the king.... in public affairs, he seemed to have no idea of any rule of right and wrong, but brute force, glossed over with a little religious hypocrisy and archiepiscopal advice.... Henry, because he did not know how to govern his own kingdom, determined to make war upon his neigh-bours. Because his own title to the crown was doubtful, he laid claim to that of France.... Henry declares his resolution 'when France is his, to bend it to our awe, or break it all to pieces' – a resolution worthy of a conqueror, to destroy all that he cannot enslave; and what adds to the joke, he lays all the blame of the con-sequences of his ambition on those who will not submit tamely to his tyranny. (Hazlitt, pp. 285-6)

The great actor of the period, Edmund Kean, only attempted Henry when he was in his final decline; unable to remember more than four consecutive lines, he was finally booed off the stage.

The increasing conservatism and antiquarianism of the Victorian age brought *Henry V* back into popularity as a patriotic pageant. The actor-manager William Charles Macready had one of his greatest successes with it in his farewell season at Covent Garden in 1839. Macready restored the choruses, delivered by an actor dressed as Time and illustrated with spectacular dioramas by the painter Clarkson Stanfield. These tableaux included the fleet leaving Southampton, the siege of Harfleur and Henry's triumphant return to London. Macready cut the lines about the 'rough cockpit' and 'wooden O'. Samuel Phelps, who played Exeter and Burgundy for Macready, carried scenic spectacle even further with his elaborate storming of Harfleur at Sadler's Wells in 1852.

The grandest of the Victorian productions was that of Charles Kean at the Princess's Theatre in 1859. Kean was a Fellow of the Royal Society of Antiquaries and a specialist in what he called 'the illustration of Shakespeare', a task he described with the lofty rhetoric of the British Empire:

> Impressed with the belief that the genius of Shakespeare soars above all rivalry; that he is the most marvellous writer the world has ever known; and that his works contain stores of wisdom, intellectual and moral, I cannot but hope that one who has toiled

for so many years, in admiring sincerity, to spread abroad amongst the multitude these invaluable gems, may, at least, be considered as an honest labourer, adding his mite to the great cause of civilization and educational progress. (Cole, p. 340)

The passage above appeared in the playbills for *Henry V*, which Kean chose as his farewell production at the Princess's. The fulsomeness of Kean's biographer, writing the following year, gives an indication of the tone of the production: '[Henry's] short reign may be looked on with unmingled satisfaction, as an epoch of glory.... The remembrance of past heroism is a wholesome spur to national pride, a sound guarantee for the future' (Cole, pp. 341-2).

Kean's production used barely half the text, but none the less ran more than four hours. He played a stolid, stalwart Henry himself, and his wife played the Chorus as Clio, Muse of History. His staging was of an unprecedented scale, using literally hundreds of extras for the siege of Harfleur. This episode was one of the highlights of the production:

> The assault on Harfleur, which opens the third act; the desperate resistance of the French garrison; the close conflict on the ramparts; the practice of the rude artillery of the day, with the advance of other besieging engines; and the final entry of the victorious assailants through the breach, – formed together the most marvellous realization of war, in its deadliest phase, that imitative art has ever attempted. (Cole, p. 344)

Despite its antiquarian specificity ('the rude artillery of the day'), the battle had a contemporary resonance in the years following the Crimean War: Cole reports that Kean's staging 'vividly embodied the carrying of the Malakoff' (p. 344).

Kean's other spectacular innovation was his staging of Henry's return to London, described in the fifth-act Chorus. Kean had introduced a pageant of the deposed Richard and triumphant Bolingbroke riding through the streets in his 1862 *Richard II*; for *Henry V* he elaborated this idea into a huge crowd scene at London Bridge, with Henry entering on horseback while virgins flocked round him and angels showered him with gold (Brennan, p. xix). Despite these hagiographic touches, the scene had all the archaeological specificity of Kean's other work: his biographer praises him for 'carefully following the account of an eye-witness, whose MS. has been preserved' (Cole, p. 346).

Another production in the spectacular tradition was Charles

Calvert's in Manchester in 1872. Theatre historian Richard Foulkes points out that in many respects Calvert's production was the first to acknowledge the anti-war aspects of the play. Calvert had himself been recently active in raising funds and public sympathies for victims of the Franco-Prussian conflict, presenting, as a benefit, a series of tableaux depicting the horrors of war and the blessings of peace. As Foulkes points out, 'The Victorian theatre's preoccupation with antiquarianism is often equated with a total inability to make links between contemporary events and Shakespeare's plays. But in 1872 not even the most blinkered antiquarian could have been unaware of the parallel between recent events and King Henry's expedition to France' (p. 28). The French were suddenly victims rather than enemies: and Calvert's production to some extent reflected this. For once, Henry's threats to Harfleur retained the 'shrill-shrieking daughters' and 'naked infants spitted upon pikes', rendered with such conviction, according to Foulkes, 'that the horrors in store were powerfully impressed not only on the inmates of Harfleur, but also upon the audience, many of whom must have found themselves recalling reports of the Franco-Prussian war' (p. 29). Calvert cut 1200 lines, but he kept such potentially negative moments as the executions of the traitors, Bardolph and the French prisoners. Finally, Calvert followed Kean in presenting a tableau of Henry's return to London, but his crowd had a very mixed response to the returning conqueror, leading the *Examiner and Times* critic to speculate that many were either 'faithful adherents of Richard the Second or members of the peace party' (Foulkes, p. 32). The returning soldiers were wounded and fatigued, and crowds of women anxiously scanned their faces looking for their menfolk. An illustration of Calvert's tableau prominently features a soldier and a circle of townsfolk gathered around a fainting woman who has just learned of the death of a loved one. In contrast to Kean's heroic pageant, Calvert's production was informed by a realistic attitude to war shaped by contemporary events.

Calvert's production was exported to New York and eventually played at Drury Lane in 1879. The leading role was taken over by George Rignold, a matinée idol who took a more traditional, heroic line on the part, riding a white horse called Crispin during the battle scenes. The heroic interpretation was given renewed prominence during the Boer war. In 1900 Lewis Waller, Frank Benson and Richard Mansfield all gave productions competing in

1 Lewis Waller as a heroic Edwardian Henry V, *c.* 1910.

their patriotic fervor, and Sidney Lee published an article called 'Shakespeare and Patriotism' which made the French responsible for the atrocities threatened by Henry at Harfleur:

> It is only when a defeated enemy declines to acknowledge the obvious ruin of his fortunes that a sane and practical patriotism defends resort on the part of the conqueror to the grimmest measure of severity. The healthy instinct stiffens the grip on the justly won fruits of victory. (quoted in Sprague, p. 95)

Lewis Waller's reading of the part was 'that of an Edwardian romantic-declamatory actor who never merely stepped on the stage but hurtled upon it; an uncomplicated blazon' (Trewin, p. 148). Benson's production was so celebratory of Englishness that Max Beerbohm compared it to a university cricket match: 'One was constantly inclined to shout, "Well played, sir! Well played *indeed!*"' (Beaumann, *RSC*, p. 43). And Richard Mansfield, an American, chose the play because of

> its virile and healthy tone (so diametrically in contrast to many of the performances now current), the nobility of its language, the breadth and power of which is not equalled by any living poet, the lesson it teaches of Godliness, honour, loyalty, courage, cheerfulness and perseverence, its beneficial influence upon young and old; the opportunity it affords for a pictorial representation of the costumes and armour, manners and customs, of that interesting period. (pp. xi–xii)

Mansfield' s cuts are subtle but telling. Williams's image of the 'arms and legs and heads chopped off in a battle' joining together and accusing the King is neatly excised from the middle of his speech. The first order to kill the prisoners – before the massacre of the boys – is likewise removed. In his introduction Mansfield rather charmingly acknowledges the distaste with which modern spectators may view Henry's words and actions. Referring to the 'Upon the King' speech, he concedes that, 'As ninety-nine out of a hundred men sweat in the eye of Phoebus all day and wind up days of toil with nights of sleep, we cannot expect much sympathy from them for the lamentations of Henry'. However, he says, 'we must remember that when Shakespeare wrote, affairs were managed rather differently', and he feels it his duty to make Shakespeare's Henry more palatable: 'no matter how great the author, the actor must often disguise him and in a manner excuse him to his audience'. Mansfield relies on the notion that in the

[23]

past Henry's actions would have had a uniformly favourable response: 'He tells God that he has five hundred poor in yearly pay and that he has built two chantries and will do still more if God will help him to thrash the French. This was all then the custom of those times' (pp. xiii–xiv). To Mansfield there is no question that the play is intended to teach a 'lesson' of 'Godliness, honour, loyalty, courage, cheerfulness and perseverance', and anything about it that prompts a different response does so because of our own misunderstanding, and should be eliminated or 'excused'.

Mansfield's perception that some people would respond negatively to Henry was borne out in the criticism of the period. Shaw, in *Our Theatres in the Nineties*, condemned Shakespeare for attempting 'to thrust such a Jingo hero as his Harry V down our throats' (Sprague, p. 95). Walter Pater and W. B. Yeats both preferred Richard II to Henry V, Yeats calling Henry 'a ripened Fortinbras' who is 'as remorseless and undistinguished as some natural force' (Beaumann, *Henry V*, p. 12 and Sprague, p. 96). Yet this negative criticism had little effect on stage productions, which tended to remain in the grand heroic vein. One important exception was William Poel's experiment with open staging in 1901, using a full text, a bare stage and a brisk and modest Chorus dressed like an Elizabethan student. After the First World War, views of the play began to darken even further; in 1919 Gerald Gould first asserted that *Henry V* is ironic, 'a satire on monarchical government, on imperialism, on the baser kinds of "patriotism," and on war' (Brennan, p. xxxix). Laurence Olivier's 1937 Henry at the Old Vic, on which he based his film interpretation, was considered grave and underplayed by contrast to the prevailing tradition: he was noted by *The Times* for his thoughtfulness and lack of rant (7 April 1937). As I shall discuss in the next chapter, his film version combines many aspects of the heroic, pictorial Victorian tradition with an awareness of the problems the text presents, beginning the move toward a complex twentieth-century Henry.

CHAPTER II

This star of England:
Laurence Olivier (1944)

Laurence Olivier's film *Henry V* provides an inevitable starting point for a discussion of modern performance interpretations of the play. This film is the most widely seen and influential performance of the century; virtually all the subsequent productions discussed in this book consciously positioned themselves against it. While it is also, in terms of textual licence and directorial intervention, one of the most radical revisions, it carries on a performance tradition that is both conservative and patriotic. As a wartime commission dedicated to the British forces of the D-Day landings, Olivier's *Henry V* unquestionably has an ideological component, but its exploration of the theatrical and cinematic media makes it a fascinating and complex film as well as a rousing patriotic adventure story.

The fact that Olivier's version of *Henry V* is a film necessarily involves it in aesthetic problems different from those faced by stage interpretations. A film director has at his or her disposal a much different range of techniques and methods for implementing the interpretation intended. Chief among these is a much closer control over the audience's point of view. Every theatregoer sees a different play, even within one performance; every filmgoer sees essentially the same film, even years after it was made. Of course, the element of reception remains crucial, because the film-maker cannot guarantee that each viewer will interpret a given shot in a given way; but he or she has much greater control over what the viewer is actually interpreting. A theatre director can call attention, by a gesture, to the response of one of the characters on stage to a given line; but the film director, with a reaction shot, can prevent the viewer from looking at anything else. Combined with the specificity of the camera eye is its mobility: it can approach an actor or object from any angle, direction or distance, and can record the action in a limitless number of locations.

The primarily visual nature of the film medium offers the possibility of replacing verbal elements in Shakespeare's text with cinemagraphic ones: in their films of *Hamlet*, both Grigori Kozintsev and Franco Zeffirelli show Ophelia's drowning and the letter-switching that dooms Rosencrantz and Guildenstern. The technical capabilities of the medium allow very intimate acting in amplified closeups, extensive use of exactly timed music, and such effects as voice-over for the soliloquies in Olivier's *Hamlet*, or the blurring of focus just preceding the appearance of the Ghost. The possibilities of editing and montage allow sudden transpositions of space and time, as in Olivier's Agincourt charge and Branagh's Falstaff flashbacks, both to be discussed later. However, Elizabethan dramaturgy, with its frequent, fluid scene changes, is in some ways closer to the cinema than to fourth-wall naturalistic drama. Olivier has argued that 'Shakespeare, in a way, "wrote for the films." His splitting up of the action into a multitude of small scenes is almost an anticipation of film technique, and more than one of his plays seems to chafe against the cramping restrictions of the stage' (Olivier, *Henry V*, foreword).

There are unquestionably differences between film and Shakespearian theatre which will affect a director's choices. The greater possibilities for visual expression, and the corresponding audience impatience with extensive passages of text, necessarily bear on any film adaptation of Shakespeare. Similarly, films generally aim for a wider audience less aware of the text and production history, and they are packaged and marketed in a different way. Nevertheless, there are enough connections between the media to make translation possible, and to make the interpretive enterprises equivalent.

Critical attention to Olivier's *Henry V* has been divided between its use of the film medium and its ideological tendencies; in fact, of course, the two are intertwined. The choices made in translating a play to the screen are bound up with the choices made in interpreting that play. When the film was first shown in Britain in 1944 and in America in 1946, critics placed less emphasis on its ideological content than on its status as a film version of Shakespeare, from some points of view the first successful one. The critical debate centred on the film's translation between media rather than on interpretive choices. London theatre critic James Agate bemoaned the film's use of mobile cameras and location shooting: 'All the early part struck me as enchanting. But when the film flew, so to speak, out of the window, Shakespeare, as far as I am concerned, walked out of the door' (*Times*, 3 December 1944). Roger Manvell, by contrast, regretted that 'this film could not make full use of the resources of the cinema since it was bound to the verbal wheel of Shakespeare's text written for a rhetorical theatre' (Geduld, p. 76). On the other hand, James E. Phillips praised it for 'the success with which an appealing and even exciting show is made out of material not generally regarded as the most promising Shakespeare wrote' (Geduld, p. 80). Andre Bazin went so far as to say that 'there is more cinema, and great cinema at that, in *Henry V* than in 90% of original scripts' (Bazin, p. 116).

In the 1960s and 1970s critics began to place more emphasis on the film's 'propagandistic' purpose and the extent to which it neutralised the (newly rediscovered) darker aspects of Henry's character: 'The *raisons d'être* [of Olivier's film] are the prestige of Shakespeare, a big battle, a rousing jingoism, and a shaky parallel to contemporary events' (Durgnat, *Mirror, p.* 109). The film's most virulent critic, Gordon Beauchamp, complained that 'Olivier has systematically and tendentiously gutted *Henry V*', leaving a 'pasty patriotic ragout' (p. 228). More recently, there has been a swing back in the other direction, with many critics asserting that the film's primary concern is not with war and patriotism but with the nature of theatrical and cinematic art. Ace G. Pilkington argues that the film 'makes possible a revised evaluation of the play itself, suggesting that it is not exclusively or even primarily about war and that the speeches of Henry and the Chorus have more to do with theatrical than patriotic victories' (p. 129). The Marxist critic Graham Holderness has observed how the film's emphasis on theatrical and cinematic artifice destabilises the apparently traditional reading of the King. As Holderness writes, 'The decision to incorporate into the film devices and aesthetic strategies derived from the dramatic technique of the Chorus provides the film with an ideological tendency which is quite different from – potentially contrary to – its ideology of patriotism, national unity, and just war' (*Shakespeare's History*, p. 186).

This range of readings attests partly to the inevitable historical oscillation of interpretation. It also underlines the way interpretation is a function of emphasis. The various critics understand the film differently according to which elements of it they choose to weigh most heavily. Those reading it as propaganda focus on its presentation of Henry and the war, and its elimination of discordant elements. Other critics find a more subtle form of patriotism in the presentation of an idealised Merrie England in the framing scenes of Shakespeare's Globe: 'If there is a part of the film Olivier consciously shaped to help the war effort, it is this England of the mind, this homage to Shakespeare, rather than any specific additions to or deletions from the text' (Pilkington, p. 114). Ralph Berry agrees that 'The propaganda is of an extraordinarily subtle and advanced quality, relying like all good propaganda on positive assertions' (*Changing Styles*, p. 68). Other critics who question the film's propaganda role focus on the parts of the film dealing not with the war but with the nature of Shakespearean drama and its relation to cinema: 'Preoccupation with Henry's war makes us forget how great a part of the film's experience these other things are, how long and elaborate the Globe sequence is, or how prominent a role Chorus and his language play throughout' (Silviria, p. 90). As Holderness argues, 'to see the film as concerned simply to offer a "straight" patriotic version of *Henry V* is to interpret selected parts rather than the film's significant whole' (*Shakespeare's History*, p. 190).

My own reading of the film attempts to take all these different elements into account. I think *Henry V* is a brilliant and sophisticated film that, while carrying over the play's exploration of role-playing and reality in an exciting and original way, nevertheless presents a progression toward the unity, in an ideal Henry, of an ideal England. While Olivier to a considerable extent acknowledges the divisions and complexities in the text's style and substance, the film works to reconcile those divisions (play/history, theatre/cinema, King/common man, war/peace, England/France, even, perhaps, male/female) in the figure of Henry/Burbage/Olivier, who emerges unbesmirched as the Star of England. Further, Olivier's treatment of the play has had profound effects, one way or the other, on every major English-language version since.

The film's most immediately distinctive feature is its structure. It begins in Shakespeare's London at a performance in the Globe, moves through a series of theatrical indoor sets to location shooting for the battle of Agincourt, and then in a more condensed way reverses the process. Despite the elegant symmetry of this structure, the transitions of style are not rigid or fully ordered; while there is a general movement toward cinematic naturalism, both 'theatrical' and 'cinematic' elements are evident throughout, and some of the transitional scenes are rather a hodge-podge. The script is severely cut: of the more than 3000 lines of the Folio text, only 1505 remain in Olivier's screenplay. Harry Geduld divides the cuts into six categories, many with ideological implications:

> (1) background, including both antecedent action and foreshadowing of events that follow the action of the play; (2) much elaboration of idea, argument and detail; (3) all suggestions that England is endangered by internal conspiracy or that Scotland is a potential threat; (4) much material involving the comic characters; (5) passages and incidents revealing aspects of Henry's character unlikely to be attractive to modern audiences; (6) miscellaneous material involving the French, including lines that show the French nobles to be more spirited, worthy adversaries than the rather weak, brash figures they are made to appear in the film. (p. 48)

Pilkington has objected that not all these cuts are necessarily ideologically motivated: 'it is obvious that if one is willing to cut more than half the play, a great many lines must vanish from somewhere' (p. 112). The exclusion of the Scottish question can certainly be justified on dramatic grounds, as can that of the comic material; and while the French king is certainly weakened, Dale Silviria convincingly argues that in the night scene before Agincourt, Olivier's French are more serious and impressive than Shakespeare's (pp. 94-5). Nevertheless, it is clear that many of the cuts – the traitors scene, the execution of Bardolph, Henry's boasting, the order to kill the prisoners, the joke on Williams – have the effect of neutralising a potentially negative reading of Henry.

The film opens with a handbill, blowing in the sky, advertising a performance at the Globe playhouse on 1 May 1600 of *Henry V* by 'Will Shakespeare'. The camera pans down to an aerial shot of a model of Elizabethan London based on the Visscher engraving, focusing first on the Tower. The sky is blue, the distant hills green, the Thames glassy, and the roofs of London red under picturesque little wisps of white smoke. The camera tracks back over London Bridge toward the south-west, revealing the Globe and the 'Beere bayting' house. The latter, in the foreground, seems at first to be the focus of attention, but then the camera moves to the right and focuses in on the Globe, where a tiny flag is hoisted to announce the performance. The holiday occasion, pristine weather and toy-kingdom quality of the model prepare us for the idealised version of Elizabethan London that the Globe scenes give us. The elegiac quality of the shot would have been all the more poignant to a London film audience of 1944, who had seen many such aerial city views in newsreels of bomb devastation (Davies, p. 30).

The Globe, revealed in a long mobile shot that descends into and pans round its interior, is a detailed evocation of the ordered yet vigorous society idealised in Tillyard's notion of 'The Elizabethan World Picture'. All the levels of this harmonious commonwealth are present, from the buxom orange-seller to the haughty nobleman who declines her wares and goes to take his seat on the stage. The Globe audience, diverse and energetic, represents the first celebration of a quality of Englishness that Olivier will return to throughout the play. As Jack Jorgens notes, 'Our impression of the English is bound up with Olivier's robust reconstruction of the Globe with its dynamic actors and vigorous audience. It is a bustling, lively, democratic place in the sense that commoners, gentlemen and nobles watch the same play – a quality which carries over into Henry's fellowship with his soldiers in France' (p. 123). Nevertheless, James Agee is not wrong to feel the quaint Globe scenes are presented in a 'subtly patronizing way', in their treatment of both audience and performance (p. 208). Olivier is at least partly interested in contrasting the coarse but vigorous theatre of the past with the subtler, more versatile modern cinema.

The Chorus, Leslie Banks, plays his opening speech in a grand rhetorical style with many a flourish. Midway through the speech, however, Banks approaches the camera, which has come to rest in a position from which none of the Globe audience is visible, and addresses it directly with the line 'On your imaginary forces work' (I.Chorus.18). Here William Walton's symphonic score is heard for the first time, in contrast to the period fanfares we have heard (and seen) played by the Globe's musicians. For a moment the Globe framework is transcended, the Globe audience is forgotten, and the Chorus's words assume naturalistically spoken immediacy and musically underscored importance in the language of contemporary cinema. The moment passes quickly, but it establishes a distance between the cinematic style used later in the film and the overblown acting of the Globe.

The playhouse audience remains an important feature when the play proper begins with the scene between Canterbury and Ely, played on the balcony. The audience's laughter, coughs and mocking interjections continually remind us of their presence, and when Canterbury mentions Falstaff in interpolated lines from *2 Henry IV*, we see them roar with approval in a high-angle shot from Canterbury's point of view. They loudly boo Falstaff's banishment, an interesting choice which places them, at least initially, at odds with the reformed Henry. He is first introduced to us backstage after a Hogarthian but wholesome scene of hurried actorly preparations. As a procession of lords and clerics files past in a fanfared entrance, Olivier/Burbage steps into the left fore-ground and nervously clears his throat before following them on to welcoming applause. The initial presentation of the King as a nervous actor allows some space for Holderness's critical reading of Henry as theatrical player-king. On the other hand, it serves to point up the parallel projects of Burbage, Henry and Olivier in undertaking a difficult challenge against the odds.

Aside from the celebration of an ideal England and the empha-sis on theatricality, the most important interpretive choices in the Globe sequence involve the 'Salic Law' speech. Olivier presents the two bishops as comically incompetent actors, with Felix Aylmer's pedantic, forgetful Canterbury playing straight man to Robert Helpmann's fey and feckless Ely. Canterbury's validation of Henry's claim to France is obscured by slapstick buffoonery involving a huge pile of documents, which all three actors end up scrabbling on their knees to sort out. Henry's intermittent attempt to interrupt the Archbishop causes a moment of confusion as to whether the free-for-all might not be some intended part of the broad Globe performance, but, given that the bishops' offstage behaviour is equally bumbling, it seems that we are meant to be witnessing a genuine stage disaster. The effect of this sequence is certainly to distract attention from the flimsy legal justification of Henry's claim to France, and many critics have interpreted this as its intention: as Ralph Berry observes, Ely is 'Olivier's agent for obscuring the *Realpolitik* of I,i and I,ii.... It is a superbly comic expedient, and it completely dissolves the serious intent of the scene' (*Changing Styles*, p. 68). On the other hand, Geduld (pp. 28-9), Pilkington (pp. 112-14), Silviria (pp. 83-6) and Davies (p. 27) have all acknowledged other possible interpretations, chiefly to do with Olivier's exploration of the differences between theatre and cinema. As Geduld argues, the comic bumbling is part of 'a deliberate "put-down" of theatre in favor of film as a medium for the kind of dramatic work that is being presented' (p. 28). What-

2 The Salic Law scene in the Globe Theatre, from Laurence Olivier's 1944 film of *Henry V*. Felix Aylmer as Canterbury, Olivier as Henry, Robert Helpmann as Ely

ever its intentions, the effect is to obscure Canterbury's specious justification for Henry's war, as Geduld acknowledges: 'By the time the French ambassador arrives, somehow or other Henry's forthcoming campaign seems to have been "justified" without our noticing precisely how' (p. 29).

Actually, Olivier takes care to give Henry at least cinematic justification. After Canterbury has finished his disquisition, the lengthy last part of which has been given in a single front shot, we suddenly hear Exeter's voice from off screen: 'Gracious Lord, stand for your own.' The camera cuts to a new angle, one we have not previously seen, and one which again occludes the sense of the theatrical occasion. The shot is a medium closeup of Nicholas Hannen's Exeter, a noble, persuasive figure in a dark red velvet doublet (the richest colour yet seen in the film), as he continues his speech urging Henry to invoke the spirit of his 'mighty ancestors'. At the mention of Edward, the Black Prince, the camera cuts back to Henry in close up, and we see the effect this invocation has on him. Another cut reveals the richly costumed and stately figures of Salisbury and Westmoreland as they urge Henry to emulate 'the former lions of [his] blood'. Suddenly a group of grave and noble men, strongly framed in richly coloured shots apparently miles from the silly clerics and jeering groundlings, are asking their sovereign to lead them in a heroic enterprise for the glory of England. Peter Donaldson notes how in this scene Olivier anticipates Robert Weimann's theory of the *locus* or upstage structure as the specific, ceremonial background to serious events and the *platea*, or forestage, as an unlocalised site for clowning and playing to the audience (p. 5). The cinematic shots of Exeter and the lords introduce the serious, more realistic world of the film's later scenes.

Henry's speech to the French ambassador is another instance of Olivier transcending the Globe framework. Agee admitted that here, 'in flashes', Olivier acknowledged 'that the Elizabethan stage at its best was in its own terms as good as the theater or the screen can ever hope to be' (p. 208). Olivier begins the speech seated in his throne in closeup – again, the cinematic perspective. In response to the Dauphin's joke, Olivier gives a wry, naturalistic half-smile that would have been imperceptible to most Globe spectators. Then, in one of Olivier's most celebrated cinematic effects, the camera tracks backward as Olivier builds his speech in tones of rising anger. Olivier explained to Roger Manvell how he got the idea for this technique:

The film climax is the close-up; the Shakespearean climax is a fine gesture and a loud voice. I remember going to George Cukor's *Romeo and Juliet*. As a film director he did what seemed the right thing when he took the potion scene with Norma Shearer – he crept right up to a huge head, the ordinary film climax.... At the moment of climax she was acting very smally because the camera was near. That was not how it should have been. So the very first test I made for *Henry V* I tried to see how it would work in reverse. It was the scene with the French Ambassador, and as I raised my voice the camera went back – the exact opposite technique to that in *Romeo and Juliet* – and I have done that ever since. (Manvell, pp. 37-38)

The back-tracking camera allows a proper 'Shakespearian' (i.e. theatrical) climax within the cinematic medium. It has a further effect beyond that, as Graham Holderness notes:

The movement from close-up to long-shot doesn't just allow scope for the actor to intensify his performance; it also, more fundamentally, increases the size and multiplies the content of the frame: it supplies more abundance of visual detail thereby bringing more objects, images and characters into significant relationship. (*Shakespeare's History*, p. 189)

Holderness argues that in this case the long-shot, which shows Henry playing flamboyantly to his onstage and offstage audiences, questions the King's authority by revealing him as a theatrical showman. At any rate it does place Henry's rhetoric back in the context of an Elizabethan stage performance. Indeed, for much of the opening sequence, the interaction of actors and audience – the theatrical event itself – is the primary subject matter. These scenes serve to get the action off to a vigorous start without getting caught up in the political background to the war; they serve to overstate the theatricality of the performance and so prepare the way for a favourable reception of the cinematic naturalism to follow; and finally, they serve to present the lively, integrated English society that Olivier celebrates in its fifteenth-, sixteenth- and twentieth-century manifestations.

As already noted, Olivier cuts much of the material relating to the comic characters. These cuts are dramatically justifiable, as much of the humour is difficult to communicate to a modern audience, particularly a film audience with little or no knowledge of the *Henry IV* background. What remains of Pistol and his crew can be divided into three segments, each of them serving different purposes. The initial scene serves to further flesh out Olivier's picture of Merrie England in the Globe; the death of Falstaff introduces a minor key which will be heard again on Agincourt Eve; and Pistol's antics in France help to set off the bravery and good nature of the rest of the English force.

The first comic scene, II.i, is the last set in the Globe. It calls attention to the earthier elements of Olivier's England. It begins in a sudden downpour, a realistic corrective to the cloudless sky of the opening model shot. Stagehands strew straw on the stage, the boy hangs a sign announcing the Boar's Head and a coarse curtain is drawn over the ornate backdrop of the court scenes. Nym and Bardolph play in a broad grotesque style, with the latter affecting a comic stutter. But it is Pistol and his wife, a boy Quickly, who fully set the tone for the scene, playing directly to the audience and laughing at their own bawdy jokes. Robert Newton's Pistol is particularly flamboyant, leering and goggling indulgently to the groundlings. Audience reaction helps carry the scene by functioning like a sit-com laugh-track. The scene becomes about the Globe environment itself: the chief action is between the players and the groundlings rather than between the characters on stage. Irrepressible vitality and a great capacity for rough but harmless fun are foregrounded as predominant characteristics of the English folk. At the mentions of Falstaff's illness, Walton's cinematic score intrudes, hinting of sentiment to come; but the scene ends with the players bowing to loud applause rather than with any sombre note. The lively atmosphere of the Globe cannot take death too seriously.

Accordingly, the scene concerned with Falstaff's death is played in a very different style. It is set in and in front of a studio Boar's Head which quotes the Globe façade in general structure but is much more naturalistic. It is also the only night scene in the film except for the Agincourt Eve sequence. It begins with the camera tracking in through the open window of the upper story to show an old, delirious Falstaff lying in bed in a candlelit interior reminiscent of Dutch painting. Falstaff sits up and utters a few lines from *2 Henry IV*, ending with 'My King, my Jove, I speak to thee, my heart'. Olivier's voice, echoing in Falstaff's memory, is heard off-camera, as we track in to see Falstaff's reaction to the 'I know thee not, old man' speech. After, 'I have turned away my former self / So shall I those that kept me company', Falstaff sinks back, fumbling with the sheets. The camera cuts to a low angle-shot showing Quickly – now a woman, Freda Jackson – reacting to the dying Falstaff. The film's shift to conventions of realism, necessary for the darkening tone, is marked by the gender-switch of the performer.

Shakespeare's actual scene II.iii is played in the street in front of the inn. It is a very static scene, with the actors posed in an emblematic grouping of solidarity in grief. Quickly plays the speech absolutely straight, very movingly, and avoids the innuendoes of the final lines. The emphasis on loss and sorrow seems strange in the midst of a colourful patriotic pageant, and many critics have commented on the way this scene qualifies the apparently traditionalist reading of the play. As Silviria notes, 'The death of Falstaff represents the one time that Olivier not only lets stand an equivocal aspect of Shakespeare's Henry but actually amplifies the damaging evidence' (p. 106). Falstaff does not appear at all in Shakespeare's play, and certainly not Henry's harsh rejection of him; what effect do they have inserted here? Graham Holderness feels that 'the immediate juxtaposition of this colourful pageant [Henry's departure from Southampton] with the melancholy chiaroscuro of Falstaff's death supplies an undertone of calculated cruelty to Henry's extravagant display of theatrical virtuosity' (*Shakespeare's History*, p. 191). The scene certainly indicates that there are human costs to Henry's enterprise, although (since the rejection takes place off screen) they are never too closely associated with Henry himself.

The remainder of the film shows us very little of these characters, although Pistol's leek-eating scene is retained. It is set up by Pistol's cowardly behaviour at Harfleur, where Fluellen beats him into the breach with his sword. Their other encounter, when Pistol pleads with Fluellen for Bardolph's life, was scripted but not shot; in the end Olivier cut Bardolph's death altogether (Pilkington, p. 106). In general, the accounts of cowardice and viciousness among Pistol and his crew are much reduced: the le Fer scene is gone, as is the boy's speech condemning their thievery, along with most other references to looting. Pistol's main function in the French scenes is as a contrast character, the exception who proves the rule: as the Constable is the only brave Frenchman, Pistol is the only cowardly Englishman. A comparison of the leek scene in the original treatment with the finished film suggests a general tidying-up. According to the treatment,

'The extent of after-battle looting is obvious', with both Fluellen and Gower 'tricked out' in clothes recognisable as belonging to the French lords, and Fluellen beats Pistol until he bleeds from the head and mouth (Pilkington, p. 105). In the film, only Pistol has looted (he wears the Constable's breastplate), and the beating is a cartoon comeuppance. The treatment reads like a more contemporary version, emphasising the brutality of the whole English army; in the finished film Pistol's misbehaviour and good-natured punishment serve to point up the honest, sportsmanlike values of the other soldiers.

The movement out of the Globe comes just after the first Falstaff scene, when the film begins a series of transitional scenes, mixing theatrical and cinematic conventions, before arriving at the realistic location shooting of Agincourt. The Chorus begins to phrase his speeches more naturalistically, and they come in shorter and shorter segments, as he loses his presence as mediator and becomes a cinematic voice-over. His presence, indeed, begins to become superfluous, as the film shows what he had asked the theatre audience to imagine. The last we see of him is in the speech describing the English fleet. At the beginning of the speech he is floating in a dark, misty void; at 'You stand upon the shore and thence behold / A city upon th'inconstant billows dancing' (III.Chorus.14-15) he turns his back to the camera and disappears, as a model shot of the fleet becomes visible through the mist.

The shot then dissolves to a vista of the French King's hilltop palace, and subsequently to an interior therein. The visual style for both is taken from the illuminations, by the brothers Limbourg, in *Les Très Riches Heures du duc de Berri*. This quotation is almost immediately wittily acknowledged when the French king, in his first speech, directly addresses the Duke of Berri (a 'ghost character' in Shakespeare's text), who is standing at a lectern, presumably inspecting his new book of hours. All of the French court scenes have the posed, graceful, fragile quality of medieval illuminations. As Ralph Berry notes, 'The stylized pictorial arrangements and their languid movements and poses identify the spirit of Charles VII's court: it is bored, overcivilized, decadent, a world away from the passion and vitality of the English' (*Changing Styles*, p. 69). Olivier spares no pains to contrast the French and English, following historical tradition in making the King, who in Shakespeare is a commanding figure, into a witless weakling. The Dauphin and lords are equally ineffectual – Orleans is first seen playing with a child's toy – and the only Frenchmen of spirit are Leo Genn's brave Constable and Ralph Truman's noble Montjoy. The contrast between nations is further stressed when Exeter, robed in rich red against the prevailing blues of the French, enters to issue his ultimatum in grave and measured tones.

Making the French weak but fairy-tale beautiful serves Olivier in two ways. It makes the English victory not only inevitable but necessary – these people obviously aren't fit to govern their country. Indeed, since the French seem to be *only* aristocrats, Henry's war assumes an element of class conflict, with the diverse and inclusive English society taking on the snooty French. The elegance and beauty of the French, however, make them a desirable addition to the English mixture, and their very lack of martial vigour makes this assimilation possible. As Berry notes, 'There is, at bottom, no enemy' (*Changing Styles*, p. 68). Raymond Durgnat points out how this fact complicates any easy reading of the film's propagandistic wartime associations: 'the English are the English but Agincourt is D-Day where the French are Germans until Henry courts Katherine, whereupon the French are probably the French' (*Films and Feelings*, p. 262). Actually, the French are far too likable to be the Germans, and Henry's courting of Katherine, and the uniting of the kingdoms, are made inevitable almost from the beginning. After Henry takes Harfleur – without uttering any of the text's threats about 'shrill-shrieking daughters', 'reverend heads dashed to the walls' or 'naked infants spitted upon pikes' (III.iii.35-8) – he walks past the pop-up book castle's wall and looks out over the verdant French countryside. Through a series of dissolves to Walton's music, the camera seems to lift Henry's gaze first to the distant French palace and then to the garden terrace where we see the Princess for the first time. It is as though fate, and film technique, are drawing them together.

Henry's gaze at the Princess is returned at the end of the scene. Before the English lesson, Katherine looks down into a courtyard to see Montjoy escorting Exeter and his party out through the gates. Their presence motivates Katherine's sudden interest in learning English. The scene is played with delicacy and charm as the ladies cut roses from the garden. At the end, Katherine looks over the walls to see the English party disappearing in the distance. This look could be read different ways: perhaps it indicates

[38]

her concern over the English, antlike in the distance, creeping into the 'best garden of the world' (V.ii.36). Nevertheless, a major effect of her gaze over the walls is to mirror, and in effect to answer, Henry's earlier look; Walton's gentle music supports this interpretation. By playing up the beauty of France and linking Henry with Katherine visually and musically, Olivier stresses the union of England and France rather than their discord – a meaningful interpretive choice in 1944.

Olivier's performance in the name part was essentially taken over from his stage performance for Tyrone Guthrie in 1937; he acknowledges in *On Acting* that this was the Henry 'which I was later to film' (p. 61). In preparing for the role, Olivier was reluctant to go for heroism:

> I didn't think it was the play for me at that time. It seemed wrong, I was frightened of the heroism. England had completely changed in the 1930s: the whole atmosphere of the country, which was frequently mirrored in the theatre, was against heroics. (p. 58)

After unsuccessfully attempting a low-key Henry, Olivier was persuaded to heroics by Guthrie and Ralph Richardson. Of the former, Olivier recalled that 'he pointed me in the direction I had fought against, and he was right'. But Olivier tried to avoid 'showing off; I played the man like a trumpet as clearly and truthfully as I knew how' (p. 61). In the film, Olivier achieves a mixture of heroism and sensitivity that hits all the grand notes of the role but deftly parries modern accusations of bombast with many subtle and deeply felt moments. The high rhetoric is played to the full in many cases. For the speech to the French ambassador, the Globe setting allows Olivier to go right over the top, playing directly to the galleries and ending with a bow. In 'Once more unto the breach' Olivier (again aided by the receding camera) is equally full-throated, but his giving the speech while managing a restive horse adds a note of naturalistic spontaneity. The martial rhetoric is unbated; and indeed, Olivier's acting annotations to this speech, quoted in *On Acting*, show a canny political insight remarkably in tune with modern interpretations of Henry as the manipulative player-king:

> *Change the tune to as natural a one as is humanly possible... Now take them with you, they want to come, climb the ladder... Now, like any good politician, speak to them collectively in such a way that they think you are speaking to them individually.* (pp. 62-3)

3 Olivier's Henry V at the Battle of Harfleur

These notes were published years after the event, of course, but they match up with Olivier's performance. The subtext of political manipulation which animates the lines cannot be detected in the face of the sincere and valiant king on the screen, however; Olivier/Henry is too good an actor to let it show through.

The high rhetoric of the tennis-ball and breach speeches is counterbalanced by many intimate and sensitive moments elsewhere in the film. Peter Donaldson has linked the sensitivity of Olivier's Henry with the film's other transgressions of gender boundaries:

Olivier's *Henry V* also intimates an integration of the feminine within the king's personality.... For this Henry V outward success is matched by an inward integration of a 'feminine' capacity for tenderness, nurturance, and intimacy. (pp. 14-15)

The *locus classicus* for these qualities in the film is the Agincourt Eve sequence, to be discussed below. But Olivier includes other such moments. He cuts the traitors at Southampton, but leaves Henry's enfranchisement of the slanderous prisoner, now an act of pure benevolence. Likewise, Henry carefully instructs Exeter to 'Use mercy to them all' at Harfleur, even though he has not threatened them with anything else. When Montjoy threatens him from horseback with the French king's message, the camera cuts to a medium close up of the standing Henry at the reference to 'his own person, kneeling at our feet, but a weak and worthless satisfaction' (III.vi.132-3). Olivier's expression is not of anger or defiance, but of quiet wonder, an awed recognition and acceptance of the course to which he has committed himself.

Along with martial valour and sensitivity, Olivier manifests other qualities peculiar to British conceptions of heroism in the first half of the twentieth century. His casual flair as he tosses his crown on to the back of his throne, his good sportsmanship in flinging a bag of coins to Montjoy, his unflappable cheerfulness at the beginning of the Crispian's Day speech: all suggest a uniquely English notion of grace and courage, extending in popular depictions from the Raj to the RAF, and later mercilessly parodied by Monty Python. As Harry Geduld observes, Olivier 'apotheosizes most of the public school virtues that were supposed to have built the British Empire' (p. 53). James E. Phillips, in a highly perceptive article written for *Hollywood Quarterly* just after the film's American release in 1946, points out how Olivier has altered and in some ways reduced Shakespeare's complex portrait of a successful Renaissance Prince to make Henry a modern movie hero of immediate and wide appeal.

He has assurance, poise, and self-confidence in every situation, whether it be attack or retreat in war or in love.... [He] carries himself with authority and dresses impressively.... Without sacrificing dignity or authority, he maintains the proper comradely relationship with subordinates and inferiors. In a word, he is a figure completely recognizable and understandable today. (Phillips, quoted in Geduld, pp. 53-4)

Olivier creates an irresistibly attractive leader within the conventions of modern films. What he leaves out is the sense of a man who has to make difficult decisions with painful consequences, to execute his friends, to meet atrocity with counter-atrocity, to maintain in blood a cause he gravely doubts is just. Olivier's cutting of the traitors, Bardolph's death, the Harfleur threats, the prisoner massacre and the guilty prayer for undeserved victory severely reduces his material for giving depth, complexity and scope to the character. However, in one of the film's most effective sequences, on the night before Agincourt, Olivier uses his limited materials to the full to flesh out his hero.

The Agincourt Eve sequence is one of the longest and most detailed in the film; it is lightly cut and given disproportionate importance compared to its status in the original text. The Chorus, heard in quiet, naturalistic voice-over, is divided into two sections prefacing the French and English scenes individually. A long-shot shows us the two camps with flickering fires; the camera tracks in to the French tents. The scene between the French lords is static and gravely played, with long pauses suggesting anxiety beneath the jocular words. Leo Genn's Constable is particularly impressive in this scene, almost immobile, absently demolishing the Dauphin like a preoccupied man swatting a fly. His stoical demeanour does more than Shakespeare's text toward creating audience sympathy for the doomed French; when the Dauphin remarks that some of the stars on his armour will fall tomorrow, Genn grimly replies 'That may be' as though looking into his own grave. In this scene at least, Olivier's treatment of the French is more liberal than Shakespeare's.

During the next section of the Chorus speech – 'The country cocks do crow, the clocks do toll' (IV.Chorus.15) – the camera tracks over to the English camp. In this section the camera is much more mobile, gliding among the torchlit tents as though representing Henry's point of view. As the Chorus describes 'The royal captain of this ruined band' (29) visiting his troops, the camera tracks up to a miserable and frightened soldier warming himself by a brazier. A shadow falls across him, he turns his head and the camera swings to take up his point of view, looking after the departing Henry and his guard. Geduld argues that the subjective camera in the English camp, contrasting with the stasis of the French scene, 'increasingly emphasize[s] Henry's intimacy with his men, his personal involvement in their fates, his identification with them' (p. 41). On the other hand, the expression of mute awe and apprehension on the face of the young soldier, as Henry's shadow falls ominously across him, suggests a more complex reading. As Silviria has observed, 'Nothing as easy as the putting on of a comforted expression occurs…. Olivier shows the salutary effect Henry's presence produces in his men but also how not even his caring majesty can erase the night's terrors completely' (p. 118). Olivier's visual image here qualifies the Chorus's rhetoric; he cuts the choral assertion 'That every wretch, pining and pale before, / Beholding him, plucks comfort from his looks' (IV.Chorus.41-2).

A brief exchange with the nobles follows, with Henry and Erpingham sharing a joke that only momentarily lightens the atmosphere. Although he clearly asks for Erpingham's cloak in order to conceal his identity, Olivier plays 'I and my bosom must debate awhile' with grave, quiet sincerity – his primary purpose is solitary meditation, not spying on his troops. After the episodes with Pistol and Fluellen – both played with Henry mainly off screen – the camera tracks to the soldiers round a brazier in darkness, their faces lit by the fire. Olivier clearly differentiates the three soldiers. Williams is a strong, belligerent man in his prime. Bates is older, a weathered, bearded Yorkshireman, fiercely loyal to the King while acknowledging that Williams's criticisms have merit. In an effective reassignment, Olivier gives Williams's speech about 'all those legs and arms and heads chopped off in a battle' to Brian Nissen's Court, a grave, guileless country lad. As Peter Donaldson notes, 'Olivier's amplification of Court's part has the effect of isolating the moral seriousness of these lines from the testy, almost cynical challenge to the king's motives Williams goes on to make ("Ay, he said that to make us fight harder, but when our throats are cut…." [IV.1.199-200])' (p. 17). Olivier's sharp reply to Court – much abbreviated from Shakespeare – seems inadequate, and leaves Henry with a good deal of moral ground to make up. After Williams and Henry quarrel, Bates drags Williams away into the darkness, leaving the boy Court asleep by Henry's side. The camera closes in on Henry's pallid face, framed by his dark cloak and the black night, for 'Upon the King'. The speech is given quietly in an amplified voice-over, while Henry's face subtly registers the emotional shifts – the technique used for all the soliloquies in *Hamlet*. Midway through the speech, on the reference to the sound sleep of the 'wretched slave', the camera tracks back to reveal the sleeping Court, over whose head Henry raises a paternal hand as if to stroke him. This gesture, rather than his earlier speech, is Henry's real response to the frightened boy.

For the end of the speech, when speaking of the peasant rising to 'help Hyperion to his horse', Henry turns to look back at the dawn beginning to glimmer in the night sky, suggesting peace and hope. As Donaldson observes,

> In the play text the king's meditation leads not to peace with himself but to the guilty memory of his father's theft of the crown and an unsuccessful attempt to pray. But in the film the scene works to restore the fellowship breached by Williams' challenge and to show the king in harmony with himself, pious and confident. (p. 18)

Olivier certainly reduces Henry's conflict by cutting the prayer and by implying fellowship, or at least the desire for it, in the image of Henry and Court; but I would argue that Olivier plays an inner unrest in these scenes that is not fully resolved until the Crispian's Day speech. Olivier thoroughly milks the few lines of the prayer that remain:

> O God of battles, steel my soldiers' hearts,
> Possess them not with fear, Take from them now
> The sense of reckoning lest the opposèd numbers
> Pluck their hearts from them.

(Olivier, *Henry V*, p. 62)

It is as though he is playing the entire Shakespearian scene with the few lines of it that he includes. Between the time he kneels down, prompted by the sight of soldiers hearing Mass, and the time he rises, Olivier shows a depth and range of emotion unexplained by his lines. This inner journey, which seems to bring Henry closer to peace but which opens a window on some great sorrow – *may* correspond to the suppressed material in the text, involving Henry's guilt and fear. It certainly does so structurally: without the intense unspoken emotion Olivier portrays, the prayer as he retains it would seem ridiculously perfunctory. As played in the film, it adequately prepares the final note of 'The day, my friends, and all things stay for me'. The result – playing the *effect* of moral conflict without any evidence of personal guilt – is like that of the earlier moments at Southampton and Harfleur when Henry is merciful without any suggestion that he could be otherwise. Olivier has it both ways, and thus is able to achieve a deeper, more sensitive and in some respects unfathomable characterisation within the boundaries of the clean, bright, faultless hero his actions in the film proclaim him to be.

Olivier's battle sequence has been discussed in exhaustive detail elsewhere (see Geduld, Silviria, Pilkington), so I will note only a few points relating it to Olivier's mythologising project. Shakespeare shows little of the battle, apologising for the inadequacy of 'four or five most vile and ragged foils, right ill-disposed in brawl ridiculous'; in a wide-screen Technicolor film, however, the battle is necessarily a prominent feature. Olivier's battle serves to demonstrate two points: how, in technical terms, the English won; and why, in moral and cinematic terms, they deserved to win. The first point is ignored by Shakespeare, perhaps in order to emphasise the miraculousness of the victory, but was well known to any English schoolboy in 1944: the English won by holding their line behind a row of stakes and by raining arrows on the advancing French forces. Olivier illustrates this tactic in the famous charge sequence with William Walton's music building to the climactic moment when the English arrows are loosed and the French horsemen thrown into confusion. But the more important aspect of Olivier's battle is its illustration of why the English *deserved* to win. Olivier partly works from material Shakespeare provided: by excising the killing of the French prisoners but retaining the massacre of the boys, Olivier establishes the moral superiority of the English. A shot of the Dauphin looking after the distant leaders of the massacre and then turning his horse in distress from the field suggests that even the French generals acknowledge that they don't deserve victory. But aside from such text-based material, Olivier morally justifies the English victory by purely cinematic means familiar from Western films. The English are presented as the underdogs, outnumbered and steadfast, holding their ground, as it were, behind the circled wagons, while the French horsemen appear in a strong and threatening position on the ridge of a hill. In the language of the Western, the 'good guys' are clearly established. Further, the French are arrogant and overdressed and deserve to be taught a lesson. The famous shot of an armoured French knight being lowered creakily on to his horse from a crane is an emblem of doomed hubris. According to cinematic conventions, the French would have to be either more humble or more terrifying to suggest even the possibility of their victory.

[45]

The climax of the battle, following the discovery of the slaughtered boys, is a single combat between Henry and the Constable. The film has taken pains to establish the Constable as the one Frenchman who might be a worthy opponent. Olivier sets up the combat in a highly conventional way. The Constable's horse and armour are black, whereas Henry is brightly clad on a white charger. A closed, pointed visor gives the Constable a fierce and inhuman appearance, as well as disguising Leo Genn's stunt double; Olivier very pointedly does his own stunts, equating actor with role in his willingness to take risks along with his men. The Constable, typically, gets the upper hand at first, knocking Henry's sword out of his grasp, but at the last moment Henry strikes him to the ground with a single blow of his fist. In depicting the triumph of the unarmed, threatened underdog, Olivier makes Henry's combat metonymic of the whole English victory as well as instantly readable within cinema fight conventions.

Olivier deliberately avoided any suggestion of wounds or blood, giving his battle a formal, storybook quality in its visual texture:

> I showed no bloody gashes. The bright mediaeval costumes tended, too, to emphasize the formal elements and patterns of the battle. But to be true to the film's overall style the battle should have been fought on green velvet – and that, clearly, was impracticable. (Olivier, *On Acting*, pp. 172-3)

Olivier's comment highlights the often-overlooked point that the switch from theatrical studio sets to outdoor location shooting did not necessarily mean a movement to greater realism. Olivier couldn't use green velvet, but he found the closest natural substitute in the green fields of Ireland, and shot only on sunny days to give the scenery and costumes the greatest possible brilliance. Indeed, the unnatural brightness and verdancy of Agincourt field caused Orson Welles to remark that *Henry V* was a film in which, as far as he could see, 'one minute the characters conversed on a stage, the next they rode out in full armour on to a golf course' (Collick, p. 50). Olivier's battle does feel more like a sporting event than a war, and this ties in well with its propagandistic celebration of Englishness: it shows, as it were, the battle of Waterloo being won on the playing fields of Eton.

The wooing of Katherine achieves two purposes for Olivier: it provides some graceful romantic comedy to consolidate his happy ending and complete its picture of his ideal hero, and it serves a political purpose in rehabilitating France and emphasising Anglo-French unity, an important issue in the closing years of the Second World War. Elegantly staged in a book-of-hours interior, the scene lets Olivier show off the dashing and romantic persona that had given him success in Hollywood. His wooing is easy and confident, his French is good and the doll-like Katherine of Renée Ascherson never really stands up to him. Only occasionally does Olivier acknowledge the political imperative behind the marriage. He does include Burgundy's plea for peace, over a tracking shot of the disordered but still fertile French countryside, ending with two unkempt French urchins. The effect, however, is not to remind the audience of the havoc wrought by Henry's army, but rather to suggest France's need for Henry's paternal care. Henry's terse reply to Burgundy – 'You must buy that peace / With full accord to all our just demands' (V.ii.70) is softened to 'you must gain that peace'. Later, in the scene with Katherine, Olivier includes one acknowledgement that the wedding is a matter of politics and war and that all the cards are in Henry's hands. When Henry asks if she will have him, Katherine replies somewhat coyly and proudly, 'Dat is as it sall please de roi mon pere' (261). Olivier looks off toward the room in which the treaties are being drawn up, and replies with a slight steely edge to his voice, 'Nay, it will please him well, Kate, it shall please him, Kate'. The king her father has no choice in the matter. The shot serves to remind Olivier's audience of what Shakespeare's would have thoroughly understood: that this marriage isn't simply a matter of true love.

For the most part, however, Olivier presents the marriage as a symbol of peaceful and fruitful alliance between England and France, with England, of course, in the dominant masculine role. While Katherine accepts Henry's kiss, 'patiently, and yielding', the film cuts to a close up of their joined hands, with the signet rings of England and France together. Indeed, the end of the film works quite hard to emphasise peace, unity and stability, to counter the effects of discord created by the war and to a certain extent by Olivier's stylistic experimentation. After the final lines in the French court, Henry and Katherine walk upstage, away from the camera, in a tableau suggesting marriage, and we are back in the Globe theatre, with Henry/Burbage in heavy makeup. But Katherine, while in the wig and costume of the boy player, seems still to be the actress Renée Ascherson, though it's hard to tell. The return to the Globe has not totally destroyed the illusion of the cinema. In a final shot tracking away from the couple, the female Katherine has been replaced by a boy – and, as Peter Donaldson has noted, the sexiness of the earlier shot has been replaced with stately formality (pp. 11-12). Donaldson concentrates on this moment's relation to the gender dynamics of the film, but it also represents a general tendency to break down boundaries as the film ends. When the medieval Princess of France appears on the Globe stage and *then* dissolves into an English working-class lad, historical, geographical and gender divisions – as well as those between theatre and cinema – are themselves dissolved into a timeless vision of unity and peace, far from European wars, ancient or modern. The film has in the end been less about beating the French than about achieving this final unity, this utopian 'England of the mind', as Pilkington calls it (p. 114).

Olivier's film looks back to the eighteenth- and nineteenth-century tradition of a faultless hero; but it goes beyond it in its self-conscious treatment of the film medium and in its inclusion of some hints of a darker, more modern reading, notably in the sombre adagios of Falstaff's death and Agincourt Eve. Nevertheless it is an almost entirely positive film – rather than a tub-thumper about the English crushing the evil French, it is much of the time a vision of England's virtues in peace as well as war. The harmonious picture of Englishness represented by the Globe theatre and the graceful courage and benevolence of Olivier's Henry make the film patriotic without being war-mongering. To directors later in the century, however, Olivier's film came to represent all they wanted to react against: it was the 'traditional' reading that they set out to revise. I have argued that Olivier's *Henry V* is subtler and more sophisticated than the heroic stage tradition out of which it came. Nevertheless, as the twentieth century progressed, the film's bright and positive presentation of Henry, his nation and his war could no longer go unqualified.

CHAPTER III

We band of brothers:
Terry Hands (1975)

Terry Hands's 1975 *Henry V* was, for several reasons, the most important British production of the play since Olivier's film. It marked a turning point in the stage history of the play as well as that of the Royal Shakespeare Company. While the play had had two important productions at Stratford since the Second World War – in 1951 and 1964 – both had been part of cycles whose central emphasis reduced the importance of *Henry V*. The first cycle, overseen by Anthony Quayle, was largely an illustration of John Dover Wilson's thesis about the necessity of Falstaff's rejection; after that event was accomplished *Henry V* seemed an afterthought, and Richard Burton received less notice as King than he had as a thoughtful young prince. The 1964 production was added to fill out Peter Hall and John Barton's *Wars of the Roses* series; *Henry V* was overshadowed by the civil wars that followed it, though Ian Holm's tough, weary Henry suggested a new approach to heroism and signalled a change of direction for the play. But Hands's 1975 *Henry V*, though later joined by *Henry IV* and *The Merry Wives of Windsor,* stood initially on its own in a very high-profile position. It was the opening play of the RSC's centenary season, at a time of crisis for both the country and the company. As such, it provides a vivid example of the ways a production's meaning is generated in a complex negotiation between text, interpretation, audience expectations and the social, political and economic circumstances of the production.

Hands's production is the first explicitly 'anti-war' revision of the play that I will consider. It was not the RSC's first; Hall's production, in 1964, had taken a strongly anti-war line in keeping with the generally nihilistic political views of Jan Kott, which informed the whole cycle. Holm's doubling of Henry with Richard III can hardly have been coincidental, given Kott's view of history as a cyclical, and cynical, 'Grand Mechanism' (Kott, p. 10). Physically small and unromantic in bearing, Holm's Henry was scarcely distinguishable from his shell-shocked troops. The Chorus was flashy and grandiloquent; Hall's programme notes asserted that 'the play is a criticism of the Chorus' view of the story' (quoted in Brennan, p. xxviii). While Hall's production expressed Vietnam-era cynicism, Hands's needed a more positive approach to regain widespread support for the RSC in an era of budget cuts. Put simply, the goal of the production was to condemn war while keeping the play's celebratory, even patriotic aspect. Hands solved this problem by representing the war not as conflict with an enemy, but as an occasion for spiritual struggle and growth, both within Henry and within the whole English army. The principal metaphor Hands used for the interdependence achieved by Henry and his men was not combat but theatre itself. Hands explored a non-illusionistic performance style the company had been developing since 1970, focusing on the theatrical event rather than the grim campaign it represented, and Alan Howard's bravura performance of spiritual agonies and final self-awareness embodied the decade's general shift from the political to the personal. Disturbing aspects of the war – the traitors, the execution of Bardolph, the killing of the prisoners – were reintroduced to show, as it were, that the company had nothing up its sleeve; but their potentially disruptive effects were minimised and they were subordinated to the King's spiritual struggle.

The RSC chose *Henry V* to open the 1975 season for four main reasons. First, Hands felt that initially presenting *Henry V* on its own, rather than as part of a chronological cycle, might encourage critical reappraisal (Beaumann, *RSC*, p. 326). Second, the play was a rousing crowd-puller which would make a good kick-off to the centenary season (Beaumann, *Henry V*, p. 14). Third, the RSC, along with the rest of the country, was in grave financial trouble, threatened by inadequate grants and facing the closure of its theatres. Hands saw *Henry V* as a metaphor for the company's own condition: 'It is about improvisation, interdependence, and unity: three essential qualities if the company was to surmount its present difficulties' (Beaumann, *Henry V*, p. 14). Finally, Hands felt that the conception of theatre expressed in the choral speeches could provide the company with the artistic direction it had been groping throughout the 1970s to find.

The unique historical position of this production, opening a commemorative season for the RSC at a time when the company was compelled to justify its existence and redefine its artistic path, meant that great cultural significance was accorded to its treatment of the play. The production's critical, popular and commercial success – it played for four years, touring Europe and America – demonstrated that Hands's reading had struck a strong chord in the *Zeitgeist*, and assured it of 'definitive' status. The production's almost mythical importance was consolidated by a commemorative edition of the play, prepared by Sally Beaumann, which included photos, interviews with the company and an annotated copy of the prompt text. Alan Howard became, for the next several years, the world's foremost Shakespearian actor; Terry Hands had ensured for himself the eventual sole directorship of the RSC; and all subsequent English productions of *Henry V* had to contend with the memory of this production as well as Olivier's film.

The historical and cultural background of the production is worth considering in detail, as it affected not only the company's artistic choices but the way they were perceived. In 1975 Britain was in its worst domestic crisis since the war. The breakdown of consensus that had begun with disillusionment with Harold Wilson's Labour government continued to splinter British politics; Edward Heath's Conservative economic policies between 1970 and 1974 failed to curb inflation and unemployment and resulted in a crippling miners' strike; Scottish and Welsh separatism were on the rise, as was the crude, racist nationalism of the National Front; and in 1974 the IRA began a year of unprecedented mainland violence culminating in the November Birmingham pub bombings (Marwick, p. 226). Inflation provided Britain's worst problem, exceeding twenty per cent throughout 1974, and creating a crisis in (among other things) funding for the arts (Beaumann, *RSC*, p. 323). The Arts Council's sizable grant to the RSC was unable to keep pace with rising costs; at the same time, it made the company unpopular with smaller alternative theatres, so that the RSC, which once assumed a radical posture, was being attacked from the left. The Aldwych theatre, originally a venue for progressive new writing, was now threatened with closure and relied on starry productions like Stoppard's 1974 *Travesties*, 'essentially a West End production inserted into the RSC repertoire' (Beaumann, *RSC*, p. 1974). Hands's *Henry V* opened at a time when the RSC was shifting from the publicly funded radicalism of the 1860s to the more mainstream and privatised company of the

[51]

1980s, with its West End musicals and Royal Insurance sponsorship (Holderness, *Shrew*, p. 73). The company needed a commercial success to demonstrate its economic viability in an era of budget-cutting; it also had to reestablish its political, intellectual and artistic credibility at a moment when its institutional status made it an easy target in the theatre community.

Artistically, the company had been undergoing a period of uncertainty and stagnation; having left behind the gritty, cool, quasi-Brechtian style of the 1960s with Peter Hall's departure in 1968, it had been unable to find a suitable replacement. The one great success of the period, Peter Brook's 1970 *Midsummer Night's Dream*, had produced only limp imitations. Without a governing style or mission, by 1975 the company seemed at an artistic nadir. As Beaumann reports in her history of the RSC:

> It had two enervated Stratford seasons behind it; its continuity of work had been undermined; its continuing belief in the company principle appeared intermittent, and its tendency to go for the sure-fire one-off hit, or the instant prestige of the big-name star had become more marked. Above all its confidence in its large-theatre Shakespeare work, the foundation for the entire edifice of the RSC, seemed fitful. In the wake of the clarity, lucidity, and daring of Brook's *Dream* the company appeared to be floundering, relying too often on the hard-hitting but narrowly conceptual approach, or on décor and display. (Beaumann, *RSC*, pp. 321-2)

Beaumann's analysis is of course written in retrospect, part of the mythologising of Hands's production; but the fact remains that, given the RSC's artistic and financial disorder in the mid-1970s, the first successful production would necessarily have a wide impact on the company's future direction. Hands increased the attention on the production by connecting it with the launching of the theatre's centenary appeal, including a Royal Gala performance. Everything about the production coincided to make it a kind of showcase or advertisement for the new RSC. The challenges Hands faced were compounded by the fact that the play was *Henry V* – with its associations of nationalism and militarism – and that his company was one with a reputation for radicalism, which a few seasons earlier had produced the anti-Vietnam collage *US*. As Sinfield describes it, 'The struggle which Terry Hands faced as director was to give a positive reading of the play which was not so clumsily patriotic as to violate the company's political identity' (Sinfield, 'Royal Shakespeare', p. 172).

[52]

Hands's solution was to sidestep a political reading and focus attention on the theatrical event itself. Hands would interpret the play's action in the light of the collaborative, interdependent, courageous process needed to stage it. War and play would be metaphors for each other. At the centre of Hands's production was the emotional and spiritual growth of the uneasy, multi-faceted, role-playing king of Alan Howard. Hands recognised the applicability of his reading to the RSC's present crisis, making an explicit comparison to Olivier's film:

> It is not the first time the play has been called upon in such a situation. In 1945 Laurence Olivier's film had served to stimulate the nation as a whole. The problems of that time were specifically national and so the 'patriotic' element in the play was specifically emphasised.

Hands, however, wanted to stress not the nationalist, military, 'patriotic' element of the play but the

> specific unity... of individuals aware of their responsibilities, both to themselves and to each other, voluntarily accepting some abdication of that individuality in a final non-hierarchic interdependence – a real brotherhood. (quoted in Beaumann, *Henry V*, p. 15)

Despite Hands's avowal of specific rather than national concerns, Ralph Berry rightly notes that 'the last clause sounds oddly reminiscent of an argument in favour of an incomes policy or a voluntary pay code – matters much on the national mind in 1975' (Berry, *Changing Styles*, p. 78). In accordance with contemporary concerns, the emphasis of the production was not on the war of aggression against a foreign enemy but on the overcoming of domestic disharmony.

Hands drew his stylistic approach from the Chorus's opening exhortation to 'Piece out our imperfections with your thoughts', and imagine the visual spectacle which the actors only describe (I.Chorus.23). 'We could abandon the artistic strictures of "naturalist" theatre, with its cinematic crowds and group reactions, and focus on each actor as an individual', Hands wrote in his introduction to the published text.

> We could reduce the conflict of text and decor, and trust in the ability of wooden floors ... to transform themselves from boards into billows at a leap of the audience's imagination. We felt we were doing what many people in the theatre had been longing to do for years. Start from scratch. (quoted in Beaumann, *Henry V*, pp. 16-17)

The set designed by Abdel Farrah suited Hands's anti-illusionist style. 'I felt that what we wanted to create was not a box of illusions, but something that freed the audience's imaginations and made them conjure their own illusions', Farrah said in an interview (Beaumann, *Henry V*, p. 31). Accordingly, the entire stage of the Royal Shakespeare Theatre was redesigned to focus attention on the actor. All the masking was stripped away, leaving the plain brick of the back wall and proscenium arch visible to the audience. The stage was made of bare black boards running toward the house, with a deep thrust and a steep one-in-twelve rake. 'It was a stage designed to launch the actors into the audience', said Farrah. 'The comment that pleased me most was that it was like the great deck of an aircraft carrier.' The actors were nakedly exposed, forced to create a convincing sense of place and action through performance alone: as Farrah expressed it, 'It wasn't a stage where you could hide weakness' (Beaumann, *Henry V*, p. 31).

There were a few dramatic modifications to this basic empty space. The middle of the stage rose up to a near-vertical wall for the breach scene at Harfleur, then lowered to discover Katherine of France standing shyly behind it. A brilliant heraldic canopy was flown in for the royal embarkation; it descended to the stage for the Agincourt scenes, its drab backing representing the muddy desolation of the English camp. The costumes, also designed by Farrah, underlined the emphasis on theatrical representation. The actors were on-stage warming up in rehearsal clothes when the audience entered the theatre; the play was performed without period costume until the French ambassador arrived in medieval robes. The subsequent costumes, as in all the modern English productions here considered, stressed the difference between the two nations: the French were dressed in over-elaborate period finery and shining golden armour, while the drab English military costumes suggested the twentieth-century world wars. As Hands saw it, 'Theatrically, period costume is an outmoded convention. Used here it helps accentuate the fact that the French are frozen in an era that has already passed' (Beaumann, *Henry V*, p. 137).

The rehearsal-clothes opening was one of the most notable features of the production, although it was maligned by many critics and audience members. Some saw it as a reference to the company's financial desperation, a snide joke at the expense of the Arts Council: 'Evidently the RSC are about to show us, yah boo sucks, that cut-price Shakespeare simply doesn't work, and that if

4 The rehearsal-clothes opening of Terry Hands's 1975
RSC production, with Alan Howard as the King

the Arts Council doesn't come up with a better cheque this is how
we'll be getting our bard in the future' (Morley, *Punch*, 16 April
1975). This reading – diametrically opposed to Hands's intention –
was frequent among the critics. Only one of the opening-night
critics fully interpreted the scene as Hands intended: Gordon
Parsons wrote that 'the bare stage and overt rehearsal presentation of the opening were preparing us for a further RSC exploration of the crucial relationship between role-playing and role'
(Morning Star, 11 April 1975).

The emphasis on theatricality in the opening sequence was
matched by Emrys James's playing of the Chorus. A short, bald-
ing, round-faced Welshman in neat but casual modern black
clothes, James played the Chorus as enthusiastic and engaging.
'It's the duty of the Chorus to lure the audience into the play, to be
friendly, to relax them, so their imaginations can start working',
James said in interview. 'He reassures them, teases them. And he's
very disarming, very modest' (Beaumann, *Henry V*, pp. 62-3). John
Elsom characterised James's Chorus as 'bright-eyed and lip-licking
... an astute, admiring commentator' *(Listener,* 17 April 1975) and

Charles Lewson called him 'an avuncular Chorus of immense persuasiveness' *(Times,* 9 April 1975). James took no ironic distance from his role: 'I don't think he is partisan about the English.... I think he reports fairly exactly on the state of each side. I suppose the speeches are patriotic. I don't quite know why one should be defensive about that' (Beaumann, *Henry V,* p.63). There was no deliberate attempt by the production to criticise the Chorus or to undermine his authority. The one possible exception was when he was interrupted by Nym and Bardolph for the beginning of II.i, at which he left the stage to them with a good-natured shrug. As Hands described it, 'the play itself begins to take over. The Chorus, who has instigated the proceedings, should be shown to have lessening control over it' (Beaumann, *Henry V,* p. 120). Accordingly, it was also at this point that scenic spectacle began to replace the rehearsal-room opening: at 'English Mercuries', the heraldic canopy unfolded, music played for the first time, and a huge gun-carriage rolled on upstage. The casually dressed actors gathered around it and visibly donned their military costumes while the low-life scene took place downstage.

Aside from the bare opening and James's modern Chorus, there were other reminders of the theatrical nature of the event. Many scenes were played non-naturalistically, especially the formal French scenes, as when the King delivered his call to arms directly to the audience, in full armour, and initially, Hands notes, wearing buskins 'to increase his symbolic height and power' (Beaumann, *Henry V,* p. 158). Similarly, the traitors were announced non-naturalistically: 'Picked out by follow spots as the Chorus names them, they are figures rather than people' (quoted in Beaumann, *Henry V,* p. 127). Yet the most sustained use of the theatrical metaphor in the production was in the playing of Henry himself, and the emphasis on the roles he enacts in his development as king.

Howard's focus on role-playing was one of the features of the production most noted by critics:

> Alan Howard explored with intelligence and passion the assumption of various identities demanded of the king, returning every so often to an intense and lonely self-communion. Here was an actor playing a man playing a king: an exercise in introspection far removed from the usual recruiting poster. (Marcus, *Sunday Telegraph*, 13 April 1975)

Marcus's comments mirror Hands's emphasis on the man rather than the King, the personal rather than the political. Charles Lewson in *The Times*, characterising 'this intelligent performance' as 'a man's attempt to forge himself in the painful fires of authority and battle', noted the metaphorical importance of costume in this interpretation. He stressed the contrast between Henry's two onstage assumptions of the regalia of his roles: 'the first, with awe and terror as he takes up the Dauphin's challenge and prepares for battle in France, the second with easy confidence after he has been bloodied and before the battle of Agincourt' (*Times*, 9 April 1975). This depiction of the relation between costume and role recalls the scene in Brecht's *Galileo* wherein the Pope hardens himself to Galileo's torture while being dressed in his Papal panoply. Alan Howard felt role-playing was the key to Hal/Henry. Although he played Henry first, he informed the part with a knowledge of Hal's past:

> By *Henry V* he has become completely isolated, he is under an enormous magnifying glass.... It seemed to me that the Henry at the beginning of *Henry V* still cannot put off the masks that he was accustomed to using as Hal. It is only when ... he is forced into a corner, that the mask begins to slip – begins to fail him. If Hal were not so used to using masks, playing roles, then he would perhaps find it easier to be the straightforward warrior-king in *Henry V*, that so many commentators assume him to be. (quoted in Beaumann, *Henry V*, p. 54)

Howard implies that Henry's role-playing finally leads him into a discovery of his essential self, and this was indeed the general thrust of the production. Gordon Parsons, however, read Henry's 'growth' as ambiguous and stressed Henry's unease with his 'role':

> Alan Howard's Henry craves fellowship even, if necessary, in death, to escape the role imposed by the expectations of those about him. His success as warrior king both surprises and disturbs him. We watch a man destroying one essential self to fulfil a part and, in the process, discovering another vital but often distasteful persona. (Parsons, *Morning Star*, 11 April 1975)

Howard's moments of pain and unease were frequently marked in the production. Nevertheless, many critics felt Henry's adoption of various roles showed his multi-faceted nature in a purely positive way: 'the complete performer, at ease in every role' (de Jongh, *Guardian*, 9 April 1975); 'Here is Henry as patriot, dreamer, scholar, soldier, lover' (Barnes, *New York Times*, 24 April 1975); 'He showed every facet of Shakespeare's patriot king and silenced for the time being any doubts about the morality of that war of aggression' (Speaight, *Shakespeare Quarterly*, 9 April 1975); 'It is an exciting and virile performance of such nobility that the darker sides of Henry's character are totally obscured' (Schulman, *Evening Standard*, 9 April 1975).

While the production paid lip service to 'the darker sides of Henry's character', it certainly lent itself to this kind of unqualified positive reading of the king. Hands and Howard went to great lengths to rationalise the biggest strike against Henry, from a contemporary point of view: his initial decision to invade France. Howard provides several pragmatic reasons for the decision: avoiding a conflict with the Church, recovering his great-grandfather's lands, busying giddy minds with foreign quarrels (cf. *2 Henry IV*), consolidating his own dubious claim to the throne, living up to the reputation of his ancestors. He further insists that 'It's only when there is a sixth factor, the insult of the Dauphin, that he finally blows, and makes the decision' (Beaumann, *Henry V*, p. 55). (Howard's view conflicts with Henry's earlier assertion, included in Hands's text, that 'France being ours, we'll bend it to our awe / Or break it all to pieces' (I.ii. 224.5).) Howard goes on to explain Henry's decision in terms of the production's focus on self-realisation through role-playing:

> the most important reason of all, I think, is that war is going to force him to further self-discovery. The king at war is the next role he has to take up. Going to France is the next test of himself, in terms of the long Odyssey of self-exploration that he began long ago in the earlier plays. (Beaumann, *Henry V*, p. 55)

Howard's ultimate explanation for Henry's invasion of France – typical of the 1970s, frankly apolitical – combines two of the principal interpretive strands of the production: self-exploration and theatricality. Hands, in discussing Henry's decision, adds a third major strand, which I will refer to as the 'band-of-brothers theme'. This is at least an ostensibly political strand: the idea is that Henry, through the war with France, redefines his nation from one of medieval hierarchy to one of modern interdependence (if not equality). As Hands describes it:

> War in this sense is less 'war-mongering' than Shakespeare's dramatic pretext for assembling the elements of Henry's nation –

in one place, at one time, for examination. The metaphor serves to contrast the imposed unity of mediaeval discipline with the agreed unity of interdependence. If he can unite his 'army,' he will unite his 'country.' (quoted in Beaumann, *Henry V*, p. 19)

Accordingly, Hands saw Henry's decision to go to war as part of his programme to reform his kingdom. He tried to communicate this by making Henry stand apart and unconvinced during the Archbishop's bee speech, 'the full mediaeval statement of paternal fascism':

> Henry remained isolated from the others throughout the speech, listening detachedly to a hierarchic philosophy that kills kings, maintains unjust wealth, and makes men like the Archbishop advocate unthinking wars. By the end of the play he will have created a 'band of brothers.' (quoted in Beaumann, *Henry V*, p. 114)

Gary Taylor points out the illogic of this interpretation, given that Henry does in fact decide to attack France. Even if the audience had noticed Henry's distancing of himself from the bee speech, it could hardly find its way to the reading 'that Henry, appalled by the content of Canterbury's speech, decides that the system it glorifies must be dismantled, *by war with France*, just what the Archbishop and the nobles (=the system) want. This is simply an incommunicable interpretation' (Taylor, *Moment by Moment*, p. 156). Nevertheless, the band-of-brothers theme did significantly affect many of the production's choices, although most critical response to the play focused on the King's own transformation rather than that of his army.

Henry's uneasiness in his role was emphasised through stage business and through Howard's line readings. In discussing the role Howard emphasised the King's moments of indecision: 'If Shakespeare had wanted to show a man who was going to cut through this situation like a knife through butter, he could have done so' (quoted in Beaumann, *Henry V*, p. 55). Accordingly, Howard would often introduce a note of faltering uncertainty before, after or during some of Henry's traditionally 'heroic' speeches. In the traitors scene, for instance, he was enormously distraught by the personal betrayal of Scroop, who had been presented as merely a morality-play villain: 'it is not the traitor we are to examine, but Henry himself' (Hands, quoted in Beaumann, *Henry V*, p. 130). Accordingly, the emphasis was not on Henry's severity in condemning the traitors but on his distress; and

[59]

Henry's subsequent speeches about France were shot through, in Howard's reading, with an agony of self-doubt and inner torment. As Hands describes it, 'it is unthinkable that a man who has gone through the previous holocaust of emotions should now be cheerfully contemplating war'. Accordingly, Howard played his apparently confident lines ('we doubt not of a fair and lucky war.... We doubt not now but every rub / Is smoothèd on our way' (II.iii.184-5)) as stumbling attempts to pull himself together. Hands then had Henry's brothers, 'convinced and simpler in their responses, silently offer his sword and tabard and push him towards commitment' (p. 133). Howard made a big moment of putting on the tabard. Only then did Henry fully get into his role, leaping heroically onto the gun carriage for his final ringing couplet: 'Cheerly to sea! The signs of war advance! / No King of England, if not King of France!' (192-3).

Henry's next big moment of personal crisis was at Harfleur. The breach scene itself was spectacularly staged, with the English soldiers spilling back in retreat over the steeply raked wall, and Henry clinging to a rope on a scaling ladder to deliver his speech in a traditional heroic vein. With his speech to the governor, however, Howard made a powerful choice that reinforced the reading of Henry as an actor unhappy with his part. Howard delivered the speech full front, to a governor in the upper balcony of the Royal Shakespeare Theatre, playing to the hilt the images of horror. After the capitulation, he turned aside, nearly fainting with nausea and relief. As Harold Hobson noted in a typical response: 'it is at a great cost that Henry conquers both himself and his opponents; a cost seen most vividly when Harfleur surrenders.... He is like a man saved at the eleventh hour from hell' (*Sunday Times*, 13 April 1975).

The execution of Bardolph was a similar moment. Although it occurred off stage – subsequent productions made more of the actual killing – Henry had to give assent to the execution, rather than merely hearing it reported. A roll of drums was heard, and Exeter signalled with his sword for the hanging to proceed. Hands made much of the moments following the execution: the order forbidding plunder, and then, after Montjoy's entrance, the refusal of the noble privilege of ransom. He related these to the band-of-brothers theme:

> Henry has just executed Bardolph. He has changed the rule concerning the common soldiers' plunder.... Now he is faced with

another rule, the rule of ransom. He must change that too, if he is to convince his men that they are one army sharing one destiny. Harsh to others, he must be harsh to himself. (quoted in Beaumann, *Henry V*, p. 164)

Hands's linking of the two issues was probably more than an audience could pick up, but it was evident that the strain of Bardolph's execution carried over into the scene with Montjoy. As Irving Wardle reported:

Howard has to stand and give the execution order with Pistol looking him straight in the eye; an ordeal that shakes his nerve with the French herald. Then, in a wonderful transition, he begins a halting speech, hits by accident on a joke and a smile of surprised delight steals across his face at his own powers of recovery, and his capacity to keep on acting. (*Times*, 22 January 1976)

This 'wonderful transition' was entirely a creation of Hands and Howard: there is nothing in the text to suggest that Bardolph isn't forgotten as soon as mentioned. Howard worked out an elaborate and convincing subtext for his speeches to Montjoy which made Bardolph's death the dominant motivation of the scene, and Henry's speech of defiance an agonized inward battle. In Howard's view, 'Henry's answers to Montjoy ... exhibit very obviously his temporary loss of control, and his uncertainty about what to say or do next' (Beaumann, *Henry V*, p. 165). Henry's jokes, which could be interpreted as exhibiting arrogant confidence ('Yet forgive me, God, / That I do brag thus! This your air of France / Hath blown that vice in me' (III.vi.156-8)) were made the desperate attempts of a heartsick leader to pull himself and his men together, and 'made no effect on the tired and sullen soldiery' (Hands, p. 165). Henry's concluding statements could be played with proud, defiant authority:

Go bid thy master well advise himself:
If we may pass, we will; if we be hindered,
We shall your tawny ground with your red blood
Discolour. And so Montjoy, fare you well.

(165-8)

Howard's reading, instead, ingeniously relates them to Henry's inward agony over Bardolph's execution:

Finally, exacerbated, he repeats all these conflicting – or anyway tortuous – statements again, as if aware that he has stated them in a rambling fashion previously. That he exhibits such loss of control, and loss of skill with words, at such a vital moment, seems to me

[61]

indicative of the degree of pain he has suffered at Bardolph's execution, just before. (Howard, quoted in Beaumann, *Henry V*, p. 165)

The end of the scene, which was also the end of the act, made a point of isolating Henry from his men, counterpointing the eventual unity of the band of brothers. He remained downstage, off the fallen canopy, apart from his men, during the speech. When he returned to his army and ordered them on, they expressed mutinous reluctance, so that he made his final 'march away' an angry shouted command. At this point Hands reintroduced a 'marching song' that Guy Woolfenden had written to suggest the 'whistled soldiers' tunes' of British armies in the World Wars, with the refrain 'Deo Gracias' (Beaumann, *Henry V*, p. 47). First heard cheerfully at Southampton, it was here 'very forced and unwilling' to indicate the nadir of the army's morale. As Hands described the scene: 'Angrily he tries to make them sing their battle anthem. They pick it up reluctantly, raggedly. As they begin to move off, Henry is left to sing alone: Deo Gracias…. The simple patriotism of Southampton has become bitterly ironic' (Hands, quoted in Beaumann, *Henry V*, p. 165). Hands's stage business and Howard's acting choices in this scene all pointed up the importance of Bardolph's execution as a supreme test of the King's role-playing, and emphasised the disunity of the army that Henry would eventually make a 'band of brothers'.

The most important part of the play for Hands and Howard, given their reading of the King, was necessarily the dark night of the soul before Agincourt. This sequence both reconciled Henry to his role and allowed him to resolve the band-of-brothers theme through the notions of interdependence and personal responsibility. Hands and Howard's exploitation of the scenes of Henry's self-questioning, and their reading of his resolution of it, enabled them to make Henry an acceptable modern hero.

For Howard, the first part of the night scene was simply Henry putting on another series of disguises: 'his identity is confused again, by the adoption of masks' (p. 58). The three soldiers, led by Dan Meaden's Williams, made their points strongly, and Howard felt Henry's answers were not really adequate. He snapped at Williams on 'Your reproof is something too round', temporarily dropping his mask:

It seemed to me possible that Henry was aware of the insufficiency of his own arguments to Williams, and that this had angered him as it does people when they know they have been forced into a defence they don't totally believe. (p. 183)

For Howard, the one significant line that came out of the exchange with Williams and indicated the beginnings of a new attitude was 'every subject's soul is his own'. Howard called it 'a sudden and extraordinary admission of personal responsibility, his first articulation of that idea' (p. 58). Looked at another way, it is Henry's abdication of his responsibility for the souls (and lives) of his soldiers; but Howard supported his reading with sub-sequent choices emphasising his own responsibility.

Howard played the 'Upon the King' soliloquy as 'an angry bitter speech ... a sicking-up of everything in him' (p. 58):

> By the end of that speech he has whipped himself into a kind of fury against the notion of kingship and then against the views of a peasant who is unable to understand what a king's responsibilities are. He hits out at both and ends by saying neither is any use. (quoted in Cook, p. 67)

Having searched his kingly role and found it empty, Henry turned in panic to bargain with God, 'cravenly', in Howard's view (p. 58). B. A. Young felt Howard was 'unusually good in that hateful speech ... where he seems to be making a commercial deal with God for victory. It had almost a touch of Gethsemane about it' (*Financial Times*, 9 April 1975). Throughout the scene, Howard made the depth of Henry's anguish outweigh, and indeed feed upon, the dubiousness of his moral position.

Howard made the end of the scene – 'The day, my friends, and all things stay for me' – a moment of great personal revelation. Howard felt this line was the hinge of the play:

> miraculously, perhaps because every cell in his body has been stretched and stressed and pulverised, he hits on a simple truth.... It is the realisation that *his* soul is his own as much as Williams'; the realisation that he must stop acting, stop hiding. When he says 'all things stay for me,' I think he is saying more than that his army is waiting for its leader. He is saying that events are waiting upon his ability to become himself. (quoted in Beaumann, *Henry V*, p. 58)

Finally at one with his role, Howard's Henry was able to unite his men: the role-playing and band-of-brothers themes were resolved together. In Howard's words, 'When he makes the Crispin's Day

5   Alan Howard as Henry before Agincourt, with the stage canopy lowered, from Terry Hands's 1975 RSC production

speech the next morning it isn't just a performance any longer' (p. 58). Accordingly, Hands played this scene in sharp contrast to the scene at the breach.

It began with the English army asleep on stage. In a sequence that had been worked out through detailed improvisations, the army was roused by the Boy beating out reveille on a soup-pot. Gradually they got up, rolled up their blankets, prepared their equipment. When Henry challenged Westmoreland's wish for more men, he merely sat up from where he had been sleeping with the other soldiers. Henry gave his speech as the army assembled around the luggage cart to be given water by the Boy, Henry waiting his turn and drinking from a plain wooden mug. Henry spoke freely and cheerfully, and the speech developed naturally from the situation, never reaching the rhetorical pitch of the breach scene. The downplaying of the speech was deliberate, to delay the moment of the army's rousing itself to the battle, and to make it a collective action, not one imposed by Henry from above. The one rallying call was Henry's 'All things are ready, if our minds be so'. As Howard says, 'Henry passes on to his army the discovery he has made at the end of the night scene' about individual responsibility. Then, in the scene with Montjoy, the army finally, spontaneously drew together:

> No longer are they linked merely by such external things as birth, status or nationality; their unity and determination have become 'interior,' a state of mind, and perhaps heart... In rehearsal the company looked for ways in which this new confidence and togetherness might be expressed. (Hands, in Beaumann, *Henry V*, p. 193)

In the end, Hands made a moment out of Henry's proverb that 'The man that once did sell the lion's skin / While the beast lived, was killed with hunting him' (IV.iii.93-4). It was treated as a kind of music-hall joke, which Henry initiated and the rest of the army completed in chorus. Howard played the rest of his blustering speech tongue-in-cheek, as 'a rousing, blackly funny parody of confident kingship', which united the army in laughter: 'A music-hall moment shared by all, whatever their rank. A game covering a real brotherhood felt for the first time' (Hands, p. 193).

Once Henry had conquered his doubts and united his army, Hands had achieved the principal goal of his interpretation. His choices in the battle sequence seemed mainly designed to avoid compromising those achievements, with a secondary emphasis on war and the pity of war. Hands began the sequence with a forty-second sound montage of horses, arrows in flight, shouting and battle-sounds, with the stage in darkness except for the face of James's Chorus, ostensibly watching the battle. The Pistol/le Fer scene was played for comedy; Hands found it 'an inescapably funny scene' (p. 196). The Boy was killed on stage by three French deserters who plundered and overturned the luggage-cart. The text was rearranged so that Henry did not issue his order to kill the prisoners until after he had seen the dead Boy and said, 'I was not angry since I came to France / Until this instant' (IV.vii.57-8). Hands was frank about his intention to whitewash Henry: 'If the Boy is killed before the order to kill the prisoners is given, then Henry's action seems less harsh. If the Boy is killed after the order to kill the prisoners, Henry seems ruthless, and the killing of the Boy, and the sacking of the royal tent could be the French army's last act of revenge' (p. 199). Hands's explanation of the order, linking it to Henry's earlier refusal of the noble game of ransom, is extraordinary: 'I think Henry is determined that war shall end. I think it is at that moment – "I was not angry" – that he determines it. War must never again be a game – a game played with prisoners ransomed to fight another game' (p. 200). In other words, Henry's killing of the prisoners in a war he initiated is interpreted as an *anti-war* gesture. The absurdity of this notion demonstrates the lengths to which directors can go to rationalise their choices, and to square intractable textual material with the production's interpretive slant.

Having mitigated Henry's cruelty in the battle, Hands now sought to soften it in the following scene, the joke on Williams. First of all, he used a comic brawl to underline the transformation of Henry's army:

> The fight that begins at this point between Fluellen and Williams developed, in our production, into a general much-enjoyed brawl, with all the other soldiers, and with the king's brothers – Glouces-ter and Clarence – joining in, and being turfed aside with notable lack of ceremony.... Here, and in the following scenes, we tried to show how comradeship had brought with it a new understanding of equality. (pp. 208-9)

To achieve this goal Hands and his actors had to resort to considerable ingenuity, particularly in the King's interview with Williams, when he offers him the glove full of money:

Whether he takes it or refuses it, his action, and the way in which Henry speaks to him, have strong reverberations throughout the entire play. If Henry truly expects him to take it, he is being unpardonably patronising to one of the men who has just laid his life on the line for him. If Williams accepts it willingly, he accepts the old, hierarchic, obsequious system that makes such actions possible, at the same time. (p. 210)

Howard felt that Henry is here testing Williams – that he doesn't actually *want* Williams to take the money, but to prove his integrity by refusing it. Dan Meadon's Williams did refuse; then Howard tapped him on both shoulders with the glove, as if to knight him, after which Williams, presumably having established his integrity, accepted the money. Hands himself found this bit of business 'over-elaborate', but Howard and Meadon insisted on it, feeling any other handling of the scene would compromise one or the other of their characters. Gary Taylor points out that while this business satisfied the actors about their characters' integrity, it communicated nothing to the audience:

> I have yet to encounter anyone who understood what the tapping on the shoulders meant, or why Williams first refused the money and then, a line and a half later, accepted it. In fact, I have yet to find anyone who was bothered by his incomprehension of this sequence. (Taylor, p. 158)

In order to preserve his egalitarian hero-king, Hands cut Henry's question about what 'prisoners of good sort' were taken (since it implies that they were spared from the massacre, which historically was the case). The scene ended with another image of the spirit of brotherhood triumphing over archaic, hierarchical ways: when Henry asks for *Non Nobis* and *Te Deum*, the bookish Fluellen began a Latin plainsong, but was slowly drowned out by 'the English army gradually and irrepressibly beginning to hum their marching tune' (Guy Woolfenden, quoted in Beaumann, *Henry V*, p. 48). The final image was a nod to the pity of war: Henry and Montjoy, the last to leave, looked back together over the desolation of the battlefield. But the emphasis of the whole battle sequence was not on combat and its consequences, but on the transformation of Henry's army into a band of brothers.

The wooing scene was important to Hands and Howard as a final step in Henry's self-realisation. According to Howard, 'Shakespeare has shown us a man who has been through all sorts of physical, moral, and emotional tests; he has almost arrived at his completion. Where should he go next but into a true marriage of love and alliance with another human being?' (p. 60). Hands calls it 'Henry's third and most important battle':

> To Shakespeare, and probably his audience, life is always more important than death. And it requires its own act. Henry tries all his old roles, boy, bluff soldier, king. None of them fool the instinctive feminine wisdom of the French princess. She has learnt his language, now he must learn hers. (Hands, quoted in Beaumann, *Henry V*, p. 19)

Thus the scene, in Hands's view, is the culmination of the role-playing theme; Henry must drop his old masks and grow into the role of husband and father.

The importance of the wooing had been set up earlier, when the wall of Harfleur lowered to reveal Katherine, brightly illuminated, while Henry stood alone on the darkened forestage. Having the two characters on stage together foreshadowed their marriage, and the juxtaposition of her learning a new language with Henry's barbarous threats powerfully suggested an alternative to war.

The wooing scene began with a reminder of theatricality: Emrys James took Burgundy's long speech, as the Chorus. All references to the Duke of Burgundy were cut, and James was not so listed in the programme. The Chorus was simply taking a more active role in resolving the play: 'Since that my office hath so far prevailed / That face to face, and royal eye to eye, / You have congreeted' (V.ii.29-31). This bold and interesting choice displeased many critics, who found it, like the modern dress at the beginning, merely distracting. There was likewise an element of stylisation in the wooing scene itself, which used formal, dance-like movements between Henry and Katherine. The wooing was not presented as purely political. Ludmila Mikaël, the Comédie Française actress who played Katherine, describes the scene:

> It is not just a political match. There is development in it. I think Katherine is a match for Henry, in both senses – she is as strong a woman as he is a man, although she is young and very inexperienced.... She asks him a very challenging question – when she says, 'Is it possible that I should love the enemy of France'. Because she is strong, perhaps, something happens between them in the scene, they fall in love, whatever you want to say. (quoted in Beaumann, *Henry V*, p. 96)

[68]

The presentation of a genuine love between Henry and Katherine, 'a true marriage of love and alliance', was the final step in Hands's positive, apolitical reading of the play.

Public and critical reception of the production reveals how well Hands geared his approach to public attitudes in mid-seventies Britain. By qualifying Henry's heroism with self-doubt and moral queasiness, Hands satisfied many viewers who would normally have objected to the play as chauvinistic. The *New York Times*'s Clive Barnes felt Hands's emphasis on non-illusionistic theatricality provided 'a consistent way of keeping the wary distance of history between Shakespeare's morals and our own' (24 April 1977), and the *Yorkshire Post*'s Desmond Pratt went so far as to say 'Politics rightly take the place of pageantry – for this is an anti-war play' (10 April 1975).

Nevertheless, the production provided enough pageantry, and adequately tempered its politics, to satisfy critics with a more conservative approach to theatrical production and English history. B. A. Young of the *Financial Times* felt Howard's Henry was 'a faultless leader as immune from criticism as Churchill himself' (9 April 1975) – a comparison made by at least three other critics (*Jewish Chronicle*, 11 April 1975; *Western Daily Press*, 9 April 1975; *Evening Post*, 28 July 1976). Other critics emphasised the play's appropriateness to the country's economic and social woes:

This *Henry V* is stirring stuff, a reminder of national greatness.... Alan Howard movingly provides a portrait of English fortitude.... This is a gutsy, reviving production at a time of national adversity. And boy, do we need it. (Herbert Kretzmer, *Daily Express*, 9 April 1975)

If you're tired of the gloom and depression hanging over this country at present, go to the company's production of *Henry V* – and have a look at one of England's finest hours. (Liz Gill, *Stratford and Newham Express*, 30 January 1976)

Hands's directorial choices gave audiences the opportunity to inform the production with their own response to the subject matter of the play. Many conservative critics praised the production for what they saw as directorial restraint: 'As for Terry Hands's production, it allows the Bard to tell his stirring tale of unabashed chauvinism with a minimum of directorial interference' (Milton Shulman, *Evening Standard*, 9 April 1975). Shulman's

obliviousness to Hands's 'directorial interference' and his acceptance of the play as simply 'the Bard's' tale of chauvinism is surprising but not uncharacteristic. Indeed, more critics responded
to the conservative aspects of the play than to any of Hands's
qualifying modern attitudes, suggesting that a production must be
very bold indeed to prevent viewers from seeing what they expect
or want to see. On the aesthetic side as well, critics seemed keen to
praise the production's traditionalism rather than such innovations as the rehearsal-room opening, the intervention of the
Chorus as Burgundy, or the emphasis on convention rather than
illusion. The heraldic canopy and the golden armour of the French
were repeatedly singled out in reviews. RSC director Trevor Nunn,
laughing all the way to the bank, was merely amused by the irony:
'In box office terms, it was one of the most successful seasons in
our records. It pleased us, too, to find one of the cheapest seasons
we'd mounted in recent years hailed as one of the most spectacular' (quoted in Beaumann, *Henry V*, p. 7). Ronald Bryden was
less pleased by the company's apparent failure to communicate its
new, non-illusionistic style:

> On the whole critics and audiences seemed to go along with the
> new style of presentation while they were in the theatre. They then
> went off and praised us for the opposite of what we set out to do,
> criticising us in the margins for achieving what we intended....
> there was a certain wry comfort to be drawn from the repeated
> descriptions of one of the most experimental, complex and difficult
> productions [the RSC] had ever staged as simple, straightforward
> and ungimmicky. (Beaumann, *Henry V*, p. 248)

Nevertheless, the production did succeed in establishing the
Hands/Farrah style as the dominant one for the RSC throughout
the remainder of the 1970s. Indeed, the non-illusionistic style may
have been one of the reasons why critics and audiences were so
successful in projecting their own attitudes on to the production –
and why the production was, consequently, so successful.

A final anecdote sums up the contradictions of Hands's production, its odd intersection of radical company and patriotic play,
innovative staging and financially desperate mainstream promo-
tion. Hands arranged a Royal Gala Performance to promote the
company's centenary. Having heard rumours of the production's
radical tendencies, one company director with six tickets wrote in
alarm to Terry Hands:

I was looking forward to attending, but was horrified to learn from a friend that the performance of *Henry V* is to be given in boiler suits or some similar garb. I cannot believe this is true for such a performance, especially with Royalty present. (quoted in Beaumann, *Henry V*, p. 262)

The company gave their usual performance without alteration, although Barrie Rutter, who played MacMorris's lines about blowing up the town with IRA fervour, recalled that 'when we got to that bit I could feel them freezing in their seats. Oh-God-not-in-front-of-our-monarch vibrations came welling up out of the stalls' (quoted in Beaumann, *Henry V*, p. 84). Nevertheless, the Queen and Royal party enjoyed the production, and came backstage to visit the actors. Prince Philip even consented to write a forward to the RSC's commemorative edition of the play, in which he hoped that 'the marvellous spirit of the play' would 'give heart and courage to the band of supporters of the Theatre to overcome the menace of rising costs and inflation in the years ahead' (p. 3). Hands's groundbreaking revaluation of Shakespeare's supposed paean to monarchical nationalism had ensured the RSC of Royal patronage to help it weather its financial crisis. Jack Tinker unwittingly highlighted the ironies of the production by linking it eulogistically with the very concepts it was ostensibly criticising, both in its production style and in its interpretive agenda:

For those who demand of the beleaguered RSC: 'What are thy rents? What are thy comings-in? O Ceremony, show me but thy worth' – this evening is an eloquent answer. (*Daily Mail*, 9 April 1975)

CHAPTER IV

Flat unraisèd spirits:
BBC TV (1979)

The *Henry V* production in the BBC Shakespeare series is some-thing of an oddity in the production history of the play. While it to some extent fits into the general twentieth-century development from patriotic pageant to anti-war analysis, it incorporates vari-ous heterogeneous elements that at first appear anachronistic and irreconcilable. Its aesthetics derive from Victorian antiquarian-ism, while its medium is the studio-set television of the low-budget sit-com. Its fairly full text includes many episodes modern productions use to darken Henry's character, yet its basic inter-pretation derives from mid-century criticism that approves Henry's growth into an ideal king. Its low-key, thoughtful Henry has the contemporary tendency to downplay patriotic rhetoric, yet the series' avowed purpose resembles Charles Kean's Imperial mission to help 'the great cause of civilization and educational progress' (Cole, p. 340). This conflation of contradictory materials suggests something eclectic and challenging; it is a function of the production's consummate blandness that the interpretation seems all of a piece.

The BBC television Shakespeares have been mightily abused elsewhere (see the essays in Bulman and Coursen's *Shakespeare on Television*), so I don't want to be too hard on them here. Some are good and most are competent, and given the circumstances of their production it is perhaps unreasonable to expect more. *Henry V*, directed by David Giles, dates from the early period of the BBC series, when Cedric Messina was producer; accordingly, it lacks the more adventurous, experimental spirit of the later Jonathan Miller productions. Under Messina's tenure, the BBC Shake-speares had an aspect of cultural imperialism; in his words, 'the productions have now been sold for showing throughout the world, thus fulfilling the public broadcasting ideal behind the series – to make them available to audiences who would have no other access to Shakespeare' (Messina, p. 6). Messina's goal 'to make solid, basic televised versions of Shakespeare's plays to reach a wide television audience' was codified by the series' American underwriters, who included Time/Life, Exxon, Metropolitan Life and the Morgan Guaranty Trust company. The contracts they drew up with the BBC specified that the plays were to be set in Shakespeare's time or in the historical period they represented, that they were to be no more than two and a half hours long, and that they were to have 'maximum acceptability to the widest possible audience' (Willis, pp. 10-11). Further, the American publicity apparatus apparently claimed that the BBC Shakespeares were to be 'definitive' versions, not of an age but for all time (p. 16). The productions could hardly expect to live up to such a claim, even without the aesthetic and practical constraints imposed on them. They were adequately but not extravagantly funded, and rehearsed and taped on a fairly tight production schedule; *Henry V* was recorded in one week in June 1979. Under the circumstances, and in view of the goals set for it, *Henry V* must be reckoned a success: it is eminently 'acceptable'.

The essential interpretive choices for the production are linked to its treatment as part of a four-play cycle. Like the 1951 Stratford tetralogy, Giles's productions use the basic premise that Shakespeare's later history plays form an interlinked cycle depicting Henry's growth into ideal kingship. Lurking behind both cycles are the interpretations of E. M. W. Tillyard and John Dover Wilson, the first critics to make a strong case for interpreting the history plays as a connected series suitable for sequential production. Both critics read the plays as political lessons, arguing that Henry's rejection of Falstaff, like his defeat of Hotspur, is a necessary and valuable step on the road to heroic leadership. Anthony Quayle, who played Falstaff in both the 1951 production and the BBC series, made him an attractive but genuinely corrupt figure whom Hal must reject. Accordingly, both Richard Burton in 1951 and David Gwillim in the BBC series played Hal as a serious and sensitive young man growing into authority through hard but right moral choices. When Hal rejects Falstaff and becomes king, the central problem of this interpretation is resolved; it only remains for Henry to exercise his mature leadership, with perhaps a few regretful backward glances.

In their volumes for this series on the *Henry IV* plays, Scott

McMillin and Barbara Hodgdon discuss the essentially conservative, Tillyard/Wilson approach of the Messina/Giles productions. As Hodgdon describes it,

> Messina was entirely willing to identify Tillyard's interpretive frame – by now subjected to considerable qualification from the scholarly-critical community – with Shakespeare's voice. He talked of the histories as 'a sort of curse of the house of Atreus in English' and proposed filming them in a uniform style which would clarify continuities among them and result in an apparent totality. (Hodgdon, pp. 45-6)

Such an approach leaves little scope for investigating the problems in *Henry V*. David Giles's own comments on the play reveal an awareness of the complicated, constructed character of the King:

> You need to see all three plays ... because if you do you cannot possibly take Henry at his face value in *Henry V*.... The Chorus presents the idealised version of Henry, then we see what happens and it gives the audience the most wonderful opportunity to judge. (Fenwick, p. 23)

In fact, however, the production only humanises and sentimentalises Henry. The moments recalling Hal's earlier self merely flesh out the ideal, 'face value' King without really interrogating the Chorus's view. David Gwillim's comments on the role emphasise that, for him, producing the plays in sequence in fact *enhances* Henry's heroism:

> There are moments that fill themselves. In *Henry V* when you're told of Bardolph's death, doing the plays in sequence makes it mean a lot more. If you're just doing *Henry V* alone nobody knows that Henry has anything to do with Bardolph. You see the person fully, as Hal, as a boy, and some of that filters through and it makes it more obvious that *Henry's task is more daunting* than it seems if you only watch the play itself. (Fenwick, p. 24, italics mine)

Cedric Messina is even more emphatic about the degree to which knowledge of Henry's abandoned past reflects positively on the character.

> as he exhorts his soldiers 'unto the breach' one suddenly realises that here is a man for men, and in his dealings with the individuals his polyglot army, his earlier experiences with the ruffians, cut-purses and so forth, the companions of his roistering younger

days, he has learned the common touch. When the Chorus speaks of 'a little touch of Harry in the night,' he means that Harry understands them, their needs and their capacities. (Messina, p. 7)

For Messina and Gwillim, at least, the connections to the earlier plays of the cycle are largely a way of highlighting the humane virtues of the reformed Prince. What results, in spite of Giles's more penetrating comments, is a blandly noble, amiable Henry in a thoroughly straightforward production. This result is hardly surprising, given that, in the context of the Giles/Messina cycle, *Henry V* is a destination rather than a journey.

In accordance with the BBC's mandate, the costume designs for *Henry V* are historically accurate to a degree Charles Kean would have envied. Odette Barrow, the costume designer, enthusiastically relates the expert advice she received on medieval heraldry from Charles Kightly, an authority on Agincourt:

> it's not very easy to find out who the banner carriers in fact were at the battle and he has done that for me and sorted out their arms. Mr. Brook Little at the Royal College of Arms has been very helpful too. No one knows who the French banner carriers actually were at Agincourt, so what we've done is Mr. Kightly has made a list of people who would have been suitable as banner carriers, and who were there at the time and could have been the banner carriers, and we've selected from that list. (Fenwick, p. 20)

The slightly absurd lengths to which the producers went to achieve antiquarian accuracy in costuming are rather at odds with the play's emphasis on the processes of representation. Don Homfray, the set designer, and Giles were conscious of the problem, and at least made an attempt to incorporate some of the play's concern with artifice. As Giles said, 'If you do a realistic *Henry V* than you must cut the Chorus, and if you cut the Chorus you don't do *Henry V*' (Fenwick, p. 19). Homfray concurred: 'I'm approaching it rather as a two-dimensional thing: the Chorus is always apologising for his lack of resources, so you've got to do something really theatrical' (Fenwick, p. 20).

The 'really theatrical' approach is not much in evidence in the production, however. Occasionally, Alec McCowan's straightforward medieval Chorus will appear against a dark background, and the lights will come up when the scene begins. For the most part the settings are blandly naturalistic, low-budget studio sets: the walls look flimsy, but they don't look like they're supposed to. The ineffectiveness of Homfray's theatricality is obvious in contrast to the unpainted plywood constructions of Jonathan Miller's *Troilus and Cressida*, for instance, or the junkpile unit set of Jane Howell's *Henry VI–Richard III* productions. Together with the period costumes, the *Henry V* sets just look like an inadequate attempt at naturalism rather than a self-conscious theatrical style. Interior scenes take place amid the same set of phony stone walls, dressed differently for different locations. The opening council takes place in a quasi-medieval throne room, the Southampton scene is embellished with blowing pennants and seagull sounds, the French get a few tapestries, Princess Katherine's English lesson is given in a soft-focus studio bower, and the Agincourt scenes are played on a few square yards of freshly laid turf. For the final wooing, Henry and Katherine weave in and out of a rickety indoor gazebo, open at one side for the convenience of the camera.

The presentation is extremely conventional, mostly in midshots with a static camera that occasionally zooms in for closeups. More even than most of the other BBC Shakespeares, *Henry V* underlines the unsuitability of television as a medium for Shakespeare production. The grey-white light and chilly, flattening quality of soundstage video drains all the life out of the actors, while the mid-to-close range of the recording makes the language seem grotesquely artificial. The live presence of theatrical performance and the sensual plenitude of film can both convey the passion Shakespearean acting requires; television conveys only clinical information. One becomes acutely aware of Alec McCowen's nostrils and David Gwillim's facial mannerisms, but these corporal details don't communicate the humanity of the actors: we study them as specimens behind glass.

In some instances the closeup, talking-heads quality of the taping serves the production well. Peter Saccio has commented on the appropriateness of television for conveying the intimate machinations of power, whether ancient or modern:

> The commanding power of the television camera to guide, edit, and comment here causes political and historical processes to be seen largely as a series of private interchanges and individual responses.... The politics of Plantagenet England were the politics of a very small class, very nearly a family quarrel, as intimate as it was public.... But equally, if not more so, this backstairs notion of politics is modern. In our age of public relations and image-

building, we have good reason to suspect all public statements and to suppose that real political action takes place privately. (pp. 210-11)

The one really effective example of this approach in *Henry V* is the opening exchange between Canterbury and Ely. It begins with the two kneeling at an altar rail to pray – perhaps too obvious an image of episcopal hypocrisy. But the camera glides in to a tight closeup of the two heads as Trevor Baxter's marvellous Canterbury details with withering scorn the provisions of the Commons' bill for claiming Church lands. A distinguished white-haired gent with a face like a well-fed jackal, Baxter enjoys the irony of 'The king is full of grace and fair regard' (I.i.22) without giving away his amusement to Ely. The tight, unblinking camera catches every subtle flicker of wit and malice in Baxter's speech on the King's reformation, then cuts sharply to a reverse shot as he leans conspiratorially over to Ely to whisper 'I have made an offer to his majesty / ... As touching France' (79). As the first cut of the scene, it economically underlines the moment.

Baxter is equally good in his Salic Law speech, though this is drastically cut; but here his effectiveness is diminished by a chorus line of nobles, standing behind him but flattened into the same televisual plane, who vigorously bob and weave in what is virtually a parody of crowd-scene reaction. Particularly egregious is David Buck's Westmoreland, who wears a comic false beard and growls out his warning about the threat of Scottish invasion as though auditioning for a pirate movie. When Baxter gets the screen to himself again, for the metaphor of the well-ordered state as a beehive, his beady eagerness charges the text with excitement. His is the best performance in the production, which never recovers from his departure.

Of the other supporting performances, Tim Wylton's Fluellen is the most distinctive. Well-paired with Brian Poyser's long-suffering Gower, Wylton's Fluellen is a figure of jowly, goggle-eyed stupidity; on the stage he would probably be quite funny, but on the small screen he is merely grotesque. He undercuts the gravity of the scene in the raided English camp, munching an apple and sputtering enthusiastically about Alexander the Pig. Giles can afford to play the scene for comedy; he doesn't need the dead boys to justify the killing of the French prisoners, since Henry's bloody order passed so quickly and matter-of-factly that it is unlikely many viewers even noticed it.

[77]

David Gwillim's Henry is a gentle soul who seems to have no capacity for atrocities. With his slight build, wide mouth, big deep-set eyes and historically correct bowl haircut, he conveys a kind of earnest mediocrity, like a naive, idealistic young monk. In the first scene he seems most at home when considering the arguments of the Archbishop; when the director calls on him to toss the tennis balls playfully to his lords, the gesture seems forced and ungainly. Playfulness was never Gwillim's strong suit, even as Hal; the knowledge of his future kingship clung round him like a wet blanket. He approaches the lighter moments of the role with a curiously nodding, wagging head and a sort of thin crooked grin, but these mannerisms convey no humour, only a sort of ironic self-amusement. It seems unlikely that this lack of warmth is a deliberate choice intended to make Henry a cynical schemer, given that Gwillim and Giles bypass few opportunities for sentiment. The scene with the traitors (II.ii), for instance, is milked to the full, and not ineffectively. The TV closeup serves Giles well in catching the interplay of facial expressions as the scene develops. When Henry confronts Scroop with his personal betrayal, both are facing the camera, and the complementary expressions of anguish on their faces give the scene real emotional punch. By the end of the speech, however, Gwillim goes too far, wringing out the four repetitions of 'Why, so didst thou', in a costive squint that exhausts the viewer's sympathy (128-31).

In spite of his occasional mawkishness, Gwillim's sensitive moments mostly hold up well. In the battle orations, however, he tries with limited success to find alternatives to a traditional heroic style. The Harfleur breach scene is particularly quirky and has occasioned a fair amount of critical comment. Martin Banham, in a damning article on 'BBC Television's Dull Shakespeares', attributes Gwillim's 'uncomfortable handling' of the breach speech to the absence of a plausible army to exhort: 'no one looked more lonely and embarrassed than poor King Henry urging on invisible troops to an indistinct objective via an improbable scaffold' (Banham, in Bulman and Coursen, pp. 215, 218). Ace G. Pilkington, in a supportive chapter on the BBC production, takes issue with Banham's 'overhasty reading' and asserts that the scene is intended to show Hal's discomfort with his warrior-role: 'This explains a Hal/Henry whose voice cracks and who has run and shouted himself out of breath. Undoubtedly in the process he looks uneasy and awkward. He is meant to' (Pilkington, *Screening*

Shakespeare, pp. 95-6). There are clearly some deliberate choices involved in Gwillim's handling of the speech, but I doubt that it is 'meant to' fall quite so flat as it does, and I am not as prepared as Banham is to shift the blame away from Gwillim's Henry.

The scene seems intended to show Henry's common touch, his ability to use the playfulness of the tavern days to cajole his army into vigorous good-fellowship and bravery. Gwillim seems to be trying to *tease* his men into battle; when, for instance, he exhorts them to imitate the action of the tiger (III.i.6), he nods brightly as if to say, 'Don't be spoil-sports; won't this be a lark?'. Pilkington acutely characterises the nervously nodding Gwillim as 'like a lecturer who hopes by this means to convince his class to agree with him or at least to pretend his jokes are funny', but I doubt whether this is such a deliberate effect as Pilkington supposes (p. 94). Gwillim's pantomimic demonstration of 'hard-favoured rage' (8), waving his stiff arms up over his head, is embarrassing rather than heartening, yet his army gamely follows him. Part of the problem is Gwillim's physical awkwardness, which is exacerbated by his armour. He makes a great point of addressing his soldiers individually, yet his consequent lurching and flapping diffuses rather than sharpens his focus. At the end of the speech, he brings his voice down and glances eagerly among his men, delivering 'God for Harry … England … and … Saint … George!' as if announcing a Christmas surprise (34). There is nothing about the scene to suggest self-doubt on Henry's part, nor any deliberate criticism of his leadership methods. The speech is supposed to convince, but it doesn't.

One of the curiosities of the production is the way its inclusion of material that ought to deepen or qualify Henry's character merely reinforces its flatness. The Harfleur threats are considerably cut, but those that remain are delivered in measured tones suggesting neither bottled brutality nor desperate bluff, merely the kind of puzzled earnestness that characterises many of Gwillim's readings. The report of Bardolph's death touches a nerve, and is nicely and subtly played: Henry freezes for a moment while the camera thrusts inquisitively toward his startled, reflective face, and his line 'We would have all such offenders so cut off' is delivered with hushed gentleness (III.vi.111). Yet in the lines that follow with Montjoy, Gwillim is quickly back to his smug good humour, his lips flattening in a blandly ironical smile. In the exchanges with his commanders that close the scene he is again unflappably cheerful and modestly confident.

[79]

The argument with Williams is perhaps the most disruptive part of the production in terms of Henry's regal persona. Both Giles and Gwillim comment on the public/private opposition in the character: Giles says that 'Henry, in public, is always aware that he's in public, and is always, to a certain extent, masked', while Gwillim remarks that playing the role 'is a question of finding the human being within the demands of that public figure' (Fenwick, p. 24). Yet throughout the production, the 'private' glimpses of Hal/Henry only serve to show his suitability for his public role: he's a great king but also a sensitive young man, and there's no real contradiction between the two. In the Williams scene, however, we get something else. Henry is visibly uncomfortable as he begins his nocturnal prowl; his farewell to Sir Thomas Erpingham, 'God a mercy, old heart, thou speak'st cheerfully', is spoken *sotto voce* to himself with ironic stress on the last word, as if acknowledging that cheerfulness is sadly inappropriate (IV.i.34). When he meets the three soldiers around their fire, he gives his speech about how 'the king is but a man as I am' matter-of-factly; he is not ruminating on his own condition but feeling out his men (100-l3). Likewise, his line 'Methinks I could not die anywhere so contented as in the king's company, his cause being just and his quarrel honourable' is plainly bait thrown out to troll for treason (128-9). Williams's speech on the King's responsibility for his soldiers takes Henry aback for a moment, but when he begins to construct his answer he clearly believes himself. He even adds a note of mockery in his discussion of the likely sins of his soldiers, though he is brought up short by the memory of Bardolph on 'some making the wars their bulwark, that have before gored the gentle bosom of peace with pillage and robbery' (169-71). Henry's face takes on a look of smug satisfaction as he rationalises his foreign war as an instrument of domestic justice: 'here men are punished for before-breach of the King's laws in now the King's quarrel' (175-7).

Williams and Bates seem thoroughly convinced by his specious argument, and Henry, exceedingly pleased with himself, takes a dangerous step further to defend his own reputation: 'I myself heard the King say he would not be ransomed' (197). This proves too much for Williams, and in the quarrel that ensues Henry suddenly jumps to his feet in real and violent anger. The moment is strongly pointed, as Henry rushes into a face-off with Williams, who is restrained by Court, while the hapless Bates looks on frightened between them. For once Gwillim's Henry really is out of his depth; both his kingly composure and personal sensitivity vanish in a moment of outraged vanity. He shouts his parting line – 'It is no English treason to cut French crowns, and tomorrow the King himself will be a clipper' – not as a glib joke but as an angry threat, one which must mystify the soldiers (233-5). He then stalks off, takes a deep breath, and begins the self-analysis of 'Upon the King'.

This speech is Gwillim's best in the production. The camera work is close but undistracting, and the warm campfire lighting gives some colour to Gwillim's face and brings out the depth of feeling in his dark eyes. The material is much more appropriate to Gwillim's vocal style than the public orations are. He very clearly connects the speech back to the argument he has just gone through, plainly recalling Williams's words at several points through subtle inflections of voice and feature. For once Gwillim is not afraid to let us dislike him, as he impatiently complains of being 'subject to the breath of every *fool*' (240-1). He turns the irony upon himself with a bitter, mocking delivery of 'be sick, great greatness and bid thy ceremony give thee cure' (257-8). His descent into self-pity on the final lines about the slave's enviable lot works to Gwillim's advantage, since by dispensing with his smooth and sensitive persona, he gives Henry a place to struggle back from. The prayer scene only brings him halfway; Gwillim uses a sinking inflection on 'I have built / Two chantries', as he realises the worthlessness of his reparations (306-7). At the close of the scene, Henry is still in trouble: the wounds from the Williams argument are left unhealed.

When Henry next appears for the Crispian's Day speech, how-ever, he seems to have fully recovered his spirits. His delivery is conversational rather than oratorical, but the tone is upbeat: he exhorts his generals in the same jokey spirit he showed at the breach of Harfleur. The unease of the night scene is completely erased through the post-battle high jinks over Williams's glove. Tim Wylton's comic Fluellen comes to Gwillim's aid here; his sputtering outrage makes it impossible to take the scene seriously, so Williams's claims against Henry can't carry much weight. Williams is further diminished by being given a silly leather cap reminiscent of Snoopy-as-aviator. He gabbles his speeches rapidly in comic terror; when pardoned, he eagerly accepts Henry's offer of money and even shares a hearty laugh with Fluellen. Henry is framed in the background as Williams and Fluellen make up, his benign, smiling figure presiding over a final erasure of the tensions of the night scene. Any possible worries about Henry's character or responsibilities are forgotten in the warmth of comedy and the glow of victory.

The conventionally positive presentation of Henry is matched by a conventionally negative portrayal of the French. Giles's French are more obnoxious than Olivier's; even Montjoy is haughty and mean, pouring himself a glass of wine and laughingly delivering Grandpré's lines about 'Yond island carrions, desperate of their bones' (IV.ii.39). Giles's French King is not mad like Olivier's, but he is a bumbling incompetent who has difficulty shouting down his own lords, and who must be directed to the treaty negotiations by his Queen. The arrogance of the French men is offset by the grace and charm of the French women. Queen Isabel, a role often cut, keeps all of her lines, though she has no very pointed political dimension. Princess Katherine's English lesson is delightfully played, but with no ominous undertones; Jocelyne Boisseau seems as though she is learning the language in anticipation of a holiday in Bath. Anna Quayle's Alice is an amusing and reassuring presence, worlds away from the sphere of war and politics. For the final wooing scene, Boisseau's Katherine occasionally registers puzzled amusement at Henry's turns of phrase, but she gives him plenty of approving glances, and the outcome is never in doubt. The fairly full text gives the women in the play more lines than they often get, but it doesn't accord them any particular critical stance.

Indeed, the cutting, while not severe, has certain conventional pro-Henry aspects. On the one hand, it includes such episodes as the killing of the prisoners and the executions of Bardolph and the traitors, though these are either glossed over quickly or turned to Henry's advantage. On the other, it makes certain judicious omissions reminiscent of Olivier and his nineteenth-century predecessors. Much of the Salic Law speech is gone, suggesting that Henry has a fairly clear case; the Harfleur threats are greatly abbreviated; the coarse exchange between Burgundy and Henry, with its telling analogy between the conquest of cities and the conquest of women, is also cut. Though the text for the BBC *Henry V* is one of the least cut modern versions of the play, in production it offers few surprises or complexities.

The problem with Giles's production is precisely this: it smoothes out this thorny and uncomfortable play, making it 'acceptable to the widest possible audience' (Willis, p. 11). It refrains from jingoism with a sensitive and gentle Henry, but it mostly backs off from a penetrating analysis of Henry's character, his cause or his army. Giles may disagree with the Chorus's version of events, but he does little to qualify it or to undermine the Chorus's authority. Potentially disruptive voices are curtailed: the four British captains, the tavern crowd and even Williams are played for laughs. The production's smoothed-out aspect has in part to do with its place in the tetralogy. As part of a four-play cycle, *Henry V* must be made to fit with its companion productions. In spite of the bishops' comments on his reformation, Hal's character can't be seen to have changed too radically; Gwillim short-changes both Hal and Henry in keeping them within the same set of boundaries. The Eastcheap companions, having been played for comedy before, remain in that vein – even Pistol's final, potentially tragic speech ends with a virtual wink to the audience. The characters wore historically correct costumes in the earlier plays, so that same antiquarian accuracy must be preserved for *Henry V*, even though the text pays little heed to the historical realities of Agincourt. For Giles and Messina, *Henry V* is fulfilling a place in a story – the victorious conclusion, the promise kept – and so must conform to certain conventions and expectations.

Performance as part of a cycle doesn't necessarily constrain a production – Jane Howell's *Henry VI–Richard III* tetralogy used low-tech Brechtian designs, disjunctive stylistic levels and aggressive characterisations to keep the viewer surprised and engaged in a long and bloody family history. The BBC *Henry V* is neither original nor surprising. Its greatest fault is its bland smoothness, its apparent lack of contradiction, in spite of the manifold contradictions out of which it is built. Scott McMillin's summary of the *Henry IV* production applies equally well to *Henry V*: 'The BBC tape, correct and dull, remains on the shelf until the teacher assigns it. It is as difficult to dislike as it is difficult to view, and it makes no impact' (p. 105). By contrast, Adrian Noble's 1984 production, the next to be discussed, made a very considerable impact by playing up the text's contradictions.

CHAPTER V

Rainy marching in the painful field: Adrian Noble (1984)

Adrian Noble's 1984 Stratford *Henry V* was the first major English stage version since the enormous success of Hands's production. It proved an important milestone in the careers of Noble and the twenty-three-year-old Kenneth Branagh, and helped establish the RSC style for the 1980s. The production, like Noble's later history projects *The Plantagenets* and *Henry IV*, fused the political and personal concerns of the 1960s and 1970s and added a spiritual dimension. Bob Crowley's spare, steely, rectilinear designs reflected the strength, clarity and intelligent detail of the company's best work during this period. Noble's *Henry V* also had unique political and social resonances as the first English production since the Falklands war.

The Falkland Islands campaign was one of the most significant events for British foreign and domestic policy since the Second World War. It renewed British nationalism and assured Margaret Thatcher's Conservative government of unchallenged dominance throughout the 1980s. When Argentine forces occupied the Falklands, small Commonwealth islands off the South American coast, on 2 April 1982, Thatcher's standing among the electorate, and even within her own party, was extremely weak. Thatcher decisively mustered and dispatched British naval forces, and the ensuing conflict brought nationalist enthusiasm to levels it had not reached in decades. By May the Tories led strongly in the opinion polls; on 14 June the Argentine occupying forces surrendered, and the British troops returned to displays of flag-waving national solidarity. As a result, despite the widespread unpopularity of her economic and social programmes, Thatcher was re-elected the following year. As Arthur Marwick has noted, 'the "Falklands factor" was the critical one ... in neutralizing whatever effective resistance there might have been to the political triumph of Thatcherism' (Marwick, p. 284).

The initial response to the Falklands was jubilation, nationalism and a Conservative victory. After the troops returned home, however, left-wing criticisms of the war spread into wider discontent, as unemployment increased and the personal sufferings occasioned by the combat began to be known. Vivid accounts of the confusion of battle and the painful adjustments of return home were published, notably Robert Lawrence's *Tumbledown*. Allegations of combat atrocities on both sides gradually leaked out; the Ministry of Defence investigated reprisal killings of prisoners reminiscent of the double massacre at Agincourt *(Independent on Sunday*, 16 August 1992). In the years following the war the initial outburst of patriotic enthusiasm soured somewhat into a bitterness that permeated British artistic and intellectual life. While Noble's production never specifically alluded to the Falklands, its very historical position made associations between them inevitable. Noble's treatment of war was much harsher and more explicit than previous English productions', emphasising the brutality and misery of the soldiers, showing Bardolph's execution on stage, and using an ironic, quasi-Brechtian chorus to undercut the glory. Nevertheless, Branagh's very young King remained an attractive figure, shown growing into maturity and nobility while learning a grave lesson about the costs of war. The ideological ambiguity of the production was reflected in the response of the press, who read it in diametrically opposed ways depending on their own agendas and preoccupations.

Noble denied having a specifically revisionist intent; and indeed his comments on directing are fairly conservative. He is on record as 'loathing' post-Brechtian overlays on classical texts, and has characterised his own work as 'humanist-expressionist' (*Observer*, 27 June 1982). He is drawn to English Renaissance texts because of their generic complexity and 'refusal to be categorized' (*Times*, 3 October 1983). He disapproves of narrowing interpretive angles: 'We have to grow into Shakespeare', he writes. 'We can't make him what we want him to be.... We always have to start with what he is and not hold him down to what we are' (Noble, p. 342). This text-privileging attitude is linked to a reliance on the humanistic, archetypal theoretical approaches of Northrop Frye and C. L. Barber. Like those critics, Noble often uses the concept of a journey when discussing his productions. 'The journey of the play and the journey of the character ... is at the centre of our work in Stratford', he wrote in reference to his production of *As You Like It* (Noble, p. 339). He argues that this journey is often a physical one into another world – France in *Henry V*, Arden in *As You Like It*, Ephesus in *The Comedy of Errors* – and may allow or force a confrontation with chaos or dark inner impulses:

> In the subjective man we see the possibility of new aspects in the play as soon as we permit that chaos, that paranoia, that darker side. *Henry V* is similar there, I think, because when the king and his men leave Harfleur, they enter a long night. They enter a chaotic world where, as death seems to approach, the future is totally uncertain. *Henry V* goes into disguise, and it becomes a release for him. He learns things and achieves in that marvellous nighttime soliloquy the poise, the presence of mind, the humility, the grace to conquer chaos. So I do not believe the play is political in the sense that it is finally antiwar, but it is quintessentially Shakespearean in the sense that the pattern of chaos is overcome and disguise is a means leading to harmony. (Noble, pp. 339-40)

This reading, echoing Barber's concept of saturnalian upheaval followed by social reintegration (*Shakespeare's Festive Comedy*), reduces the war to a vehicle for Henry's spiritual journey. It is not far removed from the band-of-brothers theme stressed by Hands in his personally oriented, apolitical study of Henry's growth. Yet the apparently conservative humanism of Noble's approach, at least as he describes it, is belied by many of his productions – perhaps none so much as *Henry V*. Noble's notion of a personal, spiritual journey was certainly discernible in Branagh's grave and pious young king, but the production as a whole struck me as a harsh and distinctly Brechtian depiction of men at war in a dubious cause. The gap between Noble's rhetoric and the impact of the production is emblematic of the RSC's need to appeal to a 'universal' Shakespeare, a transcendent genius more concerned with spiritual journeys than historical realities (Sinfield, 'Royal Shakespeare', p. 176). Dominating the timeless humanism of Noble's production, however, was its tough political aspect. Several factors contributed to this side of the production: the fact of the recent war, Noble's directorial choices within scenes, Crowley's lean designs and perhaps especially Ian McDiarmid's remarkable reading of the Chorus.

While the setting was ostensibly medieval, historical specificity was subjugated to a modern, Brechtian aesthetic. Crowley's set was austere, cool and functional. A white half-curtain, like those favoured by Brecht's designer Caspar Neher, traversed the wide Stratford stage at the proscenium. The onstage seating of previous seasons had been removed, leaving an extremely wide forestage, extending to the side walls of the theatre and covered with light grey planking running horizontally across the stage. Where Farrah's vertical planking, in 1975, seemed to launch the actors into the audience, Crowley's held them up for scrutiny in friezelike groupings, an effect complemented by Noble's blocking of the court scenes. The proscenium walls were painted to match the floor up to the level of the halfcurtain, giving the effect of concrete. Above they remained bare brick. A simple door on each side provided access to the forestage.

Behind the proscenium the floor was black or very dark grey, with metal gratings running horizontally the width of the stage (these served to drain the water in III.vi, which was played in the rain). The back wall was also dark, with a door in the centre six to eight feet wide and extending to the full height of the wall. Inset in this was a conventionally sized door. When it opened, a cyclorama was visible behind it.

The stage was altered in various ways during the course of the play, with set pieces, curtains and walls introduced from above or below. The stage effects were simultaneously spare and spectacular. For the battle of Harfleur, a brass wall with three built-in ladders covered the proscenium, rising to allow the rebuffed English soldiers to stagger out beneath in a haze of spotlights and smoke. The French Princess made her first skipping entrance on to a darkened stage under a canopy of pin-spotlights suggesting soaring gothic architecture. The battle scenes were staged without any actual combat through a series of balletic countermarches employing great pennanted standards, artful lighting and volumes of smoke (Robert Bryan's lighting designs received almost universal critical approval). Scenic grandeur was reserved for the French, who in Michael Coveney's description provided 'a scintillating vision of hubristic splendour, the generals glistening in an almost oriental blare of horizontal golden spears and spangled military lapels' (*Financial Times*, 29 March 1984). The night before Agincourt the French rose on a broad narrow platform bearing human and equine armour, easy chairs and a large chess set, all in gold, in stark contrast to the 'horrid ghosts' of the English, whose smudged faces the Chorus had just been picking out with an anachronistic flashlight on the darkened forestage. The contrast between French and English was an important principle of the costume designs. The English wore textured greys with unspecific silhouettes and little ornamentation. The French, who were mostly played seriously (except for Nicholas Woodeson's petulant Dauphin), wore rich, fifteenth-century black velvet and golden armour. Just before the battle, the French generals were lowered in from the flies on a golden catwalk with blazing lights underneath, rather like the spaceship in *Close Encounters of the Third Kind*. These moments of spectacle, impressive as they were, nevertheless were contained within Crowley's overall scheme of coolness, clarity and restraint. All design elements ran the width of the stage and had the same flat, horizontal, relatively undecorated and uncoloured aesthetic.

The atmosphere of demonstration and scrutiny suggested by the set was reflected most fully in Ian McDiarmid's Chorus. The play's opening established his importance as controller and critic of the action. Dim lights rose on his ghostly figure, standing on the forestage in timeless black clothes. His rodentish face was very pale; his thin red hair slicked back. Behind him the assembled company filled the dark upstage area, evenly distributed across the wide stage. They wore the basic English costume of light grey tunics, trousers and boots – modern-looking but plausibly medieval. The effect was cool, forceful, contained and Brechtian.

McDiarmid spoke his first lines with great depth and pomp, in a manner that suggested sarcasm but didn't confirm it until he ironically dropped his voice for 'But pardon, gentles all' (I.Chorus.8). He spoke very sneeringly of 'this *unworthy* scaffold' (10). The whole speech was marked by sudden changes of inflection, intonation and tempo, often within a single line. The effect was both self-indulgent and caustically ironic – Michael Billington described McDiarmid as 'holding the more extravagant phrases up to light like a jeweller hunting flaws' (*Guardian*, 29 March 1984). Billington's phrase accurately captures the ironic scrutiny suggested by McDiarmid's performance. Michael Coveney commented at length on its importance:

> The show starts with Ian McDiarmid deflating his own rhetorical chorus act within the first speech.... He watches and he goads. He even appears to be enjoying the performance before quickly

resuming a bitchily jocose manner with a swirl of his Mephistophelian black cloak.... This most original and creative playing of the chorus is at one with a production of which it is a corporate element (*Financial Times*, 29 March 1984)

Other reviewers were more critical: Kathy O'Shaughnassy found McDiarmid's performance 'so mannered and artificial it was hard to understand' (*Spectator*, 1 June 1985). At any rate, McDiarmid's performance was central to the interpretation. Irving Wardle, contrasting Noble's production with Hands's, wrote that, while the earlier production had focused on Henry's growth to self-knowledge, the central figure in Noble's was the Chorus:

a wry commentator in timeless costume who remains onstage throughout, reflecting every queasy shift of emotion with which modern audiences view this discordant work. It is a bewitchingly varied and witty performance, but its main importance is structural. It invites the spectator not only to share the task of imagination, but also to acknowledge complicity in the play's nationalistic prejudices. (*Times*, 30 March 1984)

McDiarmid's continual sardonic presence – he never left the stage, nor was he ever acknowledged by the characters – provided a critical, cynical twentieth-century perspective on every scene. Ros Asquith felt that 'Ian McDiarmid's cynical, sophisticated chorus is so eerily attached to the proceedings that he seems to prophesy rather than explain the action – and harps on his rhetorical role with a kind of "here-we-go-again" weariness' (*Observer*, 19 May 1985). There were certainly ambiguities and apparent contradictions in the performance. If the Chorus so disapproves of the action, why does he seem to make it happen? Why is his tone so often at odds with his rhetoric? Lyn Gardner felt McDiarmid's performance underlined 'Noble's equal scorn for the French and English (all are fools tossed on the stormy sea of history)' and noted that this interpretation 'rather robs Kenneth Branagh's solid Henry of any psychological development or greatness' (*City Limits*, 24 May 1985). The two performances were certainly in opposition – critic after critic held up the two as polar figures in the production's structure – but I would argue that the dissonance between McDiarmid's knowing, cynical observer and Branagh's very earnest young king was one of the keys to the effectiveness of the production. As I discuss below, Branagh's likable Henry engaged sympathy throughout the play, but the constant presence of McDiarmid worked to disrupt or qualify audience response.

Noble's directorial choices repeatedly emphasised the pragmatic politics, emotional excesses and dirty realities of Henry's war. The opening English scenes were all played starkly against the white half-curtain. The clerics were neither bumbling buffoons nor scheming villains, but shrewd, formidable politicians. Canterbury's speech was played (by Harold Innocent in Stratford and John Carlisle in London) as a straight discussion of the facts of the succession. The mild irony of 'as clear as is the summer's sun' (I.ii.86) was intended by Canterbury rather than directed at him. The blocking in this scene did much to isolate Henry from the rest of the court, thereby emphasising the weight of his responsibility. He remained alone on one side of the stage while the nobles discussed the congruent functioning of the different parts of the state. When Canterbury concluded his bee metaphor with the execution of the 'lazy, yawning drone' (204), Brian Blessed's bear-like Exeter led a loud belly-laugh. This choice helped establish the rough, brutal attitudes of Henry's court, and prefigured the various executions to come – of the traitors, Bardolph, the French prisoners – in all of which Exeter was to play a vigorous part. Blessed's characterisation provided a useful foil for Branagh's sensitive King, doing the dirty work and liking it while Henry looked on, pained but resolute. The production suffered when the part was taken over in London by the smaller, subtler Pete Postlethwaite.

Blessed was particularly incensed by the tennis-ball insult, flinging one to the King and then angrily slamming shut the chest on 'This was a merry message' (298). Branagh himself displayed, in his speech to the French herald, a capacity for volcanic anger which became a key facet of his characterisation. This first scene communicated that Henry's war resulted from crafty greed on the part of those who stayed behind and schoolboy belligerence on the part of those who went. The final speech, however, hinted at one other motivation which proved very important: Henry's genuine belief in the divine justice of his cause.

The King's purposeful exit, 'That this fair action may on foot be brought' (310), and the rising excitement over the war which accompanies it in the text, were deftly undercut by the handling of the next chorus speech. McDiarmid was particularly mocking for

'Now all the youth of England are on fire', and played up the greed of 'crowns imperial, crowns *and* coronets, / Promised to Harry and his followers' (II.Chorus.6-11). At this point he opened a hatch on the stage floor from which the ragged Eastcheap characters emerged for II.i. The extreme tattiness of Pistol and his friends, emphasised by the blazing white lighting which came up for the scene, made a highly comic contrast to the choral rhetoric; a contrast which McDiarmid relished after the scene when he resumed the speech with 'The French, advised by good intelligence / Of this most *dreadful* preparation, / Shake in their fear' (12-14).

While the low-life characters were generally played (without great success) for boisterous and affectionate comedy, Noble also associated them with the pathos and fear of war, particularly in the departure scene (II.iii). Unlike Hands, who used Pistol's 'To suck, to suck, the very blood to suck!'(II.iii.57) as a brutal, ironic echo of the more euphemistic exit of the King and court, Noble concentrated on the sadness of parting and the fear of the unknown. The white half-curtain had been opened by this time, and the dark upstage area yawned ominously behind. The King and his army had marched into it with banners and pageantry; the Eastcheap regiment looked fearfully upstage, Pistol pushing a pram full of provisions, an outsize Mother Courage. Patricia Routledge's Quickly delivered the Falstaff speech as straight tragedy (building to an awkward climax on 'as cold as any *stone!*'). The boy wept. Nym's 'I cannot kiss – that's the humour of it' (61) was quiet, grave, and desperately sad. Sentimental music played as the men made their way through the darkness to the big door at the back of the stage, where they turned in silhouette for a last wave to Quickly. She whispered her adieu, crossed herself, and descended into the hatch, as the music swelled and the great brass wall came down for Harfleur. It was an effective and affecting moment. Michael Billington found it the keynote of the production: 'What I shall remember most from this evening is the poignant sense of loss. You see this best in the exquisitely-played scene of low-life leave-taking … the embarrassment and pain of departure' (*Guardian*, 19 May 1985).

The pathos of the low-lifes was heightened by giving them a kind of theme tune. Pistol's plainsong in III.ii and the Boy's wish to be in an alehouse in London were combined into a single song which they sang together *a cappella*: 'If wishes would prevail with me / My purpose would not fail with me / But thither should I hie.'

6   The execution of Bardolph, watched by Henry, the Chorus and the rain-soaked troops, from Adrian Noble's 1984 RSC production

This song, first heard before Harfleur, recurred through the play – hauntingly when candles were lit around the boy's corpse after Agincourt.

It was through the fate of the low-lifes that the human costs of the war were most fully brought out. The scene at the bridge over the Ternoise (III.vi) is worth considering in detail, as it is typical not only of Noble's presentation of war but of the way in which production reconfigures the text through interpretive emphasis. III.vi is basically a transitional scene between the victory at Harfleur and the impending danger of Agincourt. Henry's army, in retreat, has successfully held the bridge. Fluellen has his illusions about Pistol's valour punctured when the latter asks him to entreat for Bardolph, who is 'like to be executed' (III.vi.104). Henry communicates his defiance to Montjoy, the first of many times he will do so. Nothing else happens in the scene as written.

In Noble's production this scene was one of the climaxes of the play, coming just before the interval. It contained one of Crowley's biggest scenic effects: the entire English army huddled under tarpaulins in a line upstage, under a continual, ten-minute downpour of real water. The image quoted the trenches of Passchendaele, as well as anticipating Henry's 'rainy marching in the painful field' (IV.iii.111). When Fluellen told Henry of Bardolph's crime and sentence, the King put his hand to his head in anguish. Bardolph was brought in, guarded, downstage right. Henry faced him across the wide forestage, the rest of the army watching from their upstage line. Bardolph knelt, fixing Henry with an imploring gaze for ten or fifteen seconds of silence. With effort, Henry raised his eyes to Exeter's, who stood behind Bardolph, and gave an almost imperceptible nod. Exeter – the huge, bearded, armoured Brian Blessed – twisted a garrotte around Bardolph's neck. The strangling was slow and horrible, with bulging eyes and bloody saliva and the king fighting back tears. When released, the dead Bardolph remained kneeling, his head slumped forward. Only then did Henry come in with the line, 'We would have all such offenders so cut off' (III.vi.111).

This moment – which interrupted the textual progress of the play for a full minute – was one of the most memorable in the production. Michael Ratcliffe noted the extraordinary pay-off Noble's gamble with the scene had:

> The effect is to increase the king's humanity, not to lessen it, and
> if it be objected that to increase one man's humanity by the

termination of another's is a remarkably indulgent way of achieving that end, it is part of the intractable moral ambivalence ... generated by this remarkable play. (*Observer*, 1 April 1984)

Noble's handling of the scene allowed him to have his cake and eat it too, horrifying the audience with the brutality of military justice while making Henry seem its victim rather than its author. The scene was not yet over, and Henry addressed himself to the remainder with increased stature. Christopher Ravenscroft's Montjoy entered at the worst possible moment; Henry's terse questioning of him suggested great self-restraint. The interview established a kind of respect on both sides which developed in subsequent scenes. Henry's character was much strengthened by the growing admiration of this French herald, whom Ros Asquith found 'the noblest creature on stage' (*Observer*, 19 May 1985).

After Montjoy's exit, Branagh managed to convey both unshakable piety and despondence and exhaustion:

We are in God's hand, brother, not in theirs.
March to the bridge. It now draws toward night.
Beyond the river we'll encamp ourselves,
And on tomorrow bid them march away.

(175-8)

After taking a last long look at Bardolph, who had remained grimly kneeling on the forestage, Branagh slowly made his way up to join the troops in the rain. Ian McDiarmid pulled the half-curtain shut to heavy, distant drums as the lights went down for the interval. The muddy misery of the rain effect, the anguish of the execution, the determined defiance of Henry's speech to Montjoy, and the resigned faith of his final order gave this relatively minor scene, as played, a moral weight greater than anything that had preceded it in the play, and so made it a fitting conclusion to the first half. The production's strategy of making Henry a hero in spite of, not because of, the war was fully demonstrated in this powerful scene.

The aftermath of the battle of Agincourt was another sequence through which Noble established his unromantic, horrors-of-war reading. The battle itself was staged with lots of running and shouting on the darkened, smoky stage, with spotlights shining up through the gridded floor and martial music blaring and thundering. After the scene with le Fer (which was played for comedy), the boy was ambushed by three French soldiers. They froze in a blue down-light while the Chorus pulled the half-curtain across in front of them. In the London production, it was smeared with blood.

The killing of the prisoners was given considerable prominence. When the sound of a trumpet revealed that 'The French have reinforced their scattered men' (IV.vi.36), Henry gave the order unhesitatingly, with 'terse brutality' (Billington, 29 March 1984). 'Then every soldier kill his prisoners' was spoken with quiet, deadly firmness, and 'Give the word through!' was a vicious shout. Henry was clearly not acting in revenge for the killing of the boys, about which he did not yet know. This was the moment at which Branagh's Henry was furthest out on a limb, so far as audience sympathy was concerned. The effect was compounded when, immediately after the order was given and the forestage cleared, McDiarmid drew the curtain to reveal the carnage of the camp. This sudden juxtaposition had the effect of making Henry seem responsible for the death of the boys: the killing of the prisoners was an act of comparably inhuman brutality rather than a justifiable retaliation (or a sensible battlefield tactic). The stage was strewn with corpses, tent fabric, banners and supplies, under blue lights and a pall of smoke. Fluellen and Gower stood over the bodies in shock. Gower's 'Wherefore' was significantly excised, thus eliminating any suggestion that Henry acted in revenge. Gower snarled in simple satisfaction, 'The king most worthily hath caused every soldier to cut his prisoner's throat' (IV.vii.9-10).

Fluellen's comparison of Henry to 'Alexander the Pig' was artfully pared to avoid breaking the sense of horror and outrage. Siôn Probert's Fluellen – relatively young, handsome, long-haired and swaggering – had been fairly amusing before, but here managed to keep his character consistent without breaking the pathos of the scene. The speech was played as the confused rambling of a man in deep shock, with tears at the mention of the Wye (hinting perhaps that the boy was also Welsh). Fluellen's two moments of forgetfulness – of the names of the Macedonian river and of Falstaff – were very effective played this way. He rose to sudden anger at the discussion of the King's killing his friends; presumably this was to indicate outrage at Henry's leading men and boys to their deaths, and had little to do with Falstaff. Certainly his tearful 'There is good men porn at Monmouth' (54-5) seemed to refer again to the boy, whose hand he was holding, rather than to Henry.

Henry's entry speech, 'I was not angry since I came to France / Until this instant' (57), built to shouts as he looked at the destruction about him. On 'we'll cut the throats of those we have', Branagh grabbed a French prisoner and nearly killed him, then pushed him away in tearful frustration. This action suggested a realisation of the futility of vengeance, and was a step toward redeeming Henry for his earlier prisoner massacre. When Montjoy entered, Henry violently dragged him down into the piles of corpses, so that his shouted 'What means *this*, herald?!' referred to the murder of the boys, not merely to Montjoy's embassy (70). After Montjoy's speech, Henry replied in quiet, weary confusion, 'I tell thee truly, herald, / I know not if the day be ours or no' (85-6). When Montjoy replied affirmatively, Henry, on his knees, almost incredulous, whispered, 'Praisèd be God, and not our strength for it' (89). One by one, the exhausted soldiers flung their weapons to the steel floor with a great clanging of metal – a powerful moment noted by many critics. It was characteristic of the production, in that it was open to both anti-war and patriotic interpretations.

Henry tried to stand when asking the name of the castle, and stumbled from exhaustion; he got up and moved weakly downstage for 'Call we this the field of Agincourt' (92). While Fluellen praised the valour of the Welsh, Henry laughed and cried, his head down, and he tearfully embraced Fluellen on 'For I am Welsh, you know, good countryman' (109). After saying 'Bring me just notice of the numbers dead / On both our parts' (121-2), Henry suddenly, startlingly collapsed, Exeter barely catching him before he hit the ground. The tears and exhaustion with which Henry greeted victory were in keeping with Noble's somber treatment of war; but just as Fluellen's Alexander the Pig speech had threatened the decorum of the dead boys scene, now another ostensibly comic episode – the glove joke on Williams – rather awkwardly followed this moment of high emotion. The glove scene always has the potential for making Henry seem a smug bully, especially if the earlier argument has been serious and important, as it was. Noble cut the scene slightly and transferred the burden of the joke on to the incensed Fluellen, emphasising Henry's role as peacemaker. The glove ploy thus came across not as a cruel joke, but as a means of ensuring good fellowship among the victors; Williams retained his dignity and seemed satisfied. The tone of gravity returned for the reading of the lists of the dead. Henry was shocked into disbelief by the French list, and could barely stammer out,

'This note doth tell me of – [long pause] te – [pause] ten *thousand* French / That in the field lie slain' (IV.viii.82-3). The misery of Montjoy, whose presence isn't called for by the text, was effectively exploited during the reading of the list of the dead. He grieved personally for the Admiral of France, whose death he had not known of. Brian Masters wrote that 'Montjoy's sudden urge to leave, as the list of French dead is read out by the victorious king, is pregnant with shame and pity' (*Standard*, 17 May 1985). When Henry got to the list of English dead, the soldiers crowded round to hear. Branagh put in a note of personal grief for Davy Gam Esquire, and paused again in disbelief at 'of all other men / But – *five-and-twenty*' (107-8). Then, after a long pause, he looked up for 'O God, Thy arm *was* here', in awed amazement (108). When I saw the production in London, Branagh seemed to be adding a note of challenge to 'Take it God, for it is *none but thine*', as if blaming God for the carnage. At the scene's end the soldiers moved slowly upstage, singing a plainsong *Non Nobis*, while McDiarmid pulled a gauze traverse curtain. In the London production, the lower section of the curtain was covered with names, lettered in the style of a medieval manuscript: by its shape and purpose, it instantly suggested (to an American playgoer at least) the Vietnam memorial in Washington.

The whole sequence very powerfully dramatised the human cost of war without negating the humanity, even heroism, of the warriors. The moral and political tone was roughly equivalent to that of Oliver Stone's Vietnam film *Platoon*. The contradiction involved here, between attacking war and celebrating the qualities it brings out in those who wage it, is one faced by most modern productions of *Henry V*. Noble defends this contradiction as essential to the functioning of the play, arguing that Shakespeare's presentation of history should arouse 'almost completely contradictory feelings':

> You'll feel, if it's done reasonably well, great jingoistic pride, that kind of awful hot feeling that politicians and warmongers try to encourage in you, to give you the courage to kill your fellow man. You will experience these feelings when Henry V inspires you to war. You will also feel completely sickened by the whole business. (Berry, *On Directing Shakespeare*, 170-1)

The entire production was informed by this impulse toward contradiction. Aside from the specifically anti-war choices I have enumerated, each scene was played independently for its own effect. The low-life scenes were played primarily for comedy, the wooing scene for romantic charm, the battle speeches for heroism. The multi-faceted, complex nature of the production drew much critical praise; in Billington's words, 'It doesn't wantonly impose a point of view: it simply seeks out the variety of arguments in Shakespeare's multiangled text' (*Guardian*, 18 May 1985). In some ways, to be sure, the production thus avoided committing itself politically; it remained defensively in the shadow of Shakespeare's play. Only McDiarmid's Chorus proclaimed itself as standing apart, at an ironic distance not only from the action but from the very lines of the text.

Noble's wish to bring out the contradictory qualities in the play complemented Kenneth Branagh's approach to King Henry. 'From the beginning, we agreed that the many paradoxes in the character should be explored as fully as possible', Branagh wrote. 'That we shouldn't try to explain them' (Jackson and Smallwood, p. 97). The principal paradox – a historical as well as dramatic one – is that between Christian piety and war of aggression. Branagh stressed his 'firm belief in the *genuine* nature of Henry's humility and piety' and the 'moral gravitas' and 'genuine emotional weight' of Henry's concern for the bloodshed his invasion would cause (pp. 97, 100). 'He is a genuinely holy man and it seemed to me ridiculous to play him as some 1-D Machiavell' (p. 100). Branagh emphasised Henry's piety at every opportunity through emphatic line readings and stage business. 'May I with *right* and *conscience* make this claim?' Henry demanded of Canterbury, and his invocations of God were always charged with feeling, rather than kingly formality (I.ii.96). Aside from piety, the principle characteristics of Branagh's Henry were youth, integrity, humourless repression and a capacity for explosive emotion. Branagh felt the King was 'an intensely private man ... forced to live completely outwardly ... under pressure from all sides':

> His own personal concept of honour seemed fueled by tremendous repression. He was unable to release huge amounts of humour and indeed of violence. The responsibility of kingship which he takes so very seriously keeps all such human emotions contained, but all the more charged and dangerous. When such qualities are released we see them at their extremes. (Jackson and Smallwood, p. 101)

[98]

7   Kenneth Branagh on the walls of Harfleur,
from Adrian Nobel's 1984 RSC production

Accordingly, Branagh was very contained in the first scene, moving in a restrained, awkward manner and showing little emotional or vocal range. The directorial and acting choices emphasised Henry's isolation and capitalised on Branagh's youth (he was twenty-three, four years younger than the historical king). Canterbury's lengthy praise of Henry's statesmanship had been cut, along with much of Henry's participation in the debate on Scotland. The young king was an untested politician getting ready to make his first big move. Irving Wardle described Branagh in this scene as 'a cold, quiet figure, watching and listening and giving nothing away', then suddenly exploding into 'paroxysms of psychotic rage' in the tennis-ball speech (*Times*, 30 March 1984). The sudden violence of Henry's character was a recurring motif, as Wardle noted: 'The performance throughout presents a poised, confident mask through which panic and savagery periodically break out'. In the scene with the three traitors, Henry flew into an agonised rage over his betrayal by his 'bedfellow', Lord Scroop, flinging him to the ground and then embracing him. The note of piety was again marked when Henry, going through his catalogue of men's pretended virtues, concluded with a scream, 'Seem they RELIGIOUS? / Why, so didst thou!' (II.ii.130). The speech then cut directly to Henry's image of Scroop's revolt as 'another fall of man' (142).

Actually, the long, angry speeches in the first part of the play were those least suited to Branagh's natural abilities. He is a small, open-faced man with a voice which is strong and clear but doesn't show much range when sustained for long periods at high volume. An immensely likable actor, Branagh was most effective in showing the vulnerability and courage of the beleaguered young soldier, and in exploiting his natural boyish charm in the wooing scene. The overall impression this production gave of Henry V was thus not of a cunning politician nor a violent psychotic, but a sincere, passionate, perhaps not very smart but deeply feeling young man, going into war without fully grasping its human cost; summoning up reserves of leadership and courage through a strong faith in God, despite doubts in himself; growing into authority through a series of moral shocks, helped by luck and circumstance, but never flagging in determination. Branagh's naturally engaging, youthful and physically unthreatening presence (together perhaps with a trace of matinée-idol vanity confessed in his autobiography) tended to work against the 'professional killer of chilling ruthlessness' which he recognised as an aspect of the part (Jackson and Smallwood, 97). Branagh recounts a significant exchange with Adrian Noble during previews, 'our first real argument':

> Look, Ken ... I think that er ... I mean, the er ... performance is certainly developing enormously er ... but I do think that you must try less hard to er ...'
> 'What?'
> 'Be liked.' (*Beginning*, 148)

This note was perhaps not entirely heeded: Francis King found Branagh 'like some fresh-faced undergraduate cox determined to bring his crew to victory in the Boat Race' (*Sunday Telegraph*, 19 May 1985), and Billington was 'not sure he would be capable of the brutalities threatened before Harfleur, but it is an immensely appealing and well-spoken performance' (*Guardian*, 18 May 1985).

The appeal of Branagh's King was balanced by the anti-war thrust of Noble's production, with its emphasis on the horrors unleashed by Henry's action. The case for Henry's responsibility for the carnage – and the questions about the justice of his cause – were stated very strongly by Malcolm Storry's commanding, angry Williams. The King's counter-arguments sounded weak and glib, an effect increased by Branagh's distancing adoption of a Welsh accent for the scene. Branagh felt that Henry's replies are indeed unsatisfactory: 'I finally came to the conclusion that Henry answers no question in that scene and the "Upon the King" soliloquy emerges because of the terrible certainty of what Williams has said' (Jackson and Smallwood, p. 103). This speech, and the prayer that follows it, were central to Branagh's interpretation of the role. Doubt, isolation and loneliness, and the enormous moral as well as political responsibility of rule, were the qualities Branagh felt most basic to the King's position – he gained support for these beliefs in a discussion with the present-day Prince of Wales (*Beginning*, pp. 141-4). While 'Upon the King' was a grave, lonely meditation on his responsibility, spoken in measured tones in a spotlight, 'O God of battles' was a desperate, terrified plea. 'O not today!' was a shout of anguish, and Henry fell to his knees when hysterically recounting his acts of contrition for his ill-gotten throne: 'Five *hundred* poor I have in yearly pay' (IV.ii.304). As Alan Howard had done, Branagh played the scene in a

Gethsemane-like agony, 'the anguished fear of a young man whose mistake would cost thousands of lives', in Branagh's words. 'I wanted to infuse "and all things [stay for me]" with the dark dread of a man who would expect to go to hell and for whom the place was an absolutely real concept' (*Beginning*, pp. 137-8). Branagh's playing of this speech was one of the key moments of his performance. By the same theatrical sleight-of-hand that made long-suffering heroes out of Henry's genocidal warriors, and that made Henry seem the victim of Bardolph's execution, in this scene Henry's very doubts about his position had the effect of justifying it.

The wooing scene allowed Branagh's naturally winning qualities to shine through; at the same time, Noble qualified it with enough reminders of the savagery of the war to avoid compromising his overall political perspective. Branagh recognised the danger that the scene might break away from the rest of the production:

It was almost the greatest challenge of the performance to make credible that this was the same man whom we had seen throughout the play. In the end Shakespeare as usual provided the simplest answer, and we played the scene to the hilt on the simplest of premises, that the two characters do not speak each other's language but do literally in the course of one brief interview fall in love. This despite Henry having disposed of most of the French Royal Family. (Jackson and Smallwood, p. 104)

Just before the scene began, as Pistol made his shuffling, defeated exit from the darkened stage, the alehouse song of the dead boy was heard, very distantly. A harp picked up the tune as silent figures entered the dark area upstage of the curtain and began to light candles around the bodies which remained from the field of Agincourt. This image of waste and mourning remained visible throughout the wooing. The speech about the ruination of the garden of France was gravely delivered by an ancient Burgundy, whose voice rose to an anguished shout (slightly against the sense of the text) for 'the coulter rusts / That should deracinate such *savagery*!' (V.ii.47). Henry was formal but firm. After the French king had sadly left his daughter, the scene brightened into embarrassed comedy. Henry, looking young and handsome in a simple dove-grey tunic, began his wooing haltingly, then tossed off 'An angel is like you, Kate, and you are like an angel' with quick, self-pleased wit (110). His first 'I love you' was half-swallowed in embarrassment, as though Henry knew how outrageous it sounded, but was obliged to say it anyway.

'Clap hands and a bargain' was a desperate attempt to get this awkward situation over with (131). Both drew big audience laughs. At the end of Henry's wooing speech, Cecile Paoli's Katherine paused a long time, and removed her veil, before asking (herself as well as him) 'Is it possible dat I sould love de ennemi of France?' (175). Henry's possibly menacing reply ('for I love France so well I will not part with a village of it') was played by Branagh as if it were a genuine point in Henry's favour, and got a laugh and some applause. Branagh had the audience in the palm of his hand by this time.

Branagh made a big moment of 'by my honour, in true English, I ... [long pause] *love* ... thee', almost making us believe this improbability by seeming to realise it himself for the first time (231-2). When Katherine refused his kiss on grounds of custom, he replied, 'Oh, *Kate*', in amused frustration, as if saying, 'Come *on*'. Just after the kiss, he suddenly broke off downstage, flustered, for 'Here comes your father', getting his biggest laugh of the scene (296). Katherine was played, here as in her earlier scene, as an innocent but sexy teenager, conscious of her own attractiveness and quite interested in the young, handsome Henry. There was no suggestion, on her part, of the political imperative that lay behind the wooing.

When the nobles returned, Exeter was very angry about the king's resistance to the article naming Henry his heir, allowing Henry, by contrast, to seem gentle in his insistent request. When the article was granted, the Dauphin quietly sulked off. Having just been disinherited, he clearly could not be part of the final reconciliation, but his exit wasn't allowed to steal focus or break the generally celebratory mood of the scene. The French king was respectful and dignified in his speech giving Katherine to Henry, although he grew tearful on 'fair France' and turned away to sit down (373). As Queen Isabel had been entirely cut, her final benedictory speech was given to Henry, which made him a benevolent Santa Claus bringing peace to both nations. This conclusion was a thoroughly traditional celebration of Henry's triumphant establishment of a *pax anglica*, tempered only slightly by the sad French monarch and the faintly visible candlelit corpses.

The final Chorus speech reintroduced Noble's more ambivalent interpretation. At the final 'Amen', all but Henry and Katherine turned away upstage as the lights went down, making the upstage carnage more visible. A spot picked out Ian McDiarmid, who delivered his final lines very slowly and gravely. The weary modern perspective was insistently restated: 'they *lost France* and made our England *bleed* / Which oft ... our stage ... hath shown' (12-13). This reminder of the vanity of Henry's war and the pitilessness of history was chillingly juxtaposed to the silhouette of the boyish King and his gold-trimmed bride, so that the engaging lightness of the wooing scene didn't finally disrupt, and in some ways heightened, the effect of Noble's harsh but humanist reading.

Critical responses to Noble's production were generally positive, but varied widely in their ideas about the play, their perceptions of the interpretation and their understanding of the production's relation to historical and theatrical tradition as well as to contemporary national issues and attitudes. The theatrical sophistication of reviewers and readership – their familiarity with other productions of the play and with interpretive strategies and conventions – was certainly a factor. In general (though by no means exclusively) the national dailies paid more attention to the production's theatrical context than did the regional weeklies. Consequently, they tended to be more approving, while the locals – judging the production independently, on its merits as an evening of theatre – tended to offer sharper criticisms.

Critics were divided on their opinion of the politics of the play itself. Rosemary Say considered it a 'risky choice' for the RSC, given that 'Heroism, with blatant patriotic – and, if you like, chauvinistic – fervour storming alongside is not the stuff of the '80s, where the anti-hero is king' (*Sunday Telegraph*, 1 April 1984). Michael Ratcliffe, on the other hand, felt the play encompasses the doubts of modern interpreters:

> The RSC never fail with this piece.... [They] invariably approach it with nervous mutterings about militarism only to rediscover – surprise – that the playwright foresees all their confusions and makes them the subject of the play. (*Observer*, 1 April 1984)

Other reviewers, for praise or blame, felt Noble had worked against the grain of the text in an effort to give contemporary political relevance. David Roper in the *Daily Express* (a conservative tabloid) found Branagh an un-Shakespearian weakling 'who weeps openly on the battlefield in front of his demoralised troops.... In fairness to him, he has not been helped by his director Adrian Noble, who gives us a colourless production in what he has put forward as a post-Falklands interpretation' (30 March 1984).

Most reviewers acknowledged the importance of contemporary events and performance history: specifically the Olivier film and the Falklands war. Ros Asquith praised Noble's 'shrewd and compassionate comprehension of the work':

> He has taken many things into account – where this play sits in the nation's culture; the still-long shadow of Olivier's nationalistic film; and the staging of *Henry V* in an era in which the only antidote to Britain's fading grandeur conceivable to its leaders was the brutal adventure of the Falklands. (*Observer*, 19 May 1985)

Morley likewise called it 'a radical rethink of a play which for nearly half a century had been trapped within the memory of the stage and screen presence of our greatest living actor', and which 'simply uses the changing patriotic perceptions of modern British history' to transform the received idea of the play (*Punch*, 29 May 1985). Other reviewers, notably in the generally more conservative, less sophisticated local papers, looked on the anti-Olivier, anti-Falklands interpretation with some suspicion. While praising the production, the *Evesham Journal and Four Shires Advertiser* said that 'Those familiar with the Olivier film might find the RSC production not brazen enough, and those for whom the smell of the Falklands still lingers may find it thumps too few tubs' (5 April 1984). In other words, the recent war, for a segment of the British populace, made a *more* jingoistic production desirable. The *Rugley Advertiser*'s review exhibited a chauvinistic prejudice almost exceeding any in the play itself:

> The decadent French are victims of their own preening pomp as their gleaming golden armour sucks them into the battlefield mire. Our English underdog lads, on the other hand, have the speed and riot capacity equal to a gaggle of soccer fans on the rampage in Europe. (5 April 1984)

This statement – apparently made in whole-hearted approval – ironically foreshadowed Michael Bogdanov's more critical presentation of Henry's followers as soccer hooligans. The bloodthirsty Rugley reviewer was not satisfied with Branagh's 'flyweight' Henry, whose 'vocal power and hero charisma' he found inadequate. This critic's apparently complete unawareness of Noble's interpretive intention reveals the weight of audience preconceptions in determining the 'meaning' of a production.

Most critics, however, showed an understanding of the range of interpretive possibilities for the play and felt that Noble had taken a middle line. Paul Allen felt that Noble's use of contradictions was the key to the production's power: a power 'to confront an audience all over again with that appalling mixed emotion of wanting "our boys" to win (and even relishing the rhetoric which makes it feasible when it is Shakespeare's rather than the *Sun*'s) while recognizing the horror and futility of the war itself' (*New Statesman*, 6 April 1984). The contradictory nature of the production was perhaps its greatest strength, although it allowed a wide range of audience and critical responses. Noble's emphasis on the harsh consequences of the war did not prevent a sympathetic treatment of Henry, whose youth and religious conviction helped excuse his questionable decisions while making him an acceptable victor. With his Brechtian staging and ironic chorus, Noble unquestionably stacked the deck against a heroic interpretation: but the text itself remained, and critics who were determined to find a traditional interpretation merely dismissed McDiarmid as inadequate and the staging as colourless. The likable presence of Branagh further complicated the equation, and indeed may have been a more important factor than the play's rhetoric in generating traditional responses. In the end, most critics agreed that it was a powerful and effective production which responded to the recent Falklands conflict by stressing the awful realities of war; but how far this interpretation criticised or accepted the play's depiction of military heroism remained a matter of dispute.

CHAPTER VI

These English monsters:
Michael Bogdanov (1986)

Michael Bogdanov's *Henry V*, premiered in 1986 as one of the inaugural performances of his new English Shakespeare Company, was the most overtly political of the English productions covered by this study. Bogdanov's career as a director had been built on modern dress, left-wing productions of classics, Shakespeare particularly; and the ESC was formed as a full-scale touring company committed to this agenda. Bogdanov's intention was to make Shakespeare (and his reading of Shakespeare) relevant and accessible to people beyond the typical London theatre-going public. His focus was populist, contemporary and political:

> The plays ... are vehicles for very heated debate, or should be, about things that are happening with our world ... and it's a question of how we can actually improve the things that we find around us and how we can make this a better world to live in and give our children and grandchildren a better life ... I think that Shakespeare was writing with that in view and that we should be doing productions that make those same statements and challenge people in that way. (Bogdanov, interview)

In claiming to mirror Shakespeare's own intentions and attitudes, Bogdanov echoes Hands and Noble; but his understanding of Shakespeare is different. Bogdanov's approach to Shakespeare is predominantly influenced by the Polish theorist Jan Kott. His political analysis of the plays is drawn from Kott's notion, in *Shakespeare Our Contemporary*, of the 'staircase of power' and the continuous, cyclical nature of tyranny. Bogdanov argues that Kott's analysis is the key to Shakespeare, now as in the seventeenth century:

> The nature of kingship and power is exactly the same now as it was then: the lust for power, greed, the thing that makes brother kill

brother, mother betray son – all that scramble to the top for the crock of gold and then toppling off down the other side as someone slices off your legs from under you.... These aren't claims made by me, they can be revealed by the plays in production. (quoted in Holderness, *The Shakespeare Myth*, 92)

The Kott analysis of power was hardly new in 1986 – Peter Hall had used it for *The Wars of the Roses* in 1963 – and, as cultural materialist critics like Alan Sinfield have pointed out, it is conservative in its 'pessimistic revision of the Marxist emphasis on history' (Sinfield, 'Royal Shakespeare', p. 161). Nevertheless, Bogdanov's application of Kott's views to *Henry V* made for a production which was different in tone and intention from any previous major English production. Put simply, Bogdanov and his leading actor, Michael Pennington, made Henry an almost unqualified villain.

Aside from taking a highly critical attitude toward Henry, the production was notable for its insistent contemporaneity. Like Quayle, Hall, Hands and Giles, Bogdanov linked *Henry V* to the *Henry IV* plays in a cycle performance but with a difference. Bogdanov made *Henry V* the end of a negative historical evolution, from an England of warm tavern anarchy and courageous regional dissent to one of icy *Realpolitik* and battlefield hooliganism. The change was well marked by John Price's doubling of a brave, foolishly honourable northern Hotspur with an increasingly brutal Pistol who looted corpses on the field of Agincourt. In the case of Michael Pennington, however, preceding Henry with Hal wasn't particularly illuminating. As I observed in reference to David Gwillim's BBC performance, playing *Henry V* with the other two parts in some ways reduces the scope for Henry's characterisation. Since the audience has already seen him grow from untried youth to authoritative leader (twice), it is hard to do much of the sort of personal evolution Howard and Branagh emphasised (Howard played Hal as well, but only *after* he had developed his characterisation of Henry). Pennington's Hal was such a chilly schemer from the beginning that Henry didn't have too far to go; he dismissed Falstaff with the same sneering authority with which he would threaten the governor of Harfleur and bully the French king into handing over his daughter and his dynasty.

What carried over from the *Henry IV* plays in Bogdanov's trilogy was an atmosphere of political ruthlessness given vivid contemporary expression. While the *Henry IV* plays, contrary to

Bogdanov's usual practice, had been performed in eclectic costumes ranging from medieval to modern, the thrust was towards the present. The betrayed rebel leaders in *2 Henry IV* were executed with pistol shots to the back of the neck, and the play ended with an ominously appropriate pop song, Status Quo's 'You're in the Army Now'. This threatening modernity set the tone for the beginning of *Henry V*. The production was thoroughly contemporary, with the English going off to war in full Falklands combat gear. Bogdanov explained his choice: '*Henry V*, with its war of expediency, ruthless manipulation, bribery and corruption, palpable pacifism, the French superior in numbers but beaten by superior technology, felt modern. It should be modern' Bogdanov, *ESC*, p. 30). The only exceptions were the French; in keeping with performance tradition, they were shown to be out of date, but only by a hundred years, their 'powder-blue nineteenth-century uniforms ... echoing the futile French cavalry charges of the First World War, their battalions mown down by automatic weapons' (p. 31).

The whole cycle was intended as a comment on the domestic and foreign policy of Thatcher's Britain: 'The Henrys as a whole were a microcosm in 1400 of in fact what is still the situation in the British Isles – a divided nation with the various factions fighting against each other and particularly against Westminster rule' (Bogdanov, interview). Bogdanov was certainly responding to an urgent contemporary situation, a Britain bitterly divided and torn by violence. Discontent was particularly high in Wales, Scotland and the north of England, poor regions which had voted against Thatcher; their anger caused the 1984-85 miners' strike to erupt into frequent bloody confrontations. In 1985, racial tension and police violence caused devastating urban riots in Brixton, Toxteth and Tottenham. The worst IRA bombing in years struck a Remembrance Sunday ceremony in Enniskillen in 1987. A new kind of violence associated specifically with British nationalism made the UK notorious in Europe: football hooliganism. At Heysel stadium in Brussels on 29 May 1985, thirty-seven Italian fans were killed by out-of-control Liverpool supporters at the European Cup Final. As social historian Arthur Marwick noted, 'football hooligans abroad, ironically, saw themselves as demonstrating British might. All this was, however distortedly, in keeping with the values of the aggressive market-place and the Falklands War' (Marwick, p. 351). Bogdanov felt *Henry V* was particularly pertinent to the Falklands, 'a senseless war of expediency' fought for 'a little patch of ground that hath no profit in it but the name.... The parallels were plain. The Henrys were plays for today, the lessons of history unlearnt.... Nothing had changed in six hundred years, save the means' (Bogdanov, *ESC*, pp. 23, 25).

I will consider the theoretical implications of Bogdanov's slant later in this chapter; in practical terms, it resulted in a production with many exciting stage moments and some powerful political images, but one which for long stretches was rather lacking in dramatic interest. Like Hands and Noble before him, Bogdanov claimed to be revealing the truth of Shakespeare's text; but those sections of the text that were opposed or irrelevant to his strong political reading were merely plodded through. In discussing the cycle as a whole, *Observer* critic Michael Ratcliffe perceptively noted that 'Nine hours is a long time to spend with a director who delights in the effectiveness of the single theatrical stroke – there are many here – and has never laid claim to sustained argument or line' (*Observer*, 28 December 1986). Stretches of Bogdanov's production were lamely conventional; on the other hand, several moments were strikingly original.

As it was designed for touring, Chris Dyer's set for *Henry V* (and the earlier plays) was essentially a bare stage. Sliding scrim panels at the rear allowed strong entrances, silhouettes and cyclorama lighting effects. Two large scaffolding towers could be wheeled on from the wings, though they were little used in *Henry V*. A catwalk could be lowered from the flies. Other set pieces were wheeled on when necessary, often on visible modern trolleys. Bogdanov and his designers drew inspiration from the 'eclectic theatre of expediency as practised by the Elizabethans' for a look that was frankly functional but with a crude vitality, especially in Stephanie Howard's costumes (Bogdanov, *ESC*, p. 28). A basic collection of furniture and props served all three shows. Bogdanov and his team worked to 'create a style that was essentially rough theatre, but would add, when we needed it, a degree of sophistication' (p. 29).

The same vigorous populist approach marked the performances of Bogdanov's ensemble. The makeup of the company varied during the two years the productions were on tour, but the playing style at its best was energetic, egalitarian and brisk, with an emphasis on story-telling and an absence of subtlety. Many of the characterisations were of an almost Brechtian bluntness and reductiveness – witness (in *Henry V*) the British captains, Andrew Jarvis's splenetic, cartoonish Dauphin and all of the low-lifes except Colin Farrell's sad Bardolph. On the other hand, there were a few performances of considerable delicacy, notably John Tramper as the doomed Boy.

Given Bogdanov's highly political and blatantly theatrical approach, it is surprising he didn't do more with the Chorus. In the first year of touring, John Woodvine played it in an engaging, conversational style, basking in the audience's admiration of his superlative Falstaff (he invariably got an ovation on his first entrance, in casual contemporary clothes). He played some of the speeches with light irony, but the keynote of his performance was cordiality – he was a benevolent uncle or genial host. He had one striking moment, when he casually tossed dummy corpses about the stage to prepare the field of Agincourt: the action recalled both Bernard Shaw's Andrew Undershaft, brutally kicking a straw soldier out of the way in his munitions plant, and the grisly climax of Peter Barnes's *Laughter*, when dummies representing gassed Auschwitz inmates spill out of the filing cabinets. Barry Stanton, who succeeded Woodvine in the second tour, was conventional at best: a pudgy, droning TV opera presenter in black tie, holding a book. His speeches were flat, straightforward and boring, without a trace of self-consciousness or irony, even for a phrase like 'petty and unprofitable dukedoms'. (The one touch of wit about him was his boutonnière, a red and a white rose twisted together – the *Henry VI* plays and *Richard III* were added to the second tour.) Bogdanov admitted that 'Barry tended to get very heavy with the poetry from time to time', and that Woodvine's reading was closer to what he wanted – a reminder that many apparently interpretive aspects of a production may not coincide with a director's intentions (Bogdanov, interview).

The dominant figure in the production was Pennington's commanding, unpleasant King Henry. Pennington is an actor of great intelligence and authority, but he is not naturally sympathetic. With his domed, wrinkled forehead, deep-set eyes, natural sneer and wiry frame, he couldn't have played the boyish, charming Henry Branagh had been – not to mention the fact that Pennington was acting with the RSC when Branagh was three years old. Rather than bringing Hal forward into Henry, the ESC pushed Henry back into Hal, Pennington playing the cynical, watchful politician from his first scene in *1 Henry IV*. Bogdanov and Pennington took the character of Hal from his first soliloquy, 'I know you all, and will awhile uphold / The unyoked humour of your idleness'. Political expediency, deceitful manipulation and rhetorical skill were hallmarks of the character throughout the trilogy; as Bogdanov put it, 'He never stops talking – The Breach, St. Crispin's Day, the joyous horn-interlocking word play with Falstaff.... How can you believe this man? What a dirty rat. Michael and I went for it' (Bogdanov, *ESC*, p. 49).

In *Henry V* Pennington was absolutely convincing as a seasoned military leader: crafty, brave, authoritative and ruthless. He went to war cynically and fought it valiantly; he knew the dubiousness of his position and the personal costs of his actions, but soldiered on anyway. In discussing the role, Pennington wrote, 'What is strong in *Henry V*, and very actable, is that his sense of mission has cost him youth, ease, and spontaneity' (Pennington, *ESC*, p. 50). His Henry was not vain or glib, but grimly determined. Pennington played the part like Macbeth or Richard III when things have started to go wrong, and thus achieved a kind of impressive stature; but the crack in the mask was never wide enough to let in a redemptive quantity of audience sympathy.

The opening scene provided a good measure of the distance of this *Henry V* from previous productions. The clerics were obvious, almost moustache-twirling villains – an example of Bogdanov's nearly cartoonish emphasis on clarity. Canterbury was sneeringly ironic about how the knights would be maintained 'to the King's honour', and seemed very scornful about Henry's reformation (I.i. 12). The scene with the King and court was staged very formally, with a red cross banner hanging vertically at the back and the King in a military dress uniform at a table centre stage, flanked by columns of yes-men in smart city suits (these were changed to frock coats when *The Wars of the Roses* was added, to keep the rough historical progression of the whole cycle – Bogdanov, *ESC*, p. 103).

The whole scene had the flavour of a staged media event (one of Bogdanov's favourite ironic tricks, used for the opening of *Henry IV*, the end of *Richard III*, even the end of *Romeo and Juliet*). Henry spoke formally and hypocritically in warning the clerics about awaking his 'sleeping sword of war' (I.ii.22); his admonition that their advice be 'in your conscience washed / As pure as sin with baptism', so important to Branagh, was here cut (31-2). He asked 'May I with right *and* conscience make this claim?' with a raised eyebrow, as if troubled on a minor legal point (96). The Scottish question was discussed, but the speeches comparing statecraft with the harmonious spheres of bees and music were cut. The scene was without poetry and without debate; there was a sense of everyone agreeing, spouting platitudes, going through the necessary formalities. It was a brisk and efficient prologue to slaughter. Pennington made a conclusive moment of Henry's resolve to 'bend [France] to our awe, / Or break it all to pieces', at which the assembled court applauded (224-5). The tennis-ball gift was thus relatively unimportant, since Henry's mind had been made up from the beginning. Henry was genuinely, cynically amused by the tennis-ball joke, and pleased to have what seemed another confirmation of his right to invade France.

The briskness of the scene had a practical payoff for Bogdanov, in that it got his production off to a strong start; rather than wallowing in doubts and insecurities, his Henry got down to the business at hand. This impulse also informed the traitors scene, which – since its only value for Bogdanov was to demonstrate Henry's cruelty – was also dispatched rather quickly. It was played on the dock at Southampton, with soldiers loading equipment up a side gangplank. No time was wasted on humanising or differentiating the traitors (as Noble had done); they were cartoon conspirators in trenchcoats and broad-brimmed hats. After Henry had ironically and nastily declared their guilt, one made a break and was shot and wounded. The confessions, repentances and admissions of God's justice were all cut, as was Henry's weeping over Scroop's betrayal as 'Another fall of man' (II.ii.142). Henry had no moral conflict in this scene, merely an obstacle to get out of his way. On 'Bear them hence', the traitors were immediately forgotten (181); they were shot upstage at the end of the scene. Henry spoke 'No King of England if not King of France', with an ironic grimace, acknowledging its doggerel quality (193); as if he himself had no illusions about the patriotic nonsense he was using to gain popular support for his aggressive foreign policy.

The production's criticism of jingoism was given its most striking expression in the leave-taking scene of Pistol and his crew – the most memorable moment in the production, probably in the whole trilogy. Pistol (John Price, and after his death, John Castle and Paul Brennan) was a thuggish, long-haired biker with a swastika tattoo and, in *2 Henry IV*, a leather jacket emblazoned 'Hal's

Angels'. Nym and Bardolph were drunks in dirty raincoats. The leave-taking began with the New-Orleans-style funeral of Falstaff, which passed in silhouette across the back. Bardolph played a melancholy trombone, mourners struggled under an enormous coffin, a young, leather-clad Doll Tearsheet followed last and alone, grieving quietly. This vein of pathos continued for the fare-wells, which were accompanied by a plaintive guitar. The soldiers backed downstage in slow motion, waving goodbye as the tearful Quickly disappeared upstage, and then, when Bogdanov had screwed the sentimentality to the sticking-place, he sprang the trap. The soldiers spun around, tore open their jackets to reveal Union Jack T-shirts and began the raucous soccer chant of "Ere we go, 'ere we go, 'ere we go'. Woodvine's Chorus crossed the stage carrying a placard reading 'Gotcha!', the notorious headline with which the *Sun* newspaper crowed over the sinking of an Argentine ship. 'Jerusalem' blared out in the background as a crowd of hooligans rushed out on to the catwalk to unfold a huge banner reading 'FUCK THE FROGS'. It was an electrifying moment, and a perfect example of Bogdanov's brand of punchy, anachronistic image-making. The departure of Henry's army was given a radical re-interpretation by linking it both to the patriotic hoopla over the departure of the Falklands ships and to the chauvinistic brutality of English football hooligans on the rampage in Europe. In Bogdanov's words, the image 'grew out of a desire to bridge six hundred years of this same bigoted xenophobic patriotism' (Bogdanov, *ESC*, p. 48).

Bogdanov's productions rely strongly on this kind of big, visual or atextual statement, usually with a contemporary reference. For twentieth-century audiences, less attuned to processing densely verbal information, a powerful image can override or qualify a great deal of text. A contemporary visual quotation can, as it were, beat the text to the post, giving us an attitude toward speaker and speech before we actually hear the lines. Thus, when we see Henry standing atop a tank brandishing an M-16 to *threaten* his cowering, cursing troops back to the breach, we are disposed to doubt the sincerity of his statements about the ennobling virtues of war. Bogdanov's treatment of Grandpré's speech about the wretched estate of the English soldiers (IV.ii.38-55) provides another good example of this technique. Bogdanov lifted the speech from its context, cut the first seven lines and gave it to Montjoy, who was alone in his tent typing up a war report. Thus, instead of an

8   John Woodvine's Chorus leads Henry's hooligan followers
in Michael Bogdanov's 1986 English Shakespeare Company
production. 'Gotcha' was the headline in the *Sun* newspaper
following Britain's sinking of an Argentine ship during the
Falklands War

arrogant Frenchman crowing over the misery of his adversaries (and so deserving a poetic comeuppance), Bogdanov had a sensitive observer gravely describing the sufferings of war:

> The horsemen sit like fixèd candlesticks
> With torchstaves in their hands, and their poor jades
> Lob down their heads, drooping the hides and hips,
> The gum down-roping from their pale dead eyes,
> And in their palled dull mouths the gimmaled bit
> Lies foul with chewed grass, still and motionless.
> And their executors, the knavish crows,
> Fly o'er them all impatient for their hour.
>
> (IV.ii.45-52)

At this point Montjoy ripped the paper from the typewriter in despair:

> Description cannot suit itself in words
> To demonstrate the life of such a battle
> In life so lifeless as it shows itself.
>
> (53-5)

The French were, as is usual, historically outmoded, but aside from the Dauphin they were dignified and civilised. For their first appearance – just after 'Fuck the Frogs' – they were all in white linen, with the ladies having a *dejeuner sur l'herbe* in the background as the men sat on white garden furniture downstage, sipping wine and discussing the coming English. When Exeter entered to threaten war, he stalked straight across the white picnic blanket in his dark diplomat's suit – a powerful image of starched British imperialism invading an impressionist idyll. The second French court scene featured a slide projector showing images of Westminster, Tower Bridge, a grim northern industrial town, blond English children (for 'Norman bastards!'), Falklands soldiers and King Henry in formal regalia (at which point the Dauphin angrily tore the screen). Now dressed in grey, the French court toasted 'La France!' with champagne flutes. For the final scene, they would wear black. Michael Billington called it 'the first version I've ever seen where you wanted the French to win' (*Guardian*, 23 March 1987).

Henry's campaign was marked by efficient brutality. Instead of shouting his threats up at an invisible governor of Harfleur, as Howard and Branagh had done, Pennington sat coolly at a folding table as the governor was brought to him under an armed escort.

The governor was a proud, beaten old man with a black coat and an accent; he was accompanied by a silent comrade with beret and moustache. Their demeanour suggested both the Occupation of the Second World War and the Burghers of Calais. Henry spoke his threats calmly and nastily, to devastating effect. He underlined 'What is't to me, when you *yourselves are cause*' (III.iii.19) and spoke his final 'What say you?' (42) with a smirk that suggested an utter lack of concern with the governor's decision. The governor came forward to place his keys on the table, and was made to sign a document with a fountain pen. Henry picked up the keys, then smashed them back down with a peremptory 'Open your gates!' (51). Gun-wielding soldiers escorted them off, the comrade putting one arm around the broken governor.

At this point, Henry got up, whistled with relief and smiled nervously – he had been bluffing. After giving his orders to Exeter, he suddenly put his hand to his right side and winced with pain. It was unclear whether this pain came from a wound, the stress of the moment, or the 'sickness growing / Upon our soldiers' to which he had just referred (55-6). At any rate, it had the effect of humanising Henry slightly after a scene of really monstrous cruelty. Pennington revealed such cracks in the armour from time to time through the performance, just enough to remind the audience that Henry was in fact a human being; however ruthless his actions, they were not without costs to himself. Where the production differed from those of Hands and Noble was that the costs to himself were never made to appear greater than the costs to those around him.

The bridge scene, for instance, provided a telling contrast with the earlier productions. The emphasis was not on Henry's pain at having his old acquaintance put to death, but on Pistol's desperate, impassioned attempts to save his friend's life (even taking out money to try to bribe Fluellen). When Henry entered, Bardolph was marched across the catwalk above, shouting an interpolated 'My lord!', Henry showed a flicker of pain but held his composure under Pistol's icy glare. Almost immediately, shots were heard. Henry began quietly – 'We would have all such offenders so cut off (III.vi.111) – but built himself up through the speech. By its conclusion – 'when lenity and cruelty play for a kingdom, the gentler gamester is the soonest winner' (116-18) – he was confidently rationalising in his tough, pragmatic, soldierly way, assuring himself that his actions were all contributing to his ultimate goal. He

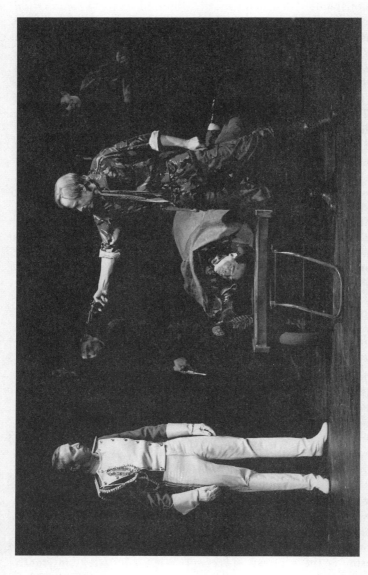

9 Henry (Michael Pennington) threatens Montjoy (Donald Gee) in Michael Bogdanov's 1986 English Shakespeare Company production

was relaxed enough to laugh at Montjoy's powder-blue uniform, and on 'There's for thy labour' (164) he gave him a tennis-ball. His threats and orders at the end of the scene reinforced the character he had built up so far: a single-minded, unscrupulous, crafty and courageous general.

One aspect of Bogdanov's populist, 'accessible' directing style is his insistent vulgarity. Despite his earnest political purposes, Bogdanov is never above going for the cheap laugh; neither was Brecht, so there's not necessarily a contradiction. Neither, for that matter, was Shakespeare, but Bogdanov usually takes textual jokes a bit further; thus, in 2 Henry IV, when Falstaff inquired of the Boy, 'What says the doctor to my water?'(I.ii.1), the bottle of urine was not only produced on stage, but Bardolph later unwittingly drank from it. There was a joke on this order in Henry V: at the beginning of the night scene before Agincourt, Pistol rushed on to defecate over a low wall of sandbags, and was thus occupied during his conversation with Henry. Bogdanov was able to get a certain amount of mileage out of this gag: it suggested (in Pistol's urgency and relief) the dysentery that historically afflicted the English troops; and it also underlined the kind of indignity involved in Henry's trying to mix with the common people (especially when Pistol angrily bared his buttocks at the end of the scene). Nevertheless, the scene became principally *about* Pistol's bodily functions, rather than Henry's inability to mix with his men; and this kind of substitution of a high-percentage visual gag or bit of stage business for a passage of text is characteristic of Bogdanov's style. Bogdanov defends himself against charges of gimmickry: 'Everything we do is selected and thought about in terms of how you communicate most directly the story of what happens in that moment of the play' (Bogdanov, interview).

The rest of the night scene went for surprisingly little, given its importance to an anti-Henry reading of the play; this was perhaps because Williams – old, fat, philosophical – lacked the moral fury needed to animate fully the speeches giving voice to the 'legs and arms and heads chopped off in a battle' (IV.i.136-7). Henry spoke his responses confidently, although at 'they have no wings to fly from God', we saw him think of his inherited guilt for the deposition and murder of Richard II (173-4). In 'Upon the King' Pennington made a lot of the pressure and stress of his responsibility. He spoke with real pain and vexation about being 'subject to the breath / Of every *fool*' (241-2). His reading of the speech suggested both a criticism of Henry – ceremony *isn't* the only advantage a king has over a peasant – and an acknowledgment that Henry's anxieties are real and his beliefs genuine, rather than mere cynical rationalisations. Henry may be fooling himself, but he isn't enjoying himself. This was another of the humanising touches Pennington gave to the part without compromising his negative reading of Henry as a ruthless politician.

Bogdanov's staging of the battle of Agincourt was close to the centre of his conception of the play and to his claim to represent Shakespeare's true intentions. In response to critics suggesting that his reading was a contemporary intervention in an essentially positive account of Henry's campaign, he said:

> People like that don't read the play ... they don't understand it, they don't know what Pistol, Nym and Bardolph stand for. They don't understand that there isn't a scene in *Henry V* about the battle of Agincourt. The only scene there is is of Pistol kicking the shit out of some poor Frenchman called Monsieur le Fer. That's the Battle of Agincourt: it's an Englishman, a liar, a cheapskate, a thief, a murderer, a lout, a bully, kicking a wounded Frenchman in the gut. That's Agincourt. (Bogdanov, interview)

In accordance with this reading, the scene was played with the utmost brutality, Pistol filling a shopping cart with plunder from dummy corpses, savagely beating le Fer, and repeatedly kicking and grabbing him in the crotch. The interpreted exchange was played completely without comedy; the boy spoke French well and was doing his best to save le Fer. His subsequent soliloquy condemning Pistol was spoken (very effectively) in tones of great moral outrage. The boy was not, however, killed on stage at the end of it. Bogdanov argues that 'It is quite clear that the French action [killing the boys] is a retaliation for the English action [killing the prisoners]' (Bogdanov, *ESC*, 47). Thus Bogdanov not only avoids the usual, pro-English interpretation, he actually reverses it. As described before, the actual killing was given a neat Brechtian realisation: Pistol, hoping for ransom, was reluctant to kill the wounded le Fer, and cut his throat only when threatened by another English soldier. The Agincourt sequence differed from Hands's, Giles's and Noble's depictions in the avoidance of anything that could be identified as heroism. While war for them was harsh but ennobling, here it was merely bombastic and sordid. Even the reading of the English dead was qualified by the presence of a soldier wrapping himself in the Union Jack and a distant chorus of "Ere we go' – another quotation of contemporary chauvinistic hooliganism.

Perhaps Bogdanov's definitive departure from the performance tradition was his treatment of the wooing of Princess Katherine, a scene he describes as 'terrifying' (Bogdanov, interview):

> We see a man who has never taken 'no' for an answer, suffered defeat in any sphere (witness his churlish revenge on the soldier Williams) determined to subdue Kate and wring acquiescence from her. (Bogdanov, *ESC*, 49)

The last phrase could be taken from any of Bogdanov's interviews about his celebrated production of *The Taming of the Shrew*, which ended with Jonathan Pryce's Petruchio having brutally 'subdued Kate' (Paola Donisetti). This similarity was not lost on reviewers; Steve Grant (*Time Out*, 25 March 1987) found that 'the final post-victory wooing of Princess Kate by the game-playing but now maturely ruthless Henry is a chilling, anti-sentimental reinterpretation splendidly reminiscent' of the sexual violence of the earlier production.

In its staging the scene recalled the opening court scene. At the back hung a blue banner with fleurs-de-lis. The characters were seated in a semicircle on simple, stylish, high-backed modern black chairs. At a table in the centre sat Burgundy, with Henry on his right hand and the French king on his left. The English officers, in red dress uniforms, and French Royal family, in mourning black, symmetrically filled out the two sides of the semicircle. As Burgundy sternly lectured them on the ravages of the war, Henry sat back in his chair and stared ahead of him, bored and annoyed. He interrupted impatiently with his harsh statement that 'You must *buy* that peace / With full accord to all our just demands' (V.ii.71). When Burgundy replied that the King had not yet made an answer to them, Henry laughed shortly and sardonically before saying, 'Well then, the peace, / Which you before so urged, lies in his answer' (75-6).

Pennington pointed the line about Katherine's being 'our capital demand' (96). In Bogdanov's description of the scene, 'She is "La Belle France" and must be forced to submit to his will. An iron will, for all that the technique is masked in flattery. Determined. Cold.... France is plundered first, then Kate' (Bogdanov, *ESC*, 49).

Kate herself was actually played as proud, spirited, flirtatious and fully conscious of the political necessity for the marriage – not a bad match for Henry. Pennington began his wooing still sitting at the table, thoroughly bored by this charade he must go through to cement his victory. However, Kate's resistance interested him; he liked a challenge. Accordingly, he eventually got up and showed more spirit, though he retained his dry tone, which worked rather well with his 'plain king' pose.

Henry's statement, 'I love France so well that I will not part with a village of it; I will have it all mine' (178-80), was cool and deadly; it (along with 'our capital demand') had been a cornerstone of the Bogdanov/Pennington reading of the scene (Bogdanov, *ESC*, p. 49). But elsewhere the scene was subtly modulated to make Henry's winning of her more plausible. Pennington had displayed another crack in the armour in the long wooing speech:

> When at the end of the play he admits to Katherine that 'a good leg will fall, a straight back will stoop, a fair face will wither, a full eye will wax hollow; but a good heart, Kate is the sun and the moon,' I tried to make the audience remember Falstaff in his high noon, a sense of fellowship Hal has lost in his destiny. The candour of his regret at this point might also make it possible for Kate, his political enemy, to begin to fall in love with him. (Pennington, *ESC*, p. 50)

While the audience could hardly be expected to think of Falstaff at this point, the sense of genuine regret came across. Further, his amused determination to express himself in French won him a measure of sympathy, from Katherine as well as the audience. In the kissing scene he was suave and sexy, but always strong and commanding; not quite the monster of Jonathan Pryce's Petruchio, but probably closer to it than to Branagh's bashful schoolboy.

When the court returned, however, Henry was all business, and this final section of the play showed Bogdanov at his best, revealing an urgent political subtext beneath the florid, celebratory rhetoric. Henry flared up in anger at Exeter's report that the King had not consented to call Henry publicly his heir. Pennington spoke angrily and strongly in asking the King to 'Let that one article rank with the rest, / And thereupon *give me your daughter*' (364-5). The King's reply, 'Take her, fair son, and from her blood raise up / Issue to me' was thus driven by a fear of blowing the whole deal; the speech was punctuated by nervous looks at the Dauphin,

who was fuming in the background at the prospect of being disinherited (366-73). The King obviously hadn't wanted wholly to
back down, but now was having to do so to salvage the treaty.
Henry accepted his offer, and went to seal the bargain with 'here I
kiss her as my sovereign queen' (376). At the kiss, the Dauphin got
up in fury and stormed out overturning his chair, and Henry angrily pulled back, the deal again in jeopardy. This time Queen
Isabel came forward, playing her blessing on their marriage as a
desperate, last-ditch attempt to smooth things over and prevent a
return to war. Henry, apparently satisfied, took Katherine's arm
and all froze in a formal, balanced grouping. The final, critical effect came not on the Chorus's last speech but after it: the lights
blazed up brightly on the 'Royal Wedding' stage picture and 'God
Save the King (Queen?)' welled up over the loudspeakers, to be
drowned out by the thunder of machine guns and helicopter gun-
ships as the scene vanished in darkness. Interestingly, when *Henry
V* was videotaped for television at one of the final performances in
Swansea, the music was merely 'Pomp and Circumstance' and the
helicopters were gone. As I shall discuss below, the radicalism of
Bogdanov's production tended to lose its force with time.

Bogdanov's interpretive approach for *Henry V* actually had two
layers: he physically updated the production to suggest links with
contemporary society and events, and he morally and politically
updated it to force the audience to evaluate actions according to
contemporary standards. The first level of updating served
Bogdanov in two ways. First, it provided clarity for his young, un-
sophisticated target audience through recognisable modern reference points: Henry's council of war is like a board meeting, the
French are effete, wine-drinking snobs, Pistol is a biker. Second,
Bogdanov's updating provided a kind of dramatic excitement and
entertainment of its own, calling attention to its own cleverness
through the disjunction of the modern image and the antiquated
language it supported (e.g. 'Fuck the Frogs', Montjoy's typewriter).
These two responses are subtly different – the second requires a
greater degree of audience sophistication – but Bogdanov
conflates the two in his defence against charges of gimmickry:

> There are those who would say that it is precisely this approach,
> not trusting the language and the situation, the need to use crass
> modern appliances such as microphones [for a press conference
> scene] that desecrates the language and distorts the plays. The de-

fence is simple. People understood.... I have to assume that an audience has no background, has not read or seen the plays, has no
knowledge of the history of England. Unless I assume this, I am
being elitist, joining that group who would ignore popular methods of communication, denying that the plays were performed for
a whole cross-section of the community, some educated, some not.
(Bogdanov, *ESC*, 43)

There is nevertheless a fine line between clarity and cuteness in
many of Bogdanov's updatings, as when Capulet, in his *Romeo
and Juliet*, got a huge laugh by calling for Peter ('What ho!') on a
desk intercom.

In many cases Bogdanov's physical updating supports his
moral/political one, but it needn't necessarily; indeed, either could
exist independently. A production of *Henry V* could combine contemporary attitudes and period dress. It would also be possible to
do the play in a modern setting but with a traditional reading of
Henry, his education in leadership and his heroism. Ironically,
this actually happened with Bogdanov's production when a
young, attractive, sympathetic leading man, John Dougall, began
alternating the part with Pennington in the second tour of the
cycle. Dougall's performance was more in the mode of Branagh's:
'I felt it was essential for me to retain the vulnerability I found in
the Prince, and carry it into the king' (Dougall, in Bogdanov, *ESC*,
p. 192). He rejected, for instance, the Harfleur tank: 'I knew I had
to get in among them and relate to them directly, trying to stop the
all too easy rhetoric of the speech' (p. 93). Pennington particularly
objected to Dougall's playing of the wooing, which he considered
'sentimentally out of key with the production, which was at pains
to underline the political expediency.... John's line on the scene
was altogether more romantic. He was on his knees, fumbling for
his French, getting his girl' (Pennington, in Bogdanov, *ESC*, p. 192).

Dougall's performance turned the production on its head:
Nicholas de Jongh wrote that 'although it looks as if Bogdanov has
done something radical with *Henry V*, the production is in truth
conservative, traditional and not that consistent' (*Guardian*, 6
February 1989). Bogdanov confessed that 'his assessment was accurate', blaming Dougall (*ESC*, p. 213); but aside from Dougall's
'matinée idol' performance which 'casts a sympathetic glow upon
the character', de Jongh picked out other hints of conservatism as
well. He specified Stanton's 'blandly conversational' Chorus; the
weak, 'forelock tugging' Williams, Bates and Court; and the con-

trast between the 'nancy boy' French, 'far behind the times', and the 'English aristocratic establishment … [who] change from their morning suits into military uniform to become true fighting men'. Other critics were equally dubious about the political effect of Bogdanov's production. Milton Shulman felt it provided 'the jingoism to satisfy any chauvinist', although he conceded that 'by dressing this production in modern clothes, Bogdanov encourages … revulsion against Henry's actions' (*Evening Standard*, 6 February 1989). Patrick Marmion felt Bogdanov's interventions were merely 'token gestures revealing the production's uneasiness with the play's message'. In a New-Historicist-style analysis of the play, Marmion astutely argued that the subversive 'seeds of doubt' contained in the text serve only as foils to the 'play's political fantasies':

> Disaffection among the troops serves to inflate the final triumph; venality among the lower orders serves to glorify the 'nobler' national sentiment; double standards in the foppish French court annul the double standards in the heroic English court. (*What's On*, 15 February 1989)

Marmion maintained that Bogdanov's directorial choices failed to support adequately the subversive elements in the text:

> One possible way to question the play's political bluff is through the 'commoners,' but Bogdanov opts for the patronising theatrical stereotype of portraying them as a farcical rabble, to be understood as such from their 'jolly' but idiotic regional accents and manners.

As a result, the play's conservative elements overcame Bogdanov's political critique, which Marmion felt was superficially applied rather than built up from the text.

Thus time, casting changes and entropy gradually brought Bogdanov's *Henry V* back to a point where it could be perceived as a traditional production (when it first opened, all the critics, whether they approved it or not, at least clearly perceived the production's political slant). The backsliding of Bogdanov's production makes clear that, although what attracted most attention was Bogdanov's surface allusion to contemporary events, it was the second layer of interpretation, the insistence on a late twentieth-century moral/political perspective, that was Bogdanov's significant interpretive departure. The technique used was essentially the same as in Bogdanov's *Shrew*: to perform events that traditionally have been applauded in such a way as to make the audience view them with revulsion. Interestingly, in both cases Bogdanov insisted that such an attitude was entirely inscribed in the text itself. He always maintained that his feminist *Shrew* was Shakespeare's: 'You can only see it as a sexist play if you misunderstand what Shakespeare has actually written' (Holderness, *The Shakespeare Myth*, p. 91). When asked whether he thought *Henry V* was an anti-war play or whether he had reinterpreted it from an anti-war perspective, he said, 'I think it's an anti-war play', mentioning the yobbishness of Henry's followers, the arguments of Williams, the killing of the prisoners, Pistol's treatment of le Fer, and Henry's capital demand for Katherine. While all of these can be used to support Bogdanov's view, the first is primarily his invention, and the last two are open to interpretation. Bogdanov insists that he is actually rediscovering the truth of the plays by redressing the imbalances of received performance tradition, notably, in the case of *Henry V*, the Olivier film:

> His film version of *Henry V* cuts the disturbing elements, the things that make you wonder whether *Henry V* really is a hymn to the glory of England.... We inherit a distorted view of these plays, which have been handed down to us through great tour de force performances. To restore these plays to their original purposes, we have to analyze every single aspect of these rather awkward parts of the plays which cannot be ignored. It's often around the edges, on the fringes, that you find these small characters, the apparently minor ones, who throw a bomb into the pool and blow all the big fish out. (Elsom, ed., *Is Shakespeare Still Our Contemporary*, pp. 19-20)

Bogdanov is certainly right that past performances emphasised and suppressed elements of the text, often for ideological purposes; but his does so no less. His stated emphasis on the 'apparently minor' characters inscribed 'around the edges, on the fringes' of the text in itself acknowledges the degree to which his interpretation reshapes the text. Indeed, since he is emphasising marginal moments and characters in opposition to both the dominant narrative thrust and the dominant performance tradition, his tactics of emphasis and suppression must be all the more vigorous than those of a 'traditional' production. While Bogdanov played a fairly full text (at least in comparison to Olivier's) he effectively negated large portions of it by layering a more high-profile extra-textual language over the top of it (for example making Henry an arrogant Rambo shouting orders from a tank at his battered foot-soldiers; imposing the roar of gunfire over the final celebrations). While Bogdanov made full use of the textual moments that support his reading, he is underselling the cleverness of his achievement by saying it's all in the text. There is textual material in *Henry V* to support interpretations that are strongly, if not diametrically, opposed, because the structural principle on which this text is organised – and the conflicting attitudes to history that lie behind it – allow such opposition. Henry's heroism is constructed through his overcoming a series of opposing forces (treacherous nobles, unscrupulous former companions, unwilling soldiers, the French themselves, Katherine), and these forces create a counter-text of dissent which Henry's rhetoric must defeat. Taking hold of *Henry V* by these competing strains of text results in two very different plays: the official and the secret versions. The text is a site of conflicting voices and ideologies; as such, it lays itself open to a range of valid interpretations, depending on which side the director takes in the struggle.

CHAPTER VII

Let there be sung 'Non nobis':
Kenneth Branagh (1989)

Kenneth Branagh's 1989 film of *Henry V* provides a compelling illustration of the way an ostensibly revisionist, 'secret' version of the play can be both challenging and conservative. Deliberately set in opposition to Olivier's film and to traditional interpretations of the text, Branagh's *Henry V* was hailed on its release as a radical, anti-war statement, courageously reversing previous notions of the play at every level. Richard Corliss called it 'an anti-war war movie' (*Time*, 13 November 1989), John Simon 'a deconstruction of Olivier's movie, Shakespeare's play, and history itself' (*National Review*, 19 March 1990). Indeed, at first viewing the two films could not appear more different. Olivier's Henry is noble and handsome, Branagh's baby-faced and dishevelled; Olivier's French are comic lunatics, Branagh's brooding and tragic; Olivier's Agincourt is fought on broad sunny fields, Branagh's in a few yards of misty mire. Yet the overwhelming impression I had from watching the two films was how much they are the same. Both try (successfully) to create Henry as a hero for their particular historical moment; and both capture and exploit the excitement of the play's narrative arc, lifting Henry through a series of challenges to the thrilling release of the climactic battle. Branagh's film differs from Olivier's in many surface details, giving a different impression of the circumstances and nature of Henry's war; but in its exploitation of the excitement of that war, and the heroism it confers on Henry, it sticks close to the dominant interpretation of the text which Olivier had popularised. As Graham Fuller astutely noted in an article in *Film Comment*, 'It is a galvanizing and accessible version but also a darkly ambiguous conflation of intoxicated jingoism and mournful disgust at the foulness of war' (p. 2). In this chapter I shall consider the cultural positioning of Branagh's film, including its relationship to Olivier's; I shall examine the film's anti-war strategy of directly involving the King in the moral and physical horrors of the war which Olivier had suppressed; and I shall contend that the film has a complementary strategy of countervailing those horrors by its unremitting personal focus on the King and his transcendence of them. In this last respect the film resembles, but goes far beyond, Noble's stage production, from which it borrows a good deal.

Branagh's stated intentions were twofold. He wanted to challenge the play's alleged jingoism by dramatising the horror of war; and he wanted to make a popular film for a mass audience. On the one hand, he wanted to make the film 'a political thriller, a warts-and-all study of leadership, a complex debate about war and the pity of war, an uncompromising analysis of the English class system and of the gulf between male and female attitudes to this type of savage conflict' (Branagh, liner notes), to present Henry as 'a man of doubt who has to suppress his own innate violence, who is volatile and unpredictable' (Branagh, quoted in Fuller, p. 7). He wanted the war to be 'a dreadful scrum' rather than 'a great Arthurian adventure.... They must have shit themselves with fear, and I wanted to convey that terror. It was worth doing this piece now ... because clearly we haven't seen enough wars to stop us from fighting' (quoted in Fuller, p. 6). On the other hand, Branagh sought 'to make a popular film that [would] both satisfy the Shakespearean scholar and the punter who likes "Crocodile Dundee"' (quoted in Fuller, p. 6). These two aims are not necessarily mutually exclusive, and to a considerable degree Branagh succeeded in both. *Henry V* did achieve popular success without resorting to the showy populism of Zeffirelli's Shakespeare movies. Yet the film shows some signs of concession to a mass audience. Branagh's cutting keeps the action moving swiftly toward the climactic battle, and his direction keeps attention focused unswervingly on the single issue of Henry's growth to maturity and heroism. The 'uncompromising analysis of the English class system and the gulf between male and female attitudes' is forgotten as Branagh concentrates on a single, accessible story:

> I feel the play is about a journey toward maturity. It is about a young monarch who at the beginning is burdened with guilt because his father has unlawfully seized the crown, who has a sometimes precarious relationship with his men but who, at the end, has learned about true leadership. (*New York Times*, 8 January 1989)

Unlike, for instance, Bogdanov's radical revision, Branagh's film finds a balance of the text's pro- and anti-war elements that allows its celebration of Henry's heroism to come through unscathed, even enhanced.

The dual nature of Branagh's film, revisionist and conservative, radical and populist, anti-war and pro-heroism, is linked to its cultural background in the England of the late 1980s. The acrid smoke of the Falklands, background to Noble's and Bogdanov's more radical productions, still permeated British intellectual and artistic life. Numerous films, plays and television programmes expressed a disillusionment with war comparable to Hollywood's delayed response to Vietnam in the early 1980s. Graham Fuller notes the number of bitter British films from the late 1980s recounting the destructive effects of the First World War or the Falklands: Derek Jarman's vivid, expressionistic film version of the Benjamin Britten/Wilfred Owen *War Requiem*; Antony Sher's *Changing Step*, about a hospital for disabled First World War soldiers; Richard Eyre's controversial *Tumbledown*, based on the autobiography of maimed and bitter Falklands hero Robert Lawrence; Martin Stellman's *For Queen and Country*, with Denzel Washington as a disaffected Falklands veteran; and Paul Greengrass's *Resurrected*, the true story of a Falklands soldier lynched by his comrades for alleged cowardice (p. 6). Branagh's film unquestionably participates in this cultural movement; as Philip French observed, it is 'made for a generation that has the Indo-China war and the Falklands campaign just behind it and is wary of calls to arms' (*Observer*, 8 October 1989).

On the other hand, another oft-noted aspect of the cultural background to the film, and to Branagh's astonishing rise to success as an actor, director, writer, producer and film-maker, is the entrepreneurial, aggressive, individualist climate of Margaret Thatcher's Britain. To link Branagh – a left-leaning populist artist from a working-class Belfast background — to the fiercely competitive capitalism of the unregulated City is perhaps unfair, but in many ways Branagh's whole approach fits very well with the attitudes underlying Thatcher's economic policies. In both the English and American presses, Branagh was often hailed (or damned) as 'a model of Thatcherite initiative in a British arts scene of radical distemper' (Corliss, *Time*, 13 November 1989), who was resurrecting the old tradition of the actor-manager in an entrepreneurial 1980s spirit. Graham Holderness astutely observes that Branagh's media identity is at least partly self-generated: Branagh

> aggressively constructs his own social persona as the tough and ambitious boy from working-class Belfast, determined to make it in the competitive market-place of the British theatre, as impatient with traditional institutions and fossilized establishments as the young shock-troops of the Thatcherite Stock Exchange. (*Shakespeare Recycled*, p. 202)

As a young star at the RSC, Branagh had strenuously objected to the unwieldy and oppressive bureaucracy of the huge, publicly funded company. 'Somehow this big machine wasn't working', Branagh writes in his autobiography. 'I felt that the size and merciless timetable of the productions was working against a consistently high quality in the work, and the burgeoning bureaucracy created tensions and fears among the members of the Company that were far from healthy' (*Beginning*, pp. 161, 166).

Branagh's decision to set out on his own, without Arts Council support, to create a self-supporting commercial company paralleled Thatcher's dismantling of Socialist infrastructure and privatisation of the gas, water and power industries. Branagh's autobiography reveals a man of great talent and ambition with an extraordinary appetite for work and a fierce commitment to an older tradition of theatre based on the actor. It also reveals a shrewd but audacious businessman and a master publicist, able to identify a niche in the British theatrical world and create a company to fill it and expand beyond it. The name Branagh chose for his company reflected his aspirations: Renaissance, 'to reflect the rebirth that was going on in the British theatre' (*Beginning*, p. 184). Enlisting prominent actors like Judi Dench and Derek Jacobi to direct plays, entrusting finances to a shrewd City stockbroker and persuading his old acquaintance Prince Charles to be the company's patron, Branagh almost instantly became the most visible figure in British theatre, selling out his early productions before they opened.

The initial decision to produce a film of *Henry V* – whatever Branagh's views on the play's attitude to war or the justice of its hero – was at least in part a deliberate attempt to invite comparison with Olivier. The sheer audacity of the project helped to gain it notoriety, although Branagh danced round the issue in interviews. 'I'm not making this film to see if I can score a draw with Olivier, but because I passionately believe Shakespeare's plays need to be constantly reinterpreted', he told Michael Billington in an interview entitled 'A "New Olivier" is Taking On Henry V on the Screen'. 'If Olivier even knows about this film, I suspect he thinks, "cheeky bastard". But the point is that, if a previous *Henry V* film had existed, it certainly wouldn't have stopped Olivier' (*New York Times*, 8 January 1989). This last comment, of course, somewhat disingenuously reinforces the comparison.

Branagh's *Henry V* is certainly distinct from Olivier's in style and tone. While Olivier's was sweeping, colourful, panoramic and self-consciously innovative, Branagh's – with a few notable exceptions – sticks to a restrained colour palette, conventional framing and editing, and closeup to medium-range shots. In accordance with Branagh's philosophy as director of the Renaissance Theatre company, the emphasis is generally on the actor: the film is filled with precise, detailed, convincingly naturalistic performances. The camera gets right in the faces of the sweaty, grimy, unshaven actors: but rather than causing them to short-change the language (as Olivier had feared Shakespearean closeups would do), it allows them to shape and mould it on a firm foundation of realistic Stanislavskian emotion. Judi Dench's weathered, tearful Mistress Quickly, Paul Scofield's grave French King, Michael Maloney's fiery and formidable Dauphin, Robert Stephens's tragic Pistol and especially Ian Holm's superb Fluellen all use the intimate camera work to their advantage in rich, powerful, immediate performances.

Branagh's intimate and naturalistic camera work is occasionally broken up by the audacious stunts of a first-time director and old-movie enthusiast, raised on Welles and Hitchcock. As in his later campy thriller *Dead Again*, Branagh occasionally can't resist going for big effects that come perilously close to the ludicrous. The effect is intensified, in both cases, by the overblown romantic scores of Patrick Doyle, which again hark back to the conventions of 1940s cinema. For the most part, however, the visual texture of Branagh's *Henry V* is immediate, gritty and realistic, albeit suffused with a slight romantic glow.

The first few scenes of Branagh's film reveal how he deliberately acknowledges and distances himself from Olivier. Branagh establishes a striking contrast of tone in the opening moments. Whereas Olivier's credits were crisply lettered on white paper against a sunny blue sky, accompanied by a cheerful angelic chorale, Branagh's are etched in fiery red on a black screen. The first phrases of the musical score are distant, ghostly fifes, but with the appearance, in large letters, of the title *Henry V*, a loud, vibrating cello chord establishes the grave, ominous, yet romantic tone that will mark the opening scenes, and indeed much of the film.

Derek Jacobi's Chorus begins with a touch of camp irony – another Branagh characteristic – by striking a match in the darkness for an imposing 'O for a muse of fire', then echoing down metal steps to switch on the lights of a movie soundstage (I.Chorus.1). Jacobi recites an abbreviated version of the prologue while moving among the clutter of properties, mirroring and parodying Olivier's backstage Globe sequences. Half-constructed set pieces and flats stand in for the 'wooden O', but the lines about imagining horses are necessarily cut. Shakespeare's appeals to the imagination are superfluous in a deliberately realistic film, and the speech seems left in only because it is famous, and because the soundstage setting is a clever way of quoting but diverging from Olivier. Nowhere else in the film is there any self-consciousness about the medium. Olivier's Globe scenes revealed the King's theatrical showmanship while lowering the political stakes through knockabout clowning; Branagh moves from the opening chorus immediately into the fierce political tension of Henry's court, and swiftly puts the focus where it will be for the entire film – in the mind of the young King himself.

It is with the clerics scenes that Branagh's *Henry V* really begins. Here Branagh marks his departure from Olivier dramatically, making the initial conference a whispered affair in a dark antechamber, with Canterbury on the lookout for spies. The King's misspent youth and reformation are mentioned but quickly passed over, as the scene is cut to emphasise the bishops' desperate self-interest. Branagh felt the scene 'vitally important for establishing ... the tone of the whole first section of the film. A conspiratorial political mood; an unfriendly palace and a dark world beyond' (*Beginning*, p. 223). However, the bishops' exchanges, framed in alternating closeups, are *so* cloak-and-dagger that they become slightly, perhaps unintentionally, comic – and when the bishops make a late and bustling entrance into the next scene, they seem to be deliberately recalling Olivier's hapless clowns. Nevertheless, their treatment succeeds in establishing a world of intrigue and deceit.

The court scene begins with another of Branagh's over-the-top touches: the King appears silhouetted in a huge doorway in a floor-length robe, gliding toward the camera like Darth Vader while the music swells and crashes about him. It's an audacious, even outrageous image, and it's impossible to tell whether Branagh intends it as ironic or not – he seems to dare the audience to take it seriously. A series of reaction shots of the courtiers, in flickering torchlight, support this grand entrance and set up the scene's principal theme of Henry as the observed of all observers. Only after all are seated and the music has ceased does the camera reveal the young King, seated in the throne in a medium shot, slipping the robe from his shoulders to reveal a close-fitting velvet jacket. He looks slight, pale and extremely young, but grave and forthright. The juxtaposition of this figure with the Wagnerian hero-god of the first shot reverses the effect of Olivier's opening, where the King is seen first as a nervous actor clearing his throat offstage, before striding on to deliver his opening lines with ringing grandeur. Olivier's opening, as Graham Holderness has noted, casts suspicion on Henry's theatrical rhetoric (*Shakespeare's History*, p. 189). Branagh's opening has the opposite effect: he suggests the awe and power of the King's position, and then the earnestness and fragility of the 'solitary, pensive boy' who occupies it (Branagh, *Henry V*, p. 21). By so doing, he firmly grasps the audience's sympathies for his hero and holds on to them tenaciously for the rest of the picture. Like Olivier's, Branagh's whole project is tied up in a deep process of self-identification with Henry and his campaign: in his autobiography Branagh repeatedly equates himself with Henry, also a twenty-seven-year-old attempting an audacious, difficult project against huge odds. The film accordingly has a very personal and limited focus.

Branagh's direction and performance in this scene place attention not on the moral or political ramifications of Henry's decision about waging war, but on how Henry fares in the first public test of his leadership. Despite having taken pains to establish the ulterior motives of the bishops – here underlined by a conspiratorial nod from Exeter to Canterbury – Branagh turns the issue of Henry's decision into a personal ordeal concerning his ability to face up to his senior advisers. Remarkably, Branagh convinces the audience that Henry passes this test, despite his doing precisely what those advisers want – agreeing to invade France. A series of

10　The young King Henry at the opening of
Kenneth Branagh's 1989 film

three increasingly tight shots of Henry as he asks the bishops' advice, warns them about the gravity of war, and demands of them, 'May I with right and conscience make this claim?' (I.ii.96), makes it seem as though Henry is successfully cutting through their rhetoric to the grim heart of the matter, but the fact remains that he goes along with their plans. Montjoy's entrance with the tennis-balls provides another observer to assess, and be impressed by, the young king's stature. Branagh delivers the tennis-ball speech with measured, tight-lipped anger, and a trace of awe at the powers he is about to unleash; Christopher Ravenscroft's Montjoy, repeating his performance from Noble's stage version, gives Henry the first of several looks of surprised but guarded admiration. As the court exits to end the scene, the bishops give each other a last conspiratorial glance, but they needn't have bothered: the political causes of the war have long since been overshadowed by Henry's private struggle with his responsibility and his destiny.

Branagh's emphasis on Henry as the audience's point of focus and sympathy is continued in the traitors sequence, which he conceived as 'Hitchcockian … fast-moving, tense, and violent' (*Beginning*, p. 225). As in his stage performance, the personal betrayal by his 'bedfellow' Scroop is the keynote, resulting in a passionate, almost sexual supine embrace over a table for Henry's speech of condemnation, lapsing into tears for 'this revolt of thine, methinks, is like / Another fall of man' (II.ii.141-2). Likewise, Branagh brings Henry into the scenes with the Eastcheap characters, introducing a flashback pastiche of the good old days at the Boar's Head. In a rosy glow of good-fellowship, Robbie Coltrane's youngish, goateed Falstaff entertains his companions with jumbled fragments from the *Henry IV* plays, then warmly greets Branagh's tousle-haired Hal, who smiles indulgently but already looks pensive and out of place. Falstaff abruptly intones, 'Harry, when thou art king, banish Pistol, banish Bardolph, banish Nym, but for sweet Jack Falstaff, banish not him thy Harry's company, banish plump Jack, and banish all the world'. Hal's 'I do, I will' is only a voice-over of shocked recognition, but Falstaff seems to hear it, and rather absurdly whispers, 'But we have heard the chimes at midnight, Master Harry. Jesus, the days that we have seen.' Hal's reply, in voice-over as he backs away, is 'I know thee not, old man'. The effect of this abrupt summary of *Henry IV* is to provide audiences with the background to Falstaff's death, as in Olivier's film. But by including Henry's pained anticipation of the rejection, Branagh makes it another action that has happened to Henry rather than been carried out *by* him, another instance when the audience can sympathise with the difficult sacrifices its hero must endure.

The hanging of Bardolph, when it comes, is very much in the same style. The moment is similar to that in Noble's production, but the use of specifically cinematic techniques increases the total effect and tightens the focus on Henry. Branagh's notes in his published screenplay make the emphasis of the scene clear:

> Once again, through the unknowing *Fluellen*, a public trial of strength is provided for the *King*. Watched by his sodden soldiers, he must enforce his decree that any form of theft or pillage of the French countryside will be punished by death. Any favouritism or sentiment shown here will be disastrous for discipline amongst these poor soldiers.

> The cost to the *King* is enormous as he gives the nod to *Exeter*, who pulls *Bardolph* to his feet, throwing the rope over the overhanging branch. (Branagh, *Henry V*, p. 71)

Branagh then cuts to a flashback of rose-tinted merriment at the Boar's Head, with Bardolph, his neck playfully encircled by the arms of Nym and Falstaff, addressing to Hal Falstaff's line, 'Do not, when thou art king, hang a thief' (*1 Henry IV*, I.ii.57). Branagh's screenplay again:

> The smile on *Hal*'s face drops away.

> HAL
> No, thou shalt.

> From the shocked face of *Bardolph* at his future King's response we:
> DISSOLVE TO:
> *Muddy Track: day (real time)*

> The stricken and bloody face of the condemned man, his head in the noose.

> *Henry*, his eyes filled with tears, slowly signals to *Exeter*....

> The *King* stares at the ugly death throes of his former friend. Tears stain his cheeks. (p. 73)

Through the film medium's control of perspective, the few brief shots of Bardolph are countered by long reaction shots of Henry. While it doesn't short-change the horror of Bardolph's death, the film does keep the focus firmly on Henry. The episode is primarily, as Branagh intended, 'a public trial of strength for the *King*.... The cost to the *King* is enormous.' Branagh plays the scene beautifully, with great sadness and no trace of harshness – indeed, there is a kind of tenderness in his nod to Exeter to proceed with the execution. It is virtually impossible to hold the episode against Henry, particularly after his brave but respectful defiance of Montjoy. Branagh ends the scene with a touch of humor that gets the viewer thoroughly back on Henry's side. Just after he says to Gloucester, 'We are in God's hand, brother, not in theirs' (the French) (III.vi.175), a rumble of thunder is heard, and Henry's eyes turn wanly up to heaven as the rain begins to pour down. Branagh has made Henry's execution of his friend – potentially one of the most negative moments in the play – into a positive appeal.

It is an ironic fact about 'revisionist' interpretations that those moments when the revision has to work hardest are often the most effective. The director must sharply focus the staging techniques to engage with and overcome the traditional interpretation of the text; the resulting tension makes the moment in question especially vivid. In the case of Branagh's film, it is the moments where the film works hardest to recuperate the King – to make us like him in spite of what he's doing – that work the best. Thus, while the standard set pieces, the Harfleur breach and the Crispian's Day speech, go for surprisingly little, moments that Olivier entirely cut are very effective in winning audience sympathy for, and interest in, King Henry. The hanging of Bardolph is one example; the threats to Harfleur are another. Branagh's breach speech – traditional heroics atop an Olivier-style white horse before a garish nighttime Harfleur – is almost a complete washout. Branagh simply isn't cut out for this kind of heroic rhetoric, nor is a 1980s audience likely to be swayed by it. The ultimatum speech, however, is intensely compelling. It is delivered from the same horse, but in a low-angle close-up that emphasises both Henry's isolation and his potential destructive power. Branagh goes all-out for the brutality of the images, his sooty face twisting as he shouts 'Your naked infants spitted upon *pikes*!' (III.iii.38). His delivery is intercut with closeups of his soldiers – not a particularly 'blind and bloody' lot, but perhaps realising, with alarm, their own capacity for destruction. The scene makes Henry's catalogue of horrors seem a genuine possibility, though one he wishes to avoid. The dramatic force of the scene is intense and surprising, and is turned to Henry's advantage at the moment the governor capitulates. Henry, near collapse from exhaustion and tension, expresses relief not merely because he has taken the town, nor because he has successfully bluffed the opponent, but because he has turned aside at the last moment from a terrible course. With the relief comes a deepening of Henry's character, in his horror at what he had been on the point of doing, at an aspect of himself and his role which he had not previously examined.

Throughout the film, Branagh manages to make negative statements about war reflect positively back upon Henry. Much of the film's 'anti-war' angle doesn't come in the form of indictments of cruelty or brutality, but in a vivid and realistic portrayal of the hardships of a soldier's life: 'rainy marching in the painful field' (IV.iii.111). The mud, fatigue, unsanitary conditions and physical difficulty of moving heavy and unwieldy equipment over miles of uneven terrain are convincingly represented. Branagh's Henry is always seen to share in these hardships: he is a warrior for the working day who gets muddy along with his men. He is still set apart in some traditional ways – he alone has a white charger, he alone wears a red and blue surcoat in an army of brown. But Branagh shows Henry suffering and interacting with his men on a very personal level.

The supporting characters are made individual and distinct, and given a degree of authority which sometimes qualifies the King's without ever undermining it. The night scene before Agincourt provides a good example. The camp is awash in phony fog and blue down-light – Branagh's cinematographer failed him here, and the lack of realism weakens the scene. The three soldiers are well played and convincing, however, particularly the pudgy, crop-haired Bates of Shaun Prendergast. Michael Williams (played by the actor Michael Williams) is a smallish, middle-aged, West Country man whose bitter grief over the fate of the war's widows and orphans (and possibly his own) is allowed to score a real point against Henry. The 'legs and arms and heads' speech (IV.i.135-49) – one of the strongest challenges to Henry's authority in the play – has great force in closeup, and a reaction shot after 'some [crying] upon their children rawly left' (142-3) shows that Henry is seriously affected by it. On the point about the suffering of the soldiers and their families, the film yields to Williams's position; on the point of the king's moral responsibility, however, it jumps to Henry's aid. As soon as Williams has made the assertion that 'if these men do not die well, it will be a black matter for the king that led them to it' (146-8), the camera snaps back to Henry who, having shaken off the guilty doubts of the previous shot, pursues his self-defence with a clear conscience and hair-splitting moral precision:

> So, if a son that is by his father sent about merchandise do sinfully miscarry upon the sea, the imputation of his wickedness, by your rule, should be imposed upon the father that sent him. But this is not so. The King is not bound to answer the particular endings of his soldiers, nor the father of his son, for they purpose not their deaths when they propose their services. Besides, there is no king, be his cause never so spotless, can try it out with all unspotted soldiers. Every subject's duty is the King's, but every subject's soul is his own. (cf. 150-92)

Branagh's trimly edited version of Henry's rambling casuistry, with oracular weight given to the last line, seems an adequate response to Williams's charges. By acknowledging the widows and orphans but asserting that 'every subject's soul is his own' Branagh prevents the sequence from weakening Henry's position with his audience. The 'Upon the King' speech that follows is backed up by music which makes Henry's isolation heroic and Hamlet-like, possibly the means to greater spiritual enlightenment. David Gwillim's television version of the speech is far more honest and penetrating. The 'God of battles' prayer, however, is desperate and anguished, and ends with despair: 'The day, my friends, and all things stay for me' is spoken not with rising cheerfulness, or even stoical resignation, but with reluctance and dread (314). Unlike Olivier's, Branagh's Henry does not really believe God is on his side until *after* the battle: a fact that makes him considerably more attractive to a contemporary audience.

The film's emphasis on the personal qualities of Henry, and its subsidiary personal emphasis on his men, are used to masterful effect in the battle. Whereas Olivier had used the wide-open screen for panoramic long shots of chivalric pageantry, Branagh forces his camera into the mêlée to reveal how the various characters fare. Branagh's method was perhaps forced on him for reasons of economy, but it is very effective. Nearly every shot in Branagh's battle sequence features a recognisable character whose actions continue his personal story as the film has presented it thus far. We see Bates 'fight lustily', as he had promised to do, drowning a French infantryman in a pool of mud. We see Pistol and Nym scurrying about the field looting corpses. We see the brave young York, who had earnestly asked to lead the charge, surrounded and slaughtered, vomiting blood as he is repeatedly stabbed by French swords. In its use of mud, slow motion and music, Branagh's battle draws on many sources, including *Chimes at Midnight*, *The Seven Samurai*, *Ran* and *Platoon*. What makes it distinctive, however, is the degree to which Branagh personalises it. A comparison of the opening moments of the two battle sequences strongly reveals the contrast between Olivier's and Branagh's approaches. Olivier has his tracking camera follow the galloping French charge; Branagh includes the sound of the approaching hoofs, but shows only the various reactions, in closeup, of the English soldiers as they await the onslaught.

Branagh's treatment of the battle clearly reveals his concern for how much he can and cannot get away with in his double project of presenting a realistic, brutal war while retaining, and even increasing, audience sympathy for Henry. The fighting is indeed an ugly scrum of mud and blood, but it is given humanity and pathos by the focus on recognisable individuals in brave and desperate struggle. Further, the slow motion and restrained, poignant music give an aesthetic contour to the scenes of combat, far removed from the grisly mechanised apocalypse of Welles's Shrewsbury in *Chimes at Midnight*. Most important are Branagh's inclusions and omissions. The massacre of the boys is given full play. Christian Bale's well-characterised Boy is seen running back to the camp a moment before a troop of French horsemen approach. A chorus of shrill screams alarms the English soldiers, who, led by Henry, slog desperately in slow motion through the water to the boys' aid. First to arrive are Gower and Fluellen: the camera returns to normal speed and the soundtrack drops away to an eerie hush as they stop in shock. A hand-held point-of-view shot – the only one in the film – looks unsteadily from corpse to corpse in the ruin of the camp. The two men grieve over the Boy, but there is no mention of any order to kill the French prisoners. Henry arrives and, after taking in the scene, gives vent to a building explosion of rage on 'I was not angry since I came to France / Until this instant!' (IV.vii.57-8). By the end of the line Montjoy has appeared and Henry drags him from his horse to the ground with

11   Henry after the battle of Agincourt, from Kenneth Branagh's 1989 film

a roar. 'What means this, Herald?' (69) refers to the slaughter of the boys, as in Noble's production. Montjoy tells Henry he has won, and after dully taking it in, Henry collapses with exhaustion. The massacre of the French prisoners does not take place. Within the conventions of realistically depicted warfare that Branagh has set up, it would be too much for an audience to take – it would be impossible for Branagh to rehabilitate Henry for the end of the film.

Branagh modulates the shift from the horrors of the battlefield to the political/romantic comedy of the final scene with great finesse. The post-battle scenes are crucial in the film's elevation of Henry above the horrors of war it has apparently been condemning. The reading of the lists of the French and English dead is played with great gravity and an emphasis on the personal: before and during the English list, Branagh uses several medium-closeups of English soldiers, expectant, weary, unsentimental. Branagh informs 'God fought for us' (IV.viii.122) with a bewildered awe, as if incredulous that his guilty prayer was answered. What follows is perhaps the most important sequence of the film, a four-minute, 500-foot tracking shot that takes Branagh from the mud and horror of war to a celebration of the moral growth of the King and a segue into the comedy of the final scene. It begins with the soldier Court singing an *a cappella Non Nobis*, following Henry's order. The identity of the singer is significant, as it helps to resolve the rift between Henry and his men remaining from the night scene. Moments before, Henry has silently returned Williams's glove, and the latter's low-comic take of realisation, alarm and relief nearly erases the fiercely dignified resistance he had represented earlier. If these moments represent Henry's resumption of authority over his men, however, he still has a gauntlet of visible suffering to pass through before the sins of the battle are fully washed from him. Picking up the slain Boy, he begins a slow, trudging passage across the battlefield which is also a roll-call of all the principals from the battle and a reminder of their fates: Pistol cradling the dead Nym, the nobles carrying York, the muddy and exhausted British captains, Brian Blessed's tank-like Exeter. In the background the corpses are being looted by villagers. Henry pauses briefly to look down on the dead Constable, held by Orleans, and exchanges a look of dull recognition with the bitter Dauphin, then passes on. A crowd of vengeful French widows and mothers rush at Henry; Montjoy holds them back; Henry walks on without noticing. Finally Henry reaches a cart on which are piled bodies of the dead; he climbs up, gently lays down the Boy, kisses him and stands erect, looking at the field about him.

It is a bold sequence, the most memorable in the film, and it illustrates the degree to which visual interpretation outweighs text: there is not a word of Shakespeare in it. The description of the final moment in the published screenplay reads it as a moment of defeat, loss, shame: 'We cut close on his blood-stained face, the dreadful price they have all had to pay for this so-called victory clearly etched into his whole being. His head drops as if in shame' (p. 114). But critic David Denby read it as a moment of triumph, of almost Christ-like exaltation: 'At that moment, his kingship is achieved – he has accepted responsibility for the dead, for the victory, for all of the burdens of leadership' (*New York*, 27 November 1989). Branagh may have been *acting* shame in that shot, but the film-text *says* triumph: the crucial factor is Patrick Doyle's music. During the course of the sequence, the *Non Nobis* grows from a shell-shocked *a cappella* solo to a soaring choral and orchestral celebration. The build is carefully calculated and timed to the shot: the chorus picks up the song as Henry's army begins to gather round him on the passage away from the field. *Non Nobis* is heard four times: first by the soloist, then by the chorus and soloist together, then again with the soloist harmonising above the chorus as the orchestra builds in. As the camera tracks backward away from the field, the strings ascend to positively cheerful heights, and the piece ends with a triumphant repetition of the chorus. The music pulls the film away from the muddy sorrows of the field to heavenly affirmation, divine sanction for Henry's achievement, not in winning the battle but in 'accept[ing] responsibility ... for all of the burdens of leadership'. The sequence is metonymic of the entire film's strategy for creating Henry's heroism by focusing on his personal suffering at his own atrocities. At the end of the sequence, Henry stands up from depositing the boy in the cart, and the battlefield is no longer in view, only Henry, the lone hero. The soaring music has signalled his redemption and made possible the dissolve to the French palace, where he woos Princess Katherine with boyish charm.

The wooing only confirms Henry's apotheosis. Emma Thompson's Katherine, while initially resistant, warms quickly to Branagh's engaging courtship, and the fact of their offscreen marriage reinforces the inevitability of their union. The scene is warmly lit and closely shot; after the first few moments the political context is forgotten until the comic return of the French King at 'Here comes your father' (V.ii.296). At the film's end, the qualifying lines of the Chorus, cut by Olivier, are retained ('they lost France and made his England bleed'); but they are spoken not with irony, but in sincere regret that Henry's shining moment was all too brief. In discussing the post-battle sequences in his autobiography, Branagh wrote, 'I wanted to reveal as much of the devastation as possible.... There would be no question about the statement this movie was making about war' (pp. 235-6). In fact there are a great many questions: it seems, finally, that the film endorses Henry's war as an occasion for him to earn, and display, his heroism.

Branagh's film presents itself as one thing, but at a fundamental level it is something else. On its grimy, sweaty, muddy surface it is a condemnation of war, from France to the Falklands; in its stirring heart it is a celebration of heroic individualism, from the battlefield to the Britain of the 1980s. Shakespeare's *Henry V* provides material for both projects, and the film smoothly and seamlessly welds them together. Interestingly, as I have noted above, it is at those moments when there is a conflict between Branagh's two projects – when the film labours to redeem Henry from his least attractive words and actions – that the film is strongest. Branagh's pained, sensitive, charismatic performance demands to be liked, in the face of all the horrors he lays to Henry's charge. The one horror Branagh shrank from gambling on is the massacre of the French prisoners. It would be the one atrocity from which Branagh could not redeem his young hero-king, and its exclusion reveals the limits of the film's revisionist project. Branagh's *Henry V* is the official version of the play disguised as the secret one.

CHAPTER VIII

Wish not a man from England: *Henry V* outside the United Kingdom

It is perhaps not surprising that *Henry V* has never been popular outside of England. It is a quintessentially English play, drawn from English history, focused on an English national hero and constructed out of English rhetoric. It makes technical demands – a large and virtually all-male cast, battles, long speeches – that are likely to daunt any producer without some cultural stake in the play. Barbara Hodgdon has argued that '*Henry V* becomes, in the theater, a tabula rasa for its culture's current prerogatives.... *Henry V*'s ability to serve its culture's needs and speak its nation's history makes it distinctly unusual' (p. 194). Yet the play has rarely served that function for cultures other than England. Even in the United States, where some knowledge of the story might be presupposed, performances have been only intermittent, and generally dependent on a visiting English star. Thomas Healy points out that *Henry V* 'is the only one of Shakespeare's histories to have been virtually ignored by the Slavic world', and that it has been equally unpopular on the continent: '*Henry V* in modern France would indeed be a perverse beast!' (p. 177). Surveys of Shakespearean performance in France, Italy, the Soviet Union and Romania make almost no mention of the play (See Bragaglia, Dutu, Jusserand, Collison Morley, Samarin).

Dennis Kennedy has argued that translating Shakespeare out of English language and culture can be revealing and liberating: foreign directors accept the strangeness of Shakespeare in a way that allows a more inventive contemporary engagement with the plays (*Foreign Shakespeare*, pp. 14-15). In many ways *Henry V* seems made for this kind of treatment; it is surprising that the 'secret' play has not been more popular with directors looking for ways to explore the history of nationalism and war in the twentieth century. The history plays were performed all over Europe in the postwar years as reflections of contemporary politics; Roger Planchon did a Brechtian *Henry IV* in France in 1957, Giorgio Strehler a harsh Kottian adaptation of *Henry VI* in Milan in 1965; Peter Palitzsch a *Wars of the Roses* cycle in Stuttgart in 1967. Yet *Henry V* received little attention. Only in German-speaking Central Europe and in North America was there any performance tradition for the play. These cultures, however, produced two ground-breaking productions which explored *Henry V* outside the context of English history in provocative and highly theatrical ways. These productions were Peter Zadek's *Held Henry* (*Henry the Hero*, Bremen, 1964) and Michael Kahn's *Henry V* (Stratford, Connecticut, 1969).

The German-speaking world has been a centre for Shakespeare production since the eighteenth century, when G. E. Lessing and F. W. Schiller upheld the Shakespearian dramaturgical model as a Romantic alternative to French Neoclassicism. The first complete cycle of Shakespeare history plays was given by Franz Dingelstedt at Weimar in 1864. Dingelstedt conceived *Henry V* and *Richard III* as polar opposites, icons of good and evil who were the central figures of their respective tetralogies (Potter, p. 40). This symbolic view of the character was not interrogated in the German-speaking theatre for another century, until the next full cycle of history plays, at the Vienna Burgtheater in the 1960s. Despite the persistent popularity of Shakespeare in the German-language theatre, there had been almost no twentieth-century productions of *Henry V* before the Burgtheater's. Under Leopold Lindtberg's direction, the Vienna *Henry V* took a subdued approach to military heroism, approaching the play after the ravages of two world wars. Like many English productions of subsequent decades, Lindtberg's *Henry V* eschewed militarism but presented a sensitive and charismatic hero. Henry was played by Oskar Werner, familiar to film audiences from *Jules and Jim* and *The Spy Who Came in from the Cold*. His Henry had 'great dignity, charm, wisdom, sensibility, and will power', according to Peter Weiser (Leiter, p. 222). According to Kurt Kahl, Werner 'converted the republicans in the stalls to loyalists with his confident artistry and charisma', but 'the darker shadows were not absent' from the production (*Theater Heute*, March 1961, p. 42). Teo Otto's set, of worn wood and tattered but splendid banners, suggested war's costs without denying its grandeur; as Dennis Kennedy observes, 'the Viennese were allowed to have it both ways' (*Looking at Shakespeare*, p. 215). A nuanced and highly successful production, Lindtberg's *Henry V* nevertheless fell well within the traditions of Central European Shakespeare performance and the conservative Burgtheater.

Three years later, Peter Zadek's production went further than Lindtberg's, indeed than any previous production of the play, in exploding the heroic conception of Henry and his war. *Held Henry* was an all-out assault on the whole idea of heroism, filled with anachronism and violent, cartoonish imagery. Strikingly designed and aggressively performed, it broke with both traditional Shakespearian decorum and Brechtian political analysis to give an iconoclastic contemporary take on 'Henry the Hero'.

Zadek had grown up in England after his parents fled the Nazis in 1933; he returned to Germany in 1958 as a controversial avant-garde director. Rebelling against the conservatism of both English and German Shakespeare production, he staged a series of productions in the 1960s that strove 'to popularize the plays through comedy, grotesquerie, eroticism, brutality, and highly visual imagery' (Engle, p. 94). *Held Henry* exemplified this programme.

Though Zadek did not consider himself a Brechtian director, his techniques reflect the ubiquity of Brecht's theatrical theories in postwar Germany. He chose *Henry V* partly because of its 'epic' dramaturgy of loosely connected narrative scenes 'which always have a clear goal, a point, a coherent atmosphere, so that each scene can stand alone'.

> Our ideas about the production started from this point; we tried to show how each one is a variation on the theme of heroism. And not only in the scenes where Henry appears – he's not the only hero. There's a whole row of smaller heroes. For example, the hero Pistol, the late hero Falstaff, or Fluellen, and the farcical hero, the Dauphin. The same theme is touched on again and again, always in a different form. (Wendt, p. 22)

Zadek used the Brechtian device of projected scene titles to comment on each scene's relation to the overall theme. Zadek's set designer, Wilfried Minks, created a visual interrogation of heroism by alternating two sets of portraits on the backdrops. For most of the play the action was backed by the fifty rulers of

England between William I and Elizabeth; at certain moments the royal portraits were replaced by images of various ancient and modern 'heroes', including Hitler, Churchill, Elvis Presley, Billy Graham, Wernher von Braun, Frederick the Great, Atilla the Hun and the German soccer star Uwe Seeler. Zadek and Minks created powerful visual images in interpolated transitional scenes showing the two countries preparing for war. Postwar Germany was understandably obsessed by mass psychology, and Zadek made expressive use of crowd scenes, showing the recruitment of volunteers over screaming loudspeakers, rallies of the frenzied populace, and the beginning of pogroms.

While the Second World War was an important referent for the production, the costumes came from the German Imperial period that led into the First World War. The archbishops discussed their plans while playing golf; Henry established his claim to the French crown at a conference table festooned with Union Jacks and microphones, while stenographers and secret policemen looked on. Henry's meeting with the French ambassador was a relaxed embassy party, with champagne and publicity photos; a jovial diplomatic prelude to the bloody campaign.

The use of a bare stage, a few expressive set pieces, and projected images allowed Zadek and Minks to make swift location changes and telling visual statements. The Southampton scene began at the harbour, with blue skies, crying gulls and dockworkers; but at the traitors' arrest it instantly became a show trial, with an angry projected crowd shouting for blood. The traitors' expressions of remorse, in this context, came across as 'self-criticism' of the kind demanded by Stalin. Henry's heroism was thus revealed as a public artifice constructed through coercion.

Zadek's attack on heroism was by no means limited to Henry himself, however. Pistol and his crew were repulsive louts, brutal in their squabbling, drunkenly sentimental over Falstaff, rapacious on the battlefield. Pistol robbed a wounded Monsieur le Fer and killed him with a shot to the back of the head. The four captains were dumb, stubborn British Tommies in short khaki pants with red makeup on their knees; they recalled the cowardly soldiers of Brecht's *Mann Ist Mann*. The French were stupid, arrogant and cruel: on the night before battle, they sat around a glittering Christmas tree, listening to Marlene Dietrich, unwrapping parcels from home and casually torturing an English prisoner.

Henry spent the night before battle in bed with a bored French whore, to whom he delivered the St Crispian's Day speech. He made his final address to the troops while posing for a huge equestrian battle portrait. Yet Zadek didn't present Henry in an exclusively negative light; his scenes with the common soldiers took on a kind of romantic pathos as he shared a cigarette with his men. The relationship with Williams was unusually developed, as Lois Potter discusses:

> When he and Williams agree to make their disagreement into a 'quarrel' (IV.2.204), the decision comes across as a bond of friendship which, in the context of this play, is something new and exciting for Henry. The end of his practical joke on Williams comes quickly and without the involvement of Fluellen; Williams is carried on dying and Henry identifies himself as if somehow hoping to prolong both the soldier's life and this one, rare, opportunity of human contact. Williams is equally unaware of the irrelevance of his self-justification to his present situation, and his 'I beseech your highness pardon me' (IV.8.56-7) is spoken as he dies. The intention may have been to show the two characters trapped in their social roles, but the effect was curiously moving, followed as it was by a sober Henry ordering the singing of the *Te Deum* and *Non Nobis*. Indeed, Zadek could be said to have made Henry more sympathetic than he usually is at this point, because more aware of his responsibility for the death of this particular soldier. (p. 47)

The wooing scene was also played to Henry's advantage, though it was qualified by the scenes that surrounded it. A projected image of a military parade on the Champs-Elysées necessarily recalled the Nazi occupation of Paris; Fluellen viciously beat up Pistol after posing for souvenir photographs. For the wooing itself, however, Henry and Katherine played in the manner of a romantic Hollywood film. As Zadek commented, 'This king, who otherwise can be very evil, suddenly has a charm, a glamour, there he's more in the company of James Stewart than of Stalin and Adolf Hitler' (Wendt, p. 22). Zadek played the scene to highlight this charm, but chilled it with a final projected title, 'And he died in the flower of his youth'.

Zadek's approach to Henry was deliberately inconsistent from scene to scene:

> I remember a conversation with Friedhelm Ptok, who plays the role. He said, 'Wait a minute, that's psychologically impossible. Now I'm like this, and then right afterwards I'm supposed to be like that – it's not the same character, those are quite different characters.'

And they are. I wasn't trying to be psychologically consistent, to carry out the character psychologically. Rather, it was a matter of illuminating a theme in many ways. That's why we chose the play. (p. 22)

This approach to character recalls Brecht, who believed human beings were constructed in different ways by different social relations. Yet in a *Theater Heute* interview Zadek distanced himself from Brecht, whose approach he believed to be overly cool and rational. Comparing *Held Henry* unfavourably with Planchon's *Henry IV*, the interviewer took Zadek to task for his lack of sustained political critique, his gratuitous use of contemporary references and his focus on a broad thematics of heroism rather than a historically exact examination of medieval imperialism. In response to the charge that 'You stage emotions, apolitical emotions, rather than political understanding', Zadek defended his eclectic, iconoclastic approach: 'I don't want to make theater for intellectuals.... I sense a barrier between the stage and the audience which is not to be overcome with the subtle methods of Brecht' (p. 22).

Zadek's production was important because it moved *Henry V* outside the context of English history into that of modern politics. While Zadek eschewed a clear political perspective, other than an aggressive denunciation of military heroism, his shock tactics forced audiences to consider the play in the light of their own lives and their unspeakable recent history. Zadek, himself a fugitive from the Nazis, made *Henry V* into a part of Germany's confrontation with its own past and present.

The other most important non-UK production of *Henry V* also invoked and transformed the methods of Brecht for an aggressive contemporary engagement with the play. In the case of Michael Kahn's Stratford, Connecticut production, the historical background was not the Second World War but Vietnam. Kahn's production found a uniquely American approach to a play that had long resisted meaningful interpretation outside of the English tradition. In order to understand the importance of Kahn's *Henry V*, it is worth considering the play's performance history in the United States and Canada.

North American productions of *Henry V* had generally been examples of a kind of cultural imperialism. Virtually all of the nineteenth- and early twentieth-century productions were centred on a visiting English star. William Charles Macready performed the play in 1826; George Rignold in 1874, in a touring version of Calvert's Manchester production; and Lewis Waller in 1912. All played the part in a traditional romantic vein. Rignold and Waller were both matinée idols who traded on their fame and appearance. George Odell, in the *Annals of the New York Stage*, dryly notes that Rignold achieved his success 'more by good looks than by dramatic gifts' (p. 528). Rignold was known for riding a white horse named Crispin in the battle scenes. Waller was the quintessential romantic Henry, and was routinely besieged at the stage door by female fans: 'It may be doubted whether any player in history has had such a large and fanatical female following', Hesketh Pearson reports in *The Last Actor-Managers* (p. 41). Praised in England as the 'ideal man – the happy warrior – great in thought, great in purpose, great in action' (*The Stratford Herald*, quoted in Brennan, p. xxi), Waller's Henry was equally celebrated in the United States. Charles Shattuck's account of the play's success in *Shakespeare on the American Stage* suggests that New York critics were at least as concerned with the taste of their own audiences as with the performance itself:

> *The Dramatic Mirror* observed that 'the same public which turned thumbs down on a trivial play by Edward Knoblauch could rise to enthusiastic appreciation of a rousing play by William Shakespeare' … Arthur Hornblow observed in *Theatre* magazine that 'There is a Shakespearean following in New York City, and it is a big one too… Be he high-brow or pin-head, he is a foolish theatre-goer who overlooks the opportunity to see "Henry V" so well-produced.' (p. 293)

The tone of these comments suggests a feeling of cultural inferiority in the New York theatre scene – the critics seem relieved that their audiences have the perspicacity to applaud their English betters.

For the theatre of the United States, *Henry V* has served mainly as an occasion for British performers to demonstrate their Shakespearean predominance. In Canada, by contrast, the play developed a uniquely local political importance. As a nation divided between French and English populations, and sometimes riven by cultural and linguistic conflict, Canada provides a fertile environment for *Henry V*. Modern trends in the performance of the play can be traced through a pair of productions given at the

Stratford Festival Canada in Stratford, Ontario. Ralph Berry has noted that Michael Langham's 1956 and 1966 productions 'offer a sure guide to the times' (p. 71). The former, featuring a romantic Henry from Christopher Plummer, was a positive reading of the play stressing the final Anglo-French unity; the latter, with Douglas Rain, was a grim indictment of war appropriate to the Vietnam era.

Langham's 1956 production was 'the triumph of the season' in the Stratford Festival's fourth year (Whittaker, p. xxiv). Tanya Moiseiwitsch designed the production, which played on the Festival's permanent semi-Elizabethan set. Her design was characteristically sumptuous, despite the bare stage, which was often adorned with carpets for a richer look. The French were beautifully clad in metallic blues and greens; for her language lesson, Katherine was attended by no fewer than four ladies-in-waiting, all in gorgeous gowns and wimpled headdresses. The elegant design of the production was an appropriate backdrop for the star-making performance of the twenty-six-year-old Christopher Plummer, who emerged as 'a Shakespearean actor of the first rank' (Brooks Atkinson, *New York Times*, 20 June 1956). Classically good-looking, with rich vocal resources and a wide emotional range, Plummer made Henry a fully rounded chivalric hero:

> Mr. Plummer was able to make *Henry V* seem a positive saint when confronted by his casuistical bishops, a warrior when compared with the vaunting and empty French nobles, a man of quick temper when he walked among his private soldiers, and a humble but ardent lover when he confronted Kate. (Arnold Edinborough, quoted in Berry, p. 71)

Plummer was especially appealing in the wooing scene, with a 'light, self-conscious and very funny proposal of marriage' (Walter Kerr, *New York Herald Tribune*, 20 June 1956). He was romantic without being lightweight; Herbert Whittaker felt he had 'the dangerous quality which rivets the attention' (p. xxiv). Yet by all accounts it was a thoroughly attractive heroic performance.

The innovative aspect of Langham's production was using leading French-Canadian actors from *Le Théâtre du Nouveau Monde* in Montreal to play the French characters. Arthur Colby Sprague felt this casting gave a unique balance to the play:

> Something was added, one felt, that no audience had had before, and this something, even if only latent in the drama, was both

human and exciting. It was present from the moment the ambassador entered and spoke: a contrast, as much physical as in bearing and gesture, between him and those about him at King Harry's court. One understood, in a flash, how there could have been a Hundred Years War. (Sprague, pp. 109-10)

The French were led by Gratien Gélinas, 'the outstanding personality in French Canadian theatre', who made Charles VI a frail but 'indomitable spirit', according to Herbert Whittaker: 'Here the majesty of France flashed through a weak vessel' (pp. xxiv–xxv). Though the French were accorded respect by the production, there was no corresponding criticism of the English, and in the scene before the battle the French knights displayed their traditional *hauteur*. The French presence was perhaps most important in the final scene, which emphasised the overcoming of differences. As Arnold Edinborough reported, for the Canadian audience the play 'became an extremely vital political tract as the last act slowly worked out a compromise between the beaten French and the victorious English' (quoted in Berry, p. 72). On a stage bedecked with hanging pennants, royal carpet and gloriously costumed courtiers, Henry and Katherine held hands as Queen Isabel blessed their union. It is perhaps worth noting that this benedictory role was not given to a French-Canadian actress but to one of the Festival's regulars. The effusive comments of Herbert Whittaker in a commemorative volume seem unconscious of the irony:

When Eleanor Stuart, the Festival's most distinguished actress, spoke Queen Isabel's lines, so beautifully, to unite French and English in the last scene, Shakespeare seemed to have written with an eye to this bi-lingual land. (p. xxv)

Though Langham's use of French actors added a cultural and political dimension to the production, the final effect was one of union and harmony, with the English in the dominant role.

The 1966 production provided a marked contrast. In his director's notes, Langham looked back critically at his earlier vision: 'the French/English peace conference that concludes the play was offered in a romantic vein, and many of us who are susceptible to sentimental inroads became moist-eyed at the prospect of French/English harmony'. His new production took a much harsher view, both of Anglo-French conflict in Canada and of Shakespeare's vision of war. As Ralph Berry has noted, Langham's programme notes have an almost defensive tone:

What has this jingoistic national anthem of a play to do with our age? It glorifies war, exploits the inanities of nationalism, is offensively class-conscious, and – as if to encourage philistine thinking in Canada – is patently and exultantly anti-French. Why then are we performing it? – Just to satisfy those who only think old-world Establishment thoughts? (quoted in Berry, p.72)

The programme clearly established an anti-war perspective, quoting the poetry of Wilfred Owen and including a photograph of conflict in Vietnam.

Douglas Rain, a gritty, unromantic actor, played the King as a troubled, brave, and isolated man, struggling under the responsibilities of kingship and the realities of war. He started guiltily at the Archbishop's passing reference to the usurper Hugh Capet and his uneasy heir, who 'Could not keep quiet in his conscience / Wearing the crown of France' (I.ii.7980). Deeply stung by the argument with Williams, he showed no confidence going into battle; 'How thou pleasest, God, dispose the day' was given with grim fatalism (IV.iii.132). Langham did all he could to stress the misery of war; the battles were gory, with both the English boys and French prisoners killed on stage. Henry's demoralised troops listened indifferently to his speeches, and after the battle looted the French corpses. Langham conceived of the production as a corrective to the version of events delivered by William Hutt's detached, sardonic Chorus:

> the Chorus represents the popular view, the national press so to speak: 'Time' and 'Life,' alias Hall and Holinshed? And I suggest that in this play we are invited to examine the difference between the popular myth and the truth. (Programme note)

The French were once again played by French-Canadian actors. This time, however, the final emphasis was not on harmonious Anglo-French unity but on uneasy détente, a state of affairs that persisted in Canada and that made Langham's *Henry V* an acute and troubling piece of social art.

The unique Canadian political situation gave productions there an edge that was lacking in the United States. Twentieth-century productions continued the anglophile heroic tradition; the first New York production since Lewis Waller's featured the Old Vic star Laurence Harvey in a traditional romantic performance of the role. The development of regional repertory theatres and festivals specializing in Shakespeare encouraged more home-grown productions, but these generally remained in the 'official' vein. James Ray played a positive, sincere Henry for Joseph Papp in Central Park in 1960 and again for Douglas Seale at Stratford, Connecticut in 1963. Stacy Keach and Powers Booth played charismatic Henrys at Ashland, Oregon, while Paul Rudd played a likable young King to Meryl Streep's Katherine in Central Park. In 1981, at Stratford, Connecticut, Christopher Plummer reprised the role that made him a Shakespearian star. Now fifty-one, Plummer gave the King greater complexity than in his youthful interpretation, but his doubling the role of the Chorus made the performance essentially a celebratory, virtuoso star turn. Even when performed by North American actors, *Henry V*, in the United States, has tended to be a celebration of Englishness – of the beautiful poetry of Shakespeare and the heroism of Agincourt.

The tradition of noble American Henrys culminated with Kevin Kline's performance for Wilfred Leach in Central Park in 1984. An actor of romantic good looks, intelligence and great personal charm, Kline made Henry at once humane and heroic. In a straightforward medieval production played in front of a castle unit set, Kline was full-throated in the breach, earnest in soliloquy and sexy in wooing the Princess. He interpreted the play as 'a heroic journey into manhood'; his Henry was a king for all seasons, growing into authentic greatness (personal interview, 18 December 1993). The review headlines tell the story: 'Heroism in Central Park' (*Stages*, October 1984), 'Finally, This Henry Becomes a Living, Breathing Hero' (*New York Times*, 15 July 1984), 'Kevin Kline is humane, dignified as warrior king' (*Christian Science Monitor*, 18 July 1984). Leach's production used a fairly full text, including such moments as the Harfleur threats and the killing of the prisoners, one of whom the King executed himself. Yet such moments all contributed to Kline's admirable character. Referring to Henry's cutting of le Fer's throat, Benedict Nightingale wrote, 'this is not, I think, an attempt to undermine Henry's moral credibility. On the contrary, the intention seems to be to show that he's strong enough personally to do what he bids others do' (*New York Times*, 15 July 1984). Kline confirmed this view: 'He wouldn't just give the order – he had to do it himself. He gets his hands quite dirty' (Kline, interview). Kline had created such a positive impression that even this act reinforced it; as Julius Novick commented, 'we feel it must be all right, otherwise he wouldn't do it' (*Village Voice*, 17 July 1984). Novick was one of a few critics who questioned the production's adoption of the 'official' line on Henry and called for an examination of the 'secret' play:

> surely a revival of *Henry V* in 1984 should view the play with a 1984 sensibility, should see in it what we, now, here, are especially able to see and need to see – which, I take it, are most likely to be the doubts, the qualifications, the minority reports, that are there in the midst even of this patriotic pageant of a play. (*Village Voice*, 17 July 1984)

Despite the popularity of Kline's Henry, a traditional production couldn't pass entirely unqualified; United States performances of the play had begun to contend with its secrets.

The 'secret' approach to *Henry V* was introduced dramatically to the United States by Michael Kahn at Stratford, Connecticut in 1969 in what remains the most important American production of the play. Kahn used the production, his first as artistic director, to signal a radical change of direction for the American Shakespeare Festival. As he wrote to the company after opening night, 'in one evening I feel we have erased the image of the Festival as not being a serious artistic effort' (quoted in Cooper, p. 148). Kahn's production was marked by a vivid theatrical inventiveness characteristic of the 1960s avant-garde, as well as a strong statement of opposition to the Vietnam war. A provocative and invigorating production, it generated considerable controversy and gained wide audiences through a New York transfer.

Kahn's production came at one of the most radical periods in United States social and political history. The late 1960s saw a massive mobilisation of many different segments of American society in response to United States involvement in Vietnam and social problems at home. The black liberation movement, the women's movement, the gay liberation movement and the growth of student activism all aggressively challenged social and political norms and institutions. Violence became a part of American civic life, from the assassinations of political leaders to racially charged riots in Watts and Detroit to the confrontations between demonstrators and police at the 1968 Democratic National Convention in Chicago. The fervour for change in social life was matched by a vigorous experimentation in the arts. In the theatre, work by Café

La Mama, the Open Theater, the Performance Group, and the Living Theater broke boundaries between actor and audience, text and performance, entertainment and social activism. Influenced by Brecht, Beckett, Artaud and Grotowski, American avant-garde theatre artists developed a radical arsenal of performance techniques which they used to challenge traditional assumptions about the nature of theatre and to advance their own political agendas. Michael Kahn's 1969 *Henry V* was part of this theatrical revolution, and was perhaps the single most important attempt to define a new style of Shakespearean performance for the United States in the late twentieth century.

Kahn's public pronouncements tended to downplay the anti-war approach and the theatrical hipness of the production. In an address to the company that was included in the souvenir programme and the Festival study guide, Kahn expressed his intentions in terms that don't really sound radical:

> Two really important things for those of us working on *Henry V* ... are Shakespeare's belief in the epic possibilities of the stage and his extraordinary and courageous use of a national hero to illustrate the contradictory problems of leadership. (Study Guide, p. 8)

Len Cariou's performance matched Kahn's understanding of Henry as a man of contradictions:

> a king who loves his men and yet is willing to sacrifice them; a man who at one moment can weep over the death of one of his lords and upon the next instant order the throats cut of prisoners taken in war – surely a crime against humanity even then; a man who can woo willingly and humbly at one moment and strike a hard bargain on his defeated in-laws in the next. (Study Guide, p. 8)

Cariou's Henry was clearly spoken, multi-layered and charismatic, often popular with critics who otherwise hated the production. 'In the midst of this trash of tasteless tricks,' Brendan Gill wrote in the *New Yorker*, 'Len Cariou as Henry manages to evoke quite an attractive royal person' (vol. 25, 22 November 1969, p. 178).

The production's real originality, however, lay in the way it used the radical theatre techniques of the period to present an anti-war approach to *Henry V*. Brechtian scene titles, Living-Theater-style improvisations, masks, games and mime contributed to a production that was both grounded in the Shakespearian text and alive with the energy of the contemporary theatre. The basic metaphor for Kahn's play was play: the games of power, war and love. The stage was intended to suggest a huge playground:

> The play itself is set on a stage which is a playground, which is an arena, which is a battleground. The games of this play are the games of war, of conquest, of power, of betrayal and of love – games played every day in the playground – and the space is transformed, as the playground is, into whatever or wherever the players want it to be. (Director's Note, Souvenir Program)

The game metaphor was relevant to the popular 1960s notion of theatre as play; yet it also implied a cynical commentary on America's war-games in South-east Asia. Games were used extensively in the opening sequence and returned at crucial points throughout the play. The stage was mostly bare, but with a sandbox and 'jungle gym' climbing frame at the back. For half an hour or so before the performance began, the company was on stage, dressed in colourful, casual modern clothes, playing various children's games – ball, Frisbee, wrestling, etc. The opening Chorus was divided, as were all the choral speeches, among four actors, but the whole company was involved in it. On 'O for a muse of fire, according to the promptbook, '[Michael] *Parish suddenly stands with arms above head. All fall back like spokes of a wheel still encircling Parish waving arms and legs being 'fire' and making 'fire' noises'* (p. 1). Most of the speech was illustrated in this way, e.g. 'leashed in like hounds' (*'drop to knees/crawl/pant as dogs'*), 'famine' (*'mime "starving" [silent moan]'*), 'sword' (*'collapse holding belly as stabbed'*), 'fire' (*'fall on backs become "fire"'*) and so forth (Promptbook, p. 1). The actors of Henry and the Dauphin each led a 'river of people' downstage to represent the 'two mighty monarchies' facing off. At a final whistle, the groups broke up to begin more games, singing 'Pop goes the weasel' and miming the ringing of a church bell to establish the scene between the two bishops.

Like all scenes in the play, this was given a Brechtian title by an actor who knocked two woodblocks together and announced, 'Scene One: The Church Becomes Frightened and Makes Plans'. Canterbury and Ely were grotesque, cartoonish figures like characters from *Alice in Wonderland* or children's drawings. Canterbury wore a huge hooped red gown with big yellow buttons, Ely a trailing black cassock. Their unholy scheming was observed by two figures representing Jesus and Mary, who sat on the jungle gym with hula-hoop haloes. Before the next scene Kahn

12   Len Cariou's Henry surrounded by his 'hawkish' advisers, from Michael Kahn's 1969 production in Stratford, Connecticut

interpolated a game of 'Choosing the king', in which Henry was invested with his cape and crown, and a prerecorded audio flashback of Falstaff's rejection from *2 Henry IV*.

The 'game' aspect of Kahn's production was sometimes playful, sometimes pointed. Kahn's bishops were comic figures like Olivier's; in the Salic Law speech Canterbury was continually annoyed by Ely's pedantic interruptions. But this treatment did not preclude a political edge to I.ii. The scene was entitled 'A Meeting of Hawks', and when Canterbury exhorted Henry to 'unwind your bloody flag' (I.ii.101), the King's lords, standing on barrels, began to caw and wave their arms like birds of prey. The use of the word 'hawks' alluded directly to right-wing supporters of America's Vietnam policy. The literal enactment of the metaphor gave theatrical excitement and a topical political charge to Henry's decision to invade France.

The two battle sequences likewise illustrated the way Kahn incorporated both theatrical playfulness and political critique. The siege of Harfleur was literally a game, with the English army flinging tennis-balls and tearing down the paper walls of the jungle gym. At Agincourt, the French army appeared as a huge war machine, wearing stilts and hockey padding. The French lords spoke in French, with UN-style simultaneous translators at the sides of the stage. The battle itself was stylised but savage; as Kahn's notes declare, 'There is to be no attempt to create a stage battle as we usually witness it in the Histories. It is our problem to create a new way of showing the battle in all its formality, terror, eroticism, and horror' (Promptbook, p. 61A). Kahn's scene titles convey his approach:

The Machine Creates the Believable Lie. Point of No Return.

Economic Lesson on the Battlefield.

Exeter Tells the Lie of Noble Death. War Crimes. Retribution. (Promptbook, pp. 57A–68)

The French prisoners were killed on stage, the Boy afterwards, in retaliation. During the reading of the list of the dead, actors wearing blood-splotched white masks surrounded the stage. The masks were based on those worn by Paris students after the riots of May 1968; another instance of Kahn's directly involving contemporary politics in his theatrical language (Promptbook, p. 76). These figures remained for the wooing scene, which was entitled 'The

Deal', and ringed Henry and Katherine at the end of the play. The wooing itself was played with traditional charm, and was the one part of the production that appealed to all critics, whatever their aesthetic or political slant. Following Brecht's practice, Kahn often played scenes for what he felt was their own individual quality, using only external commentary – the titles, the presence of the dead – to qualify audience response. In this respect he was true to the contradictory nature of the play, though the persistence of the ironic titles and the game metaphor made the overall thrust of the production powerfully evident.

Public and press response to Kahn's *Henry V* was intense and often violent, but most critics recognised the production's importance in the history of American Shakespeare production. 'I consider it a sort of American Krakatoa', Brendan Gill wrote of the New York transfer, 'a disaster on a hitherto unprecedented scale, in which a vulgar patronizing of Shakespeare is carried to the point where the original work of art is almost totally pulverized' (p. 178). Clive Barnes, who also disapproved of Kahn's interpretation, nonetheless acknowledged the production's vigour:

> Mr. Kahn can take plenty of heart. He is young and I think has overreached his imagination. But he has enormous talent for making Shakespeare – the lines; the individual scenes – really come alive.... It is, by and large, a worthy and stimulating '*Henry V*' that challenges its audiences. Although I have found fault with Mr. Kahn's concept, let me also express my admiration that he had a concept to offer, which, after all, others in his audience might find more meaningful. I believe we must be indiscreet with Shakespeare, but indiscreet with discretion. And if Mr. Kahn were to ask me, 'Whose discretion?' I would have no answer. (*New York Times*, 9 June 1969)

Barnes's uncertain tone, his recognition of a generational sea-change in Shakespearean interpretation, is unmistakable. Peter D. Smith had a similar response in *Shakespeare Quarterly*:

> Many who revere Shakespeare must have been (or would have been if they had seen it) deeply offended by this production, regarding it as a downright, inexcusable travesty. But in my bones I feel they are wrong. I know that the last word ought to be, 'You cannot make an anti-war Brechtian homily out of Shakespeare's hymn to the warlike Henry, without destroying everything of importance in the play.' I know that's what it ought to be; but I left the Theatre convinced that it is not. (Smith, pp. 449-50)

Kahn's production opened a new chapter in the play's history in the United States. It injected the play with the political and theatrical radicalism of the 1960s and gave it a vital contemporary life at a crucial juncture in American history. Many subsequent productions were influenced by it, or used a similar approach; none could ignore it.

Three recent American productions have all been, to some degree, in the Kahn mode, centred on the 'secret' play. None was wholly convincing, but each made interesting and original choices that illuminated certain aspects of the play. All were, to some extent, in the anglophile tradition, featuring directors or actors with British backgrounds. Yet each made attempts to relate the play to specifically American cultural concerns.

Barry Kyle's Theatre for a New Audience version of 1993, with Mark Rylance, had a director and leading actor who made their names with the Royal Shakespeare Company. Nonetheless, this inventive production brought its New York audience a contemporary approach to the play with much American applicability. The interpretation was fiercely anti-war. While costuming was eclectic, the style of the production often suggested Vietnam. Henry's confrontation with an angry black Williams recalled the racial and class tensions between officers and soldiers that divided United States forces in South-east Asia. The use of three women for the Chorus did much to impart a dissenting voice to the play, especially as they went on to play various victims of the conflict: the Boy, le Fer, etc. Their mournful presence darkened the play from the first speech, where they intoned 'Agincourt' as if saying 'Auschwitz'. The use of a female chorus shed a critical light on the play's construction of masculine heroism, and reminded the audience of a world rarely present in the text.

At the centre of the production was Mark Rylance's strange, quiet, anguished Henry. Rylance is an intensely compelling, bewildering actor, small, slight, softly spoken, but with volumes of presence and contained emotional power. He played Henry as a Hal unable to grow up, totally daunted by his new role. At the opening of the traitors scene he appeared drunk; his manic levity deepened to the grimmest misery at his betrayal by Scroop, whom he very nearly killed himself. Rylance's unhappy young King hit bottom in the night scene before Agincourt; the powerful Williams bested him in a very physical quarrel, and he had to escape by crawling into a tent which then collapsed upon him. For once 'Upon the King' didn't sound self-indulgent; Rylance, a notable Hamlet, brought Danish depths of agony to this speech, which was the centrepiece of his performance.

The battle scenes were predictably savage. After the Harfleur siege the stage remained littered with weapons, which Katherine and Alice picked up and examined during the English lesson. At Agincourt the French prisoners were roped together and shot by a firing squad of archers, in the manner of Goya's *Third of May, 1808*. The production offered Henry no opportunity for heroism, only for guilt, fear, abasement and rehabilitation. Henry knelt to both Williams and Katherine at the end of their encounters and seemed to learn lessons from each. The production expressed a clear view that Henry is not a man to be celebrated, but one who needs to be redeemed.

Ron Daniels's 1995 production at the American Repertory Theatre in Cambridge, Massachusetts was likewise in an antiwar mode, though its choices with Henry himself were less strong. Like Kyle, Daniels made his name in the British theatre, particularly with the Royal Shakespeare Company. Even more than Kyle, however, he strove to give his production a distinctly American flavour, but achieved only mixed success. Daniels's *Henry V* followed a 1993-94 production of the two parts of *Henry IV*, in which Hal and his gang were punkish layabouts in a modern urban world. For *Henry V* Daniels used the contemporary United States military as the dominant image; the English soldiery carried M-16s, sounded off in marching chants, and crawled under barbed wire at the battle of Agincourt. Daniels's depiction of rough male bravado scored some points in desentimentalising the 'band of brothers', but the play's emphasis on 'ceremony' and Henry's public role was lost in a production where the King was barely distinguishable from his platoon. Bill Camp's Henry wore his combat fatigues with conviction, but his characterisation extended little beyond the tough young officer sweatily bearing up in the field.

Apart from the military image, the production lacked cohesion. The French were the traditional decadent snobs, but they seemed to have come not only from another production, but from another planet. Clad in pastel body-suits and foothigh platform shoes, they looked like a psychedelic 1970s album cover. For the battle scenes they used big hobby horses, like those in John Barton's 1972

Richard II, which were ludicrously out of place on Daniels's Gulf War battlefield.

The one scene where Daniels's approach paid big dividends was the siege of Harfleur. Plainly defeated, Henry's troops were sprawled about the stage in a disordered camp. Near the centre stood a large tripod surmounted by horn loudspeakers. Livid and exhausted, Henry picked up a low-tech field microphone and jerked it across in front of the speakers, creating an angry squawk of feedback. He then sat down on some equipment and delivered his ultimatum, his back to the walls of the city. The distorted amplification gave his catalogue of horrors an unparalleled ugliness and intensity. His brother the Duke of Gloucester (Josh Karch), who had developed a nice characterisation as a sensitive young officer out to prevent atrocities, tried to wrest the microphone from him. The surrounding soldiers looked on, in varying degrees bloodthirsty or aghast. Though Camp later marked the speech as a bluff, the scene had the sickening tension of a potential My Lai massacre.

At the beginning of the following scene, Katherine's remark that she needed to learn English was not an offhand comment; it was prompted by a radio broadcast of Henry's Harfleur threats. Leonore Chaix's unusually resistant Katherine, though somewhat given to kittenish pouting, managed to score some political points about the relationship of the wooing to the war. Though the play ended with romance, Henry's courtship was not an easy one; the wooing scene was merely the last of the battles this young marine had to slog through.

Daniels subsequently directed the play for an RSC touring production in 1997. He switched the time period back to the WWI era but retained much of the same business, including the field-microphone for Harfleur and the hobby-horses for the French. The charismatic young actor Michael Sheen gave a notable performance as an agile, highly-strung king.

Another US production that made strong political choices was the all-female version by the Company of Women. A spin-off of the Massachusetts-based Shakespeare and Company, the Company of Women was co-produced by feminist psychologist Carol Gilligan and voice guru Kristin Linklater. Their opening production, *Henry V*, played in the summer of 1994 at Smith College and at Shakespeare and Company, and was scheduled for national and international touring in 1995. Using a cast of ten, director Maureen Shea and the Company took a strong feminist line on the play in an uneven production that was sporadically illuminating.

The purpose of the company, according to the programme notes, is 'to challenge what has been a male world of war and violence, to absorb and resound its voices and its language'. *Henry V* lends itself well to this kind of feminist critical approach. On the one hand, it is a play about the construction of male identity through war:

> And gentlemen in England, now abed,
> Shall think themselves accurs'd they were not here,
> And hold their manhoods cheap, whiles any speaks
> That fought with us upon St Crispian's Day.

> (IV.iii.64-7)

On the other hand, Henry's French adventure depends on his 'claiming from the female,' both in his lineage and in his political marriage to Katherine (I.ii.92). And while women are excluded from the male world of war, they are repeatedly present in the language of the play, from the virgins threatened at Harfleur to the 'maiden cities' jocularly discussed by Henry and Burgundy (V.ii.286-93).

Maureen Shea's production of *Henry V* succeeded intermittently in achieving the company's objective of claiming the play's language for women. Individual lines and moments often jumped out with new and surprising meanings. 'Can this *cock-pit* hold / The vasty fields of France?' (I.Chorus.11-12) came to mean, very clearly, 'Is the phallocentric world of the traditional Shakespearean stage really adequate to express the truth of what happened at Agincourt?' It was a striking and relevant rereading of the line, and got a knowing laugh from the audience. Likewise, the cornerstone of the Salic Law argument – 'No woman shall succeed in Salic land' – took on a vivid contemporary meaning.

In its overall staging, the production was an effective small-scale performance whose strengths were not directly related to the gender of the cast. The ten actors adroitly played multiple roles and inventively managed the simple onstage scenery. Some of the characterisations were clearer than others – Linklater's Fluellen was the most distinctive – but overall the story was swiftly and intelligibly told.

In spite of the production's successes, some resonances that might have been gained by casting a woman in the role of Henry were lost in Lisa Wolpe's simplified characterisation. Henry was a puppet tyrant, a caricature of destructive masculinity whose only modes of expression were anger and violence. From the tennis-ball speech forward, Wolpe's Henry shouted his/her way malevolently through scene after scene, beating up the traitors, raging at the governor of Harfleur, ranting through 'Upon the King'. The one-note quality of the performance was wearying, but for the final scene Shea and Wolpe made some very strong and compelling choices.

The imperial wooing was vividly played as political rape: in Shea's words, 'What struck us most about Henry's wooing of Katherine is that Katherine never says "yes"' (Barrett, p. 15). Henry began the scene with a predatory circling of Katherine, spitting out his lines with cocky arrogance. For the lines offering to 'buffet for my love' (V.ii.141-2) Henry backed her menacingly around the stage, threatening her with his fists. Wolpe's approach was utterly humourless and aggressive, but the audience nonetheless laughed at the jokes about loving France 'so well that I will not part with a village of it' (178-80), and about Henry's bad French. These laughs indicated just how hard a production has to work to disrupt audience expectations and play against the text. Shea's strongest choices surrounded the moment of the kiss. When Henry asked Alice, 'It is not a fashion for the maids in France to kiss before they are married, would she say?' (281-2), he walked behind Alice, grabbed her hair, kissed her in a savage dip, and dropped her on the floor. He then turned to confront the cowering Katherine. The aggressively sexual joking with Burgundy was included for once, and was powerfully effective; Katherine and Alice consoled each other tearfully as the men laughed about how 'maids, well-summered and warm kept', will 'endure handling, which before would not abide looking on' (325-9). All these moments were strongly conceived and realised, but Henry's earlier performance had an unfortunate crying-wolf effect – he had been such a tiresome ogre all along that Wolpe's choices in this scene could arouse little surprise or interest.

Beyond the moments described above, the cross-gender casting had surprisingly little effect. The production followed fairly standard modern anti-war lines. All the key moments were hit – the executions, the violent rhetoric, the bloody battles. Given the powerful choice of an all-female cast, the number of vividly original moments was disappointingly small. It may be simply that the 'secret' play has run its course; that the late twentieth-century burst of inventive political stagings has exhausted itself, and a new direction will need to be found for the play in the future.

What will become of *Henry V* in the new millennium? Without question, the play has changed its outline in the last fifty years of performance. The 'secret' play has now, as it were, become official; it is a rare production that plays Henry for untrammelled heroism. Modern performances have come close to establishing a new set of clichés. The scheming churchmen, the traitors, the hanging of Bardolph, the Harfleur threats, the Williams argument, the killing of the prisoners – these, rather than the celebratory speeches, are the high points of the play, and many productions have foregrounded them in similar ways. In most cases, these potentially negative moments are turned to Henry's advantage, so that the play overall reflects well on the warrior-king. Productions that condemn Henry whole-heartedly are rare and rarely successful. As I noted in the first chapter, the play's structure virtually demands a two-sided view. Henry's heroism is built in the face of various kinds of opposition, and those opposing voices, while they are speaking, hold the stage. Yet while drama requires conflict, it also requires heroes. At a fundamental level, the mechanism of the plot of *Henry V* works itself out through the construction of Henry's heroism. Even Michael Pennington's skilled performance in Bogdanov's production was unable to sustain a negative reading of Henry through the entire production. Productions in recent years have brought the opposing elements of the play into an equilibrium that replaces the heavily-cut texts, patriotic pageants, and spotless heroes of old. How this equilibrium may again become unbalanced – what the next paradigm shift will be – remains uncertain.

It might seem that any real change in *Henry V* performances would require a decentring of Henry as hero; but the audience would have to be offered some other focal point in his place, and the play have some narrative impetus besides his trajectory of conquest. One possibility would be a greater emphasis on the play's concern with its own making, a self-consciously theatrical approach in which the audience would identify more with the process of representation than with what was represented. The hero of such a production would be not Henry but the Chorus, along with the actors and audience. Barry Edelstein's 1993 workshop production with Julliard students had four different actors play Henry, disrupting traditional identification; the theatrical excitement of the production derived in large part from the inventiveness of the young ensemble in bringing forth 'so great an object' (I.Chorus.11) with the simplest means. Another option would be to direct attention away from Henry toward some of the other characters. In productions at the Colorado Shakespeare Festival in 1992 and the RSC in 1994, the strongest performances came from Pistol (Stephen Price and Clive Wood, respectively). The prominence of this character gave the play a different shape: the audience was repeatedly reminded that Henry's rising fortune was matched by the degradation of his former friend. An emphasis on the clowns, the soldiers, the Chorus or the female characters could disrupt Henry's trajectory of conquest and give the play a new direction that would challenge the late twentieth-century norm.

Or it may be that the pendulum will swing back toward a more traditional approach. At the end of the century, *Henry V* was again placed in a context of national celebration when it was chosen to open the newly reconstructed Globe Theatre in London in 1997. Directed by Olivier's son Richard and starring Globe artistic director Mark Rylance, this *Henry V* was a notable experiment in recreating Elizabethan performance conditions. Using a full text, an all-male cast, handmade Elizabethan costumes and a rush-strewn platform open to the elements, the Globe company achieved a broad popular success in an enterprise that had been burdened with controversy and suspicion. The audience became a major component of the production. Henry addressed the groundlings, who were often huddling under raincoats against the English weather, as his war-weary troops. The French, played as conventionally pompous, were roundly booed. Good-natured hecklers occasionally commented on Henry's warnings about the Scots or his patronising of Katherine. While this kind of interaction may have been a part of the Elizabethan theatre experience, the production was far from an archaeological reproduction. Rylance's introspective, low-key Henry was in the modern critical mode, and in fact substantially duplicated his performance for Barry Kyle in New York in 1993. Nevertheless, Rylance's remarkable ability to connect with the audience gave additional warmth to his Globe performance, and more than compensated for his rather slight figure and voice. His wooing of Toby Cockerell's coy Katherine delighted the audience and demonstrated the effectiveness of Elizabethan cross-gendering. Such historical conventions were presented earnestly but in a spirit of play, which encouraged an attitude of amused acceptance in the spectators. They embraced Rylance's Henry not jingoistically, but with a mixture of cultural pride and affectionate critique.

[169]

The Globe production in some ways brings the history of *Henry V* full circle, reasserting its original status as nationalist, celebratory popular entertainment. But the 'secret' play deserves a full hearing, especially as history continues to change around it. By the end of the twentieth century the conflict in the former Yugoslavia had again made war a central issue for intellectual debate and caused many to reconsider deeply-held beliefs. Our attitudes toward conflict, leadership and politics will no doubt need to be re-examined many times in the coming decades, and Shakespeare's *Henry V* is one of the tools we will use. The revisionist productions of the past decades have lent *Henry V* renewed political and theatrical force and revealed many aspects of the play obscured by stage tradition. *Henry V*, as we now know it, cannot be dismissed as fulsome chauvinism, nor can it be contained in a single interpretation or defined by a single production. The explorations of the second half of the twentieth century have given *Henry V* an enhanced status as a play full of problems and possibilities, a play worthy of continued reinvention.

BIBLIOGRAPHY

Agee, James. *Agee on Film*, vol. 1. New York: Grosset & Dunlap, 1969.

Arden, John. 'Playwrights and Play-Writers', *To Present the Pretence: Essays on the Theatre and its Public*. London: Eyre Meuthen, 1977.

Banham, Martin. 'BBC Television's Dull Shakespeares', in J. C. Bulman and H. R. Coursen, eds, *Shakespeare on Television*. Hanover, NH: University Presses of New England, 1988.

Barber, C. L. *Shakespeare's Festive Comedy*. Princeton, NJ: Princeton University Press, 1959.

Barrett, Susan Curran. 'In the Company of Women', *Smith Alumnae Quarterly*, vol. LXXXVI, no. 2, spring 1995.

Bazin, Andre. *What is Cinema?* Trans. Hugh Gray, 2 vols. Berkeley: University of California Press, 1967.

Beauchamp, Gordon. '*Henry V*: Myth, Movie, Play', *College Literature*, 5 (1978), 228-38.

Beaumann, Sally. *The Royal Shakespeare Company's Production of Henry V for the Centenary Season at the Royal Shakespeare Theatre*. Oxford: Pergamon Press, 1976.

Beaumann, Sally. *The Royal Shakespeare Company: A History of Ten Decades*. Oxford: Oxford University Press, 1982.

Berry, Ralph. *Changing Styles in Shakespeare*. London: George Allen & Unwin, 1981.

Berry, Ralph. *On Directing Shakespeare: Interviews with Contemporary Directors*. London: Hamish Hamilton, 1989.

Bogdanov, Michael, and Michael Pennington, eds, *The English Shakespeare Company: The Story of the Wars of the Roses, 1986-1989*. London: Hern, 1990.

Bogdanov, Michael. Interview by author. London, 19 April 1991 .

Boswell-Stone, W. G. *Shakespeare's Holinshed: The Chronicle and the Plays Compared*. London: Chatto, 1907. New York: Dover Publications, 1968.

Bragaglia, Leonardo. *Shakespeare in Italia*. Rome: Trevi Editore, 1973.

Branagh, Kenneth. *Beginning*. London: Chatto, 1989.

Branagh, Kenneth. *Henry V by William Shakespeare: A Screen Adaptation*. London: Chatto, 1989.

Branagh, Kenneth. Liner notes. Simon Rattle, cond. *Original Soundtrack Recording: Henry V*. By Patrick Doyle. EMI CDC 7 49919 2, 1989.

Brennan, Anthony. *Twayne's New Critical Introductions to Shakespeare, No. 16*: Henry V. New York: Twayne Publishers, 1992.

Bullough, Geoffrey, ed. *Narrative and Dramatic Sources of Shakespeare*, vol. 4. London: Routledge, 1966.

Bulman, J. C., and H. R. Coursen, eds, *Shakespeare on Televison*. Hanover, NH: University Presses of New England, 1988.

Campbell, Lily B. *Shakespeare's Histories: Mirrors of Elizabethan Policy*. San Marino, CA: Huntington Library, 1947.

Cole, John William. *The Life and Theatrical Times of Charles Kean, FSA*, 2 vols. London: Richard Bentley, 1860.

Collick, John. *Shakespeare, Cinema and Society*. Manchester: Manchester University Press, 1989.

Collison Morley, Lacy. *Shakespeare in Italy*. Stratford-upon-Avon: Shakespeare Head Press, 1916.

Cook, Judith. *Shakespeare's Players*. London: Harrap, 1983.

Cooper, Rowena Krensky. *The American Shakespeare Theatre: Stratford, 1955-1985*. Washington: Folger Books, 1986.

Davies, Anthony. *Filming Shakespeare's Plays: The Adaptations of Laurence Olivier, Orson Welles, Peter Brook and Akira Kurosawa*. Cambridge: Cambridge University Press, 1988.

Dollimore, Jonathan and Alan Sinfield. 'History and Ideology: The Instance of *Henry V*', in John Drakakis, ed., *Alternative Shakespeares*. London: Methuen, 1985.

Donaldson, Peter. *Shakespearean Films, Shakespearean Directors*. Boston: Unwin Hyman, 1990.

Durgnat, Raymond. *Films and Feelings*. Cambridge, MA: MIT Press, 1967.

Durgnat, Raymond. *A Mirror for England: British Movies from Austerity to Affluence*. New York: Praeger, 1971.

Dutu, Alexandru. *Shakespeare in Romania*. Bucharest: Meridiane, 1964.

Elsom, John, ed. *Is Shakespeare Still Our Contemporary?* London: Routledge, 1989.

Engle, Ron. 'Audience, Style and Language in the Shakespeare of Peter Zadek', in Dennis Kennedy, ed., *Foreign Shakespeare: Contemporary Performance*. Cambridge: Cambridge University Press, 1993, pp. 93-106.

Fenwick, Henry. 'The Production', in *The BBC TV Shakespeare: Henry V*, London, British Broadcasting Corporation, 1979.

Foulkes, Richard. 'Charles Calvert's *Henry V*', *Shakespeare Survey*, 41 (1989), 23-34.

Fuller, Graham. 'Two Kings', *Film Comment*, November-December 1989, 2-7.

Geduld, Harry. *Filmguide to Henry V*. Bloomington: Indiana University Press, 1976.

Greenblatt, Stephen. *Shakespearean Negotiations*. Berkeley: University of California Press, 1988.

Gurr, Andrew. *The New Cambridge Shakespeare: King Henry V*. Cambridge: Cambridge University Press, 1992.

Hazlitt, William. *Characters of Shakespeare's Plays*, in A. R. Waller and Arnold Glover, eds, *Collected Works*, vol. 1. London: J. M. Dent & Co., 1902, pp. 165-460.

Healy, Thomas. 'Nation and Ideology in *Henry V*', in Michael

Hattaway, Boika Sokolova, Derek Roper, eds, *Shakespeare in the New Europe*. Sheffield: Sheffield Academic Press, 1994, pp. 174-93.

Hill, Aaron. *King Henry the Fifth: or, the Conquest of France, by the English. A Tragedy*. London: Chetwood, 1723. London: Cornmarket, 1969.

Hodgdon, Barbara. *The End Crowns All: Closure and Contradiction in Shakespeare's History*. Princeton: Princeton University Press, 1991.

Hodgdon, Barbara. *Shakespeare in Performance*: Henry IV, Part Two. Manchester: Manchester University Press, 1993.

Holderness, Graham. *Shakespeare's History*. Dublin: Gill & MacMillan, 1985.

Holderness, Graham. *The Shakespeare Myth*. Manchester: Manchester University Press, 1988.

Holderness, Graham. *Shakespeare in Performance: The Taming of the Shrew*. Manchester: Manchester University Press, 1989.

Holderness, Graham. *Shakespeare Recycled: The Making of Historical Drama*. London: Harvester Wheatsheaf, 1992.

Jackson, Russell, and Robert Smallwood, eds, *Players of Shakespeare 2: Further Essays in Shakespearean Performance by Players with the Royal Shakespeare Company*. Cambridge: Cambridge University Press, 1988.

Jorgens, Jack. *Shakespeare on Film*. Bloomington: University of Indiana Press, 1977.

Jusserand, J. J. *Shakespeare in France Under the Ancien Regime*. New York: Putnam, 1899.

Kennedy, Dennis. 'Introduction: Shakespeare without his Language', in Dennis Kennedy, ed., *Foreign Shakespeare: Contemporary Performance*. Cambridge: Cambridge University Press, 1993.

Kennedy, Dennis. *Looking at Shakespeare: A Visual History of Twentieth-Century Performance*. Cambridge: Cambridge University Press, 1993.

Kline, Kevin. Telephone interview by author, 18 December 1993.

Kott, Jan. *Shakespeare Our Contemporary*. Trans. Boleslaw Taborski. London: Methuen, 1967.

Leiter, Samuel, ed., *Shakespeare Around the Globe*. Westport, CT: Greenwood Press, 1986.

Mansfield, Richard. *The Richard Mansfield Acting Version of King Henry V*. New York: McClure, Phillips & Co., 1901.

Manvell, Roger. *Shakespeare and the Film*. London: J. M. Dent & Sons, 1971.

Marwick, Arthur. *British Society Since 1945*. Harmondsworth: Penguin, 1991.

McMillin, Scott. *Shakespeare in Performance*: Henry IV, Part One, Manchester: Manchester University Press, 1991.

Messina, Cedric. 'Preface', in *The BBC TV Shakespeare:* Henry V. London: British Broadcasting Corporation, 1979.

Nagler, A. M. *A Source Book in Theatrical History*. New York: Dover, 1952.

Nashe, Thomas. *Pierce Pennilesse His Svpplication to the Divell*, in R. B.

McKerrow, ed., *The Works of Thomas Nashe*, vol. 1. London: Sidgwick & Jackson, 1910. 5 vols.

Noble, Adrian. '"Well, This Is the Forest of Arden": An Informal Address', in Werner Habicht *et al.*, eds, *Images of Shakespeare: Proceedings of the International Shakespeare Association, 1986*. London: Associated University Presses, 1988, pp. 335-42.

Odell, George C. D. *Annals of the New York Stage*. New York: Columbia University Press, 1927-49.

Olivier, Laurence. *Henry V*. London: Lorrimer, 1984.

Olivier, Laurence. *On Acting*. London: Weidenfeld-and Nicolson, 1986.

Patterson, Annabel. 'Back by Popular Demand: The Two Versions of *Henry V*', *Renaissance Drama*, New Series XIX (1988), 29-62.

Pearson, Hesketh. *The Last Actor-Managers*. London: Methuen, 1950.

Pilkington, Ace G. *Screening Shakespeare: From Richard II to Henry V*. Newark: University of Delaware Press, 1991.

Potter, Lois. 'Bad and Good Authority Figures: Richard III and Henry V since 1945', *Deutsches Shakespeare-Gesellschaft West Jahrbuch*, 1992, pp. 39-54.

Rabkin, Norman. *Shakespeare and the Problem of Meaning*. Chicago: Chicago University Press, 1981.

Rackin, Phyllis. *Stages of History: Shakespeare's English Chronicles*. New York: Routledge, 1991.

Saccio, Peter. 'The Historicity of the BBC History Plays', in J. C. Bulman and H. R. Coursen, eds, *Shakespeare on Television*, Hanover, NH: University Presses of New England, 1988.

Salgado, Gamini. *Eyewitnesses of Shakespeare: First Hand Accounts of Performances 1590-1890*. New York: Harper & Row, 1975.

Shattuck, Charles H., ed. *The John Philip Kemble Promptbooks*. Folger Facsimiles, Series I, vol. 3. Charlottesville: University Press of Virginia for the Folger Shakespeare Library, 1974.

Shattuck, Charles H. *Shakespeare on the American Stage: From Booth and Barrett to Southern and Marlowe*, vol. 2. London: Associated University Presses, 1987.

Silviria, Dale. *Laurence Olivier and the Art of Film Making*. Rutherford: Fairleigh Dickinson University Press, 1985.

Sinfield, Alan. 'Royal Shakespeare', in *Political Shakespeare: New Essays in Cultural Materialism*, ed. Jonathan Dollimore and Alan Sinfield. Manchester: Manchester University Press, 1985.

Smith, Peter D., 'The 1969 Season at Stratford, Connecticut', *Shakespeare Quarterly*, vol. 20, no. 4 (autumn 1969), 449-50.

Sprague, Arthur Colby. *Shakespeare's Histories: Plays for the Stage*. London: Society for Theatrical Research, 1964.

Taylor, Gary, ed. *The Oxford Shakespeare: Henry V*. Oxford: Oxford University Press, 1984.

Taylor, Gary. *Moment by Moment by Shakespeare*. London: Macmillan, 1985.

Tillyard, E. M. W. *Shakespeare's History Plays*. Edinburgh: T. & A. Constable, Ltd, 1944.

Trewin, J. C. *Going to Shakespeare*. London: Geo. Allen & Unwin, 1978.

Tynan, Kenneth. *Tynan Right and Left*. London: Longmans, 1967.

Walter, J. H., ed. *The Arden Shakespeare: King Henry V*. London: Methuen, 1954.

Wendt, Ernst. 'Politische Revue', *Theater Heute*, March 1964, pp. 17-23.

Whittaker, Herbert. *The Stratford Festival 1953-57*. Toronto: Clarke, Irwin & Co., 1958.

Wiles, David. *Shakespeare's Clown*. Cambridge: Cambridge University Press, 1987.

Willis, Susan. *The BBC Shakespeare Plays: Making the Televised Canon*. Chapel Hill: University of North Carolina Press, 1991.

Worthen, William B. *The Idea of the Actor: Drama and the Ethics of Performance*. Princeton: Princeton University Press, 1984.

APPENDIX

A. Some significant twentieth-century productions of *Henry V*

1900	Frank Benson	Lyceum
1900	Lewis Waller	Lyceum
1900	Richard Mansfield	New York
1901	William Poel	Stratford-upon-Avon
1920	W. Bridges-Adams	Stratford-upon-Avon
1937	Tyrone Guthrie	Old Vic
1937	B. Iden Payne	Stratford-upon-Avon
1938	Lewis Casson	Drury Lane
1944	Laurence Olivier	Film
1951	Glen Byam Shaw	Old Vic
1951	Anthony Quayle	Stratford-upon-Avon
1956	Michael Langham	Stratford, Ontario
1961	Leopold Lindtberg	Vienna
1964	Peter Zadek	Breman
1964	Peter Hall/John Barton	Stratford-upon-Avon
1966	Michael Langham	Stratford, Ontario
1969	Michael Kahn	Stratford, Connecticut
1975	Terry Hands	Stratford-upon-Avon
1979	David Giles	BBC Television
1984	Adrian Noble	Stratford-upon-Avon
1986	Michael Bogdanov	Plymouth and on tour
1989	Kenneth Branagh	Film
1993	Barry Kyle	New York
1994	Maureen Shea	Smith College and Lenox, Mass.
1995	Ron Daniels	Cambridge, Mass.
1997	Richard Olivier	Shakespeare's Globe

B. Principal actors and production staff in productions discussed

Two Cities Films, 1944

Director: Laurence Olivier   Costumes: Roger Furse
Music: William Walton

Henry V Laurence Olivier
Chorus Leslie Banks
Katherine Renee Asherson
Pistol Robert Newton
Mistress Quickly Freda Jackson
Fluellen Esmond Knight
King Charles VI Harcourt Williams

Dauphin Max Adrian
Constable Leo Genn
Montjoy Ralph Truman
Exeter Nicholas Hannen
Canterbury Felix Aylmer
Ely Robert Helpman

Stratford-upon-Avon, 1975

Director: Terry Hands   Designer: Farrah
Lighting: Stewart Leviton   Music: Guy Woolfenden

Henry V Alan Howard
Chorus Emrys James
Katherine Ludmilla Mikael
Pistol Richard Moore
Mistress Quickly Maureen Pryor
Fluellen Trevor Peacock
King Charles VI Clement McCallin

Dauphin Geoffrey Hutchings
Constable Bernard Brown
Montjoy Oliver Ford-Davies
Exeter Philip Brack
Canterbury Derek Smith
Ely Trevor Peacock

BBC Television, 1979

Director: David Giles   Producter: Cedric Messina
Set: Don Homfray   Costumes: Odette Barrow

Henry V David Gwillim
Chorus Alec McCowan
Katherine Jocelyne Boisseau
Pistol Bryan Pringle
Mistress Quickly Brenda Bruce
Fluellen Tim Wylton
King Charles VI Thorley Walters

Dauphin Keith Drinkel
Constable Julian Glover
Montjoy Garrick Hagon
Exeter Clifford Parrish
Canterbury Trevor Baxter
Ely John Abineri

Stratford-upon-Avon, 1984

Director: Adrian Noble   Designer: Bob Crowley
Lighting: Robert Bryan   Music: Howard Blake

Henry V Kenneth Branagh
Chorus Ian McDiarmid
Katherine Cecile Paoli
Pistol Bernard Horsfall
Mistress Quickly Patricia Routledge
Fluellen Sion Probert
King Charles VI Sebastian Shaw

Dauphin Nicholas Woodeson
Constable Richard Easton
Montjoy Christopher Ravenscroft
Exeter Brian Blessed
Canterbury Harold Innocent
Ely Sebastian Shaw

English Shakespeare Company, 1986

Director: Michael Bogdanov   Set: Chris Dyer
Costumes: Stephanie Howard   Lighting: Chris Ellis

Henry V Michael Pennington
Chorus John Woodvine
Katherine Jenny Quayle
Pistol John Price
Mistress Quickly June Watson
Fluellen Gareth Thomas
King Charles VI Clyde Pollitt

Dauphin Andrew Jarvis
Constable Hugh Sullivan
Montjoy Donald Gee
Exeter Morris Perry
Canterbury Patrick O'Connell
Ely Roger Booth

Renaissance Films, 1989

Director: Kenneth Branagh   Music: Patrick Doyle

Henry V Kenneth Branagh
Chorus Derek Jacobi
Katherine Emma Thompson
Pistol Robert Stephens
Mistress Quickly Judi Dench
Fluellen Ian Holm
King Charles VI Paul Scofield

Dauphin Michael Maloney
Constable Richard Eastman
Montjoy Christopher Ravenscroft
Exeter Brian Blessed
Canterbury Charles Kay
Ely Alec McCowan

INDEX

Agate, James, 27
Agee, James, 30
Agincourt Eve scene, 42-5, 62-5, 80-1, 101-2, 119-20, 139-40
Albright, Evelyn May, 10
Arden, John, 1
Ascherson, Renée, 47
Asquith, Ros, 89, 94, 105
Aylmer, Felix, 31, 32

Bacon, Francis, 6
Banham, Martin, 78-9
Banks, Leslie, 30
Barber, C. L., 85-6
Barnes, Clive, 69, 162
Barnes, Peter, 111
Barrow, Odette, 75
Barry, Spranger, 18
Barton, John, 49-50
battle scenes, 45-6, 66, 94-6, 120, 140-4, 161, 164
Baxter, Trevor, 77
Bazin, Andre, 27
Beauchamp, Gordon, 27
Beaumann, Sally, 51, 52
Benson, Frank, 21, 23
Berry, Ralph, 31, 37, 38, 53, 153-4
Betterton, Thomas, 15
Billington, Michael, 88, 98
Blessed, Brian, 90, 93, 143
Bogdanov, Michael, 4, 8, 105, 107-27, 130, 168
Boisseau, Jocelyne, 82
Booth, Powers, 156
Branagh, Kenneth, 3, 8, 84, 85, 89, 94, 96, 97, 98-103, 104-6, 108, 128-45
Brecht, Bertolt, 5, 57, 86, 87, 90,

119, 148, 149, 151, 158, 162
British Broadcasting Company (BBC), 72-3, 78
Bryan, Robert, 87
Bryden, Ronald, 70
Burbage, Richard, 14
Burton, Richard, 4, 49, 73

Calvert, Charles, 20-1, 152
Camp, Bill, 164-5
Campbell, Lily B., 5
Cariou, Len, 158
Chimes at Midnight, 141
Close Encounters of the Third Kind, 88
Company of Women, 165-7
Coveney, Michael, 88-9
Crowley, Bob, 84, 87-8

Daniel, Samuel, 6
Daniels, Ron, 164-5
de Jongh, Nicholas, 124-5
Dead Again, 132
death of Falstaff, 35-6, 114, 136
Dench, Judi, 131, 132
Dollimore, Jonathan, 6
Donaldson, Peter, 33, 40-1, 43, 44, 48
Dougall, John, 124-5
Doyle, Patrick, 132, 144
Duke of Edinburgh, 71
Durgnat, Raymond, 38
Dyer, Chris, 110

Elizabeth I of England, 10-11
Elizabeth II of England, 71
English Shakespeare Company (ESC), 107

Essex, Robert Earl of, 10-11
execution of Bardolph, 36, 60-1,
    79, 82, 93-4, 117, 137-8
Eyre, Richard, 130

Falkland Islands conflict, 84-5,
    105-6, 109, 110, 114-151 130
Farrah, Abdel, 54, 70, 87
For Queen and Country, 130
Foulkes, Richard, 21
French characters, 37-9, 54, 56,
    82, 87-8, 102-3, 115-16, 153-4
Frye, Northrop, 85
Fuller, Graham, 128, 130

Garrick, David, 18
Geduld, Harry, 29, 31, 33, 42-3
Genn, Leo, 38, 42
Giles, David, 4, 8, 72-83, 108
Gill, Brendan, 158, 162
Gombrich, E. H., 8
Gould, Gerald, 24
Greenblatt, Stephen, 5-6
Greengrass, Paul, 130
Guthrie, Tyrone, 39
Gwillim, David, 4, 73, 74-5, 76,
    78-82, 83, 140

Hall, Edward, 6
Hall, Peter, 4, 49-50, 108
Hands, Terry, 5, 8, 49-71, 107,
    108
Hannen, Nicholas, 33
Harfleur threats, 60, 79, 138-9,
    165
Hayward, John, 6, 11
Hazlitt, William, 1, 18-19
Helpmann, Robert, 31, 32
Hill, Aaron, 15-18
Hitchcock, Alfred, 132, 134
Hodgdon, Barbara, 4, 74
Holderness, Graham, 27, 28, 34,
    36, 130-1
Holm, Ian, 4, 49-50, 132
Homfray, Don, 75-6

Howard, Alan, 3, 4, 50, 51, 53, 56-
    65, 67, 108
Howard, Stephanie, 110
Howell, Jane, 76, 83

Jacobi, Derek, 131, 133
James, Emrys, 55-6, 68
James I of England, 14
Jarman, Derek, 130
Jorgens, Jack, 30

Kahn, Michael, 5, 147, 151, 157-
    63
Keach, Stacy, 156
Kean, Charles, 19-20, 72, 75
Kean, Edmund, 19
Kemble, John Philip, 18
Kennedy, Dennis, 146
killing of prisoners, 7-8, 45, 82,
    95-6, 120, 141, 155, 161, 164
Kline, Kevin, 156-7
Kott, Jan, 4, 49-50, 107-8
Kozintsev, Girgori, 26
Kyle, Barry, 163-4

Lambarde, William, 10
Langham, Michael, 153-5
Laughter, 111
Lawrence, Robert, 85, 130
Lee, Sidney, 23
Lewson, Charles, 57
Lindtberg, Leopold, 147-8
Linklater, Kristin, 165-6

Machiavelli, Niccolo, 6
Macready, William Charles, 19,
    152
Maloney, Michael, 132
Mann Ist Mann, 149
Mansfield, Richard, 21, 23-24
Manvell, Robert, 27
Marmion, Patrick, 125
Marwick, Arthur, 84-5, 109
McCowan, Alec, 75, 76
McDiarmid, Ian, 88-90, 91, 106

McMillan, Scott, 4, 74, 83
Meaden, Dan, 62, 67
Messina, Cedric, 72-3, 74-5, 83
Mikaël, Ludmila, 68
Miller, Jonathan, 72, 75

Nashe, Thomas, 9
Neher, Caspar, 87
Newton, Robert, 35
Nissen, Brian, 43
Noble, Adrian, 8, 83, 84-106, 107
Nunn, Trevor, 70

Olivier, Laurence, 1, 7-8, 24, 25-48, 53, 105, 126, 128-9, 132, 134, 140-1
Olivier, Richard, 169
Otto, Teo, 147-8

Papp, Joseph, 156
Parsons, Gordon, 57
Pater, Walter, 24
Patterson, Annabel, 10-11
Pennington, Michael, 4, 108, 111-13, 116-23, 124, 168
Pepys, Samuel, 14-15
Phelps, Samuel, 19
Phillips, James, 27, 41
Pilkington, Ace G., 27, 29, 78-9
Platoon, 97, 141
Plummer, Christopher, 153, 156
Poel, William, 24
Pratt, Desmond, 69
Price, John, 108, 113
Prince of Wales, 101, 131
Pryce, Jonathan, 121, 122

Quayle, Anna, 82
Quayle, Anthony, 4, 49, 73, 108

Rabkin, Norman, 8-9
Rackin, Phyllis, 6
Rain, Douglas, 155
Ran, 141
Ratcliffe, Michael, 93-4, 104, 110

Ravenscroft, Christopher, 94, 136
Ray, James, 156
Resurrected, 130
Richardson, Ralph, 39
Rignold, George, 21, 152
Royal Shakespeare Company (RSC), 49-53, 70-1, 86, 104, 131
Rudd, Paul, 156
Rutter, Barrie, 71
Rylance, Mark, 163-4, 169

Salic Law scene, 31-33, 77, 82, 112-13, 134-6
Scofield, Paul, 132
Seale, Douglas, 156
Seven Samurai, The, 141
Shakespeare, William
    1 Henry IV, 73-5, 83, 108, 136
    2 Henry IV, 13, 31, 34, 35, 73-5, 83, 108-9, 136
    As You Like It, 86
    Comedy of Errors, The, 86
    Hamlet, 26, 43
    Macbeth, 112
    Merry Wives of Windsor, The, 14
    Richard II, 14
    Richard III, 112, 147
    Romeo and Juliet, 34
Shaw, G. B., 24, 111
Shea, Maureen, 165-7
Shulman, Milton, 69-70
Silviria, Dale, 29, 36, 43
Sinfield, Alan, 6, 52, 86, 108
Smith, Peter D., 162
Smith, William 'Gentleman', 18
Sprague, A. C., 18, 153-5
Stanislavski, Constantin, 3
Stanton, Barry, 111
Stellman, Martin, 130
Stephens, Robert, 132
Stratford Festival Canada, 153-5
Streep, Meryl, 156

Taylor, Gary, 11, 59, 67
Thatcher, Margaret, 84-5, 109, 130-1
Thompson, Emma, 144-5
Tillyard, E. M. W., 4, 73
Tinker, Jack, 71
Truman, Ralph, 38
Tumbledown, 85, 130

Vietnam war, 3, 97 157, 159, 163

Waller, Lewis, 21-3, 152
Walton, William, 30, 35, 38-9
War Requiem, 130
Wardle, Irving, 89, 100
Weimann, Robert, 33

Welles, Orson, 46, 132, 141
Werner, Oskar, 147-8
Wilson, John Dover, 49, 73
Wolpe, Lisa, 166-7
Woodeson, Nicholas, 88
Woodvine, John, 111, 114-15
wooing of Katherine, 46-8, 67-9, 82, 102-3, 121-3, 144-5, 165-7
Woolfenden, Guy, 62
Wylton, Tim, 77, 81

Yeats, W. B., 24
Young, B. A., 63, 69

Zadek, Peter, 147, 148-51
Zeffirelli, Franco, 26, 129